Beyond Dogma

Beyond Dogma

Rumi's Teachings on Friendship with God and Early Sufi Theories

By

JAWID MOJADDEDI

OXFORD
UNIVERSITY PRESS

OXFORD
UNIVERSITY PRESS

Oxford University Press, Inc., publishes works that further
Oxford University's objective of excellence
in research, scholarship, and education.

Oxford New York
Auckland Cape Town Dar es Salaam Hong Kong Karachi
Kuala Lumpur Madrid Melbourne Mexico City Nairobi
New Delhi Shanghai Taipei Toronto

With offices in
Argentina Austria Brazil Chile Czech Republic France Greece
Guatemala Hungary Italy Japan Poland Portugal Singapore
South Korea Switzerland Thailand Turkey Ukraine Vietnam

Published by Oxford University Press, Inc.
198 Madison Avenue, New York, New York 10016

www.oup.com

Library of Congress Cataloging-in-Publication Data
Mojaddedi, J. A. (Jawid Ahmad)
Beyond dogma : Rumi's teachings on friendship with God and early Sufi theories / by Jawid Mojaddedi.
p. cm.
Includes bibliographical references and index.
ISBN 978-0-19-536923-6 (hardcover : alk. paper) 1. Jalal al-Din Rumi, Maulana, 1207–1273—Criticism
and interpretation. 2. Sufism. 3. God (Islam)—Knowableness. I. Title.
PK6482.M65 2012
297.4092—dc23 2011029081

1 3 5 7 9 8 6 4 2

Printed in the United States of America
on acid-free paper

For Negin

Contents

Abbreviations

EI2	*Encyclopaedia of Islam*, 2nd Edition
EIr	*Encyclopaedia Iranica*
EQ	*Encyclopaedia of the Qur'an*
F	Rumi, *Fīhi mā fīh*
KB	Kharrāz, *Kitāb al-Kashf wa'l-bayān* (in Sāmarrā'ī, ed., *al-Rasā'il*)
KM	Hujwīrī, *Kashf al-Maḥjūb*
L	Sarrāj, *Kitāb al-Lumaʿ fi'l-taṣawwuf*
M	Rumi, *Mathnawī*
MA	Aflākī, *Manāqib al-ʿārifīn*
R	Qushayrī, *al-Risāla al-Qushayriyya*
S	Tirmidhī, *Sīrat al-awliyā'* (in Radtke, *Drei Schriften des Theosophen von Tirmiḏ*)
T	Kalābādhī, *Kitāb al-Taʿarruf*

Note on the Text

IN VIEW OF the interest beyond the academy in Rumi and his place in Sufi mysticism as well as the wider Islamic tradition, every effort has been made to make this study accessible to as many readers as possible. Familiar names and terms are not transliterated, including Rumi, Muhammad, Konya, Baghdad, Nishapur, the Qur'an, *The Masnavi,* Hadith, Shariah and fatwa. Otherwise, the transliteration system here follows that of the new (third) edition of the *Encyclopaedia of Islam.* References to Rumi's writings are given so as to facilitate reference to existing translations, by citing the book and verse number for citations from *The Masnavi,* and mentioning, usually in the main text, the number of the chapter from which passages cited from the *Fīhi mā fīh* are taken. While the different translations of *The Masnavi* do not follow the same Persian edition by Mohammad Estelami, the difference in verse numbers is small enough for passages to be easily located. The different translations of the *Fīhi mā fīh* are of the same Persian edition prepared by Badīʿ al-Zamān Furūzānfar, and so their chapters do correspond precisely. Dates are given in the Islamic lunar Hegira years first, followed by their common era equivalents, except for the years of publication of books published in Iran, in the bibliography, where a solar Hegira calendar is used instead.

Beyond Dogma

Introduction

Out beyond ideas of wrongdoing and rightdoing, there is a field.
    I'll meet you there.[1]

This translation by Coleman Barks of the first verse of a quatrain by Rumi is now one of the favorite lines to quote in the English language, especially at weddings. When it is read in the context of the whole quatrain, it is clear that a wedding may be an appropriate occasion for it to be used, although it refers to a specific kind of wedding: that between God and the mystic in the "field beyond wrongdoing and rightdoing" (or more literally "Islam and unbelief").[2] While the above translation leaves the nature of the union ambiguous, other translations by Barks expand on this theme, such as the popular example below:

> This we have now
> is not imagination.
> This is not
> grief or joy.
> Not a judging state,
> or an elation,
> or sadness.
> Those come and go.
> This is the Presence that doesn't.[3]

Whatever objections one might have about the word-for-word accuracy of these contemporary translations by Barks, which were never intended to be literal, anyone familiar with the thirteenth-century Sufi Rumi's oeuvre will know that the message they convey is representative of it. The celebration of

God's presence and its effects in everyday life are at the root of the appeal of Rumi's poetry, and these examples indicate that the translations that are enjoyed by millions of readers in North America and beyond are not as far removed from the original on a fundamental level as some might fear.[4] What has disappeared in the effort to make these translations as transferable as possible is any sense of how Rumi's worldview is related to Islam, or any religion for that matter. This study aims to shed light on this issue that has become so contested.

In the technical terminology of the Sufis, the proximity to God that Rumi's poetry is preoccupied with is known as "*walāya*."[5] This is usually translated into English as either "Sainthood" or "Friendship with God," while the "*walī*" (pl. *awliyā'*), who has acquired such sanctity by experiencing God's presence continually, is "the Saint" or "Friend of God." The latter is preferable because it avoids the assumption of too many similarities with the Christian concept of sainthood. For instance, as the poetry quoted above indicates, Rumi's understanding of this concept is one that is far more immediately accessible and universal than Christian sainthood.[6]

As Gerald T. Elmore has explained, the Arabic root "*w-l-y*" for these Qur'anic terms denotes closeness, while cognate terms with this root in the Qur'an indicate that this closeness entails a high degree of reciprocity. For instance, God is the Friend to His servants and can use His ultimate power to protect and provide for them, while Friends of God serve as His "allies" by carrying out His wishes on Earth.[7] In Sufi understandings of Friendship with God, this relationship involves communication arriving from God to His Friends, who receive direct instructions on how to act as part of their mystical knowledge, as well as the ability to carry out the miraculous. It is therefore comparable with common Islamic notions of Prophethood. Friendship with God has of course been articulated in various ways in different historical contexts. Since this study will highlight such developments, it is preferable at this stage to limit to the points I have made any definition.[8]

It should not be too difficult to see how Friendship with God can be regarded as a central and defining aspect of the worldview of a mystic like Rumi. After all, when his poetry is not directly preoccupied with transcending superficial matters in order to reach proximity with God, or the subtleties of the intimate relationship already possessed with his Divine Friend, it tends to focus on the communication he receives through that relationship. This communication enables him to perceive the world around him also as being enchanted with the effect of God's Presence. The fact that his own biography identifies the most important turning point in his life as his encounter in Konya with a Friend of God called Shams-i Tabrīzī further underlines this point. However, it should be remembered that Rumi is in good company, because the oldest surviving Sufi writings, which date from some four centuries before his lifetime, indicate that Friendship with God had held such importance for many generations of Muslim mystics already. One could go as far as to say that it is the basis of mysticism in an Islamic context, even though "*taṣawwuf*" ("Sufism"; lit. "wearing wool"), the term derived from the attire of early mystics, is the expression that has come to be used to identify it. Sufi theorizers made this point and have continued to do so since a millennium ago.[9] A major reason why it is often overlooked is that the Arabic term *"walāya"* can also have additional sectarian connotations.[10]

These themes that are familiar to all readers of Rumi's lyrical poems and quatrains, whether in the original Persian or in popular translations, assume equal prominence in his didactic writings. This makes Friendship with God an obvious choice for any inquiry into Rumi's mystical teachings. The man whose life was reportedly transformed by a question posed about the relative status of the Prophet Muhammad and the Friend of God Abū Yazīd al-Basṭāmī (d. ca. 261/875) unsurprisingly taught about this relationship.[11] Moreoever, as the author of the work known as "the Qur'an in Persian,"[12] he shows a special interest in comparing the divine communication received by Friends of God with that of Prophets. Similarly, reports that he courted controversy with juristic scholars for his devotion to the wine-drinking Shams-i Tabrīzī[13] are consistent with his own teachings on the relevance of the Shariah for the actions of the Friends of God and those aspiring to that rank. Finally, as well as composing many memorable miracle stories, he also taught about the significance of this particular kind of manifestation of the sanctity of the Friends of God.

Rumi's didactic writings are his magnum opus, *The Masnavi*, and the collection of transcripts of his teaching sessions, known as the *Fīhi mā fīh*. As discussed in detail in chapter 1, these two works are remarkably consistent and even overlap in content. Although *The Masnavi* is many times longer than the *Fīhi mā fīh*, its poetic form imposes more constraints than the informal prose of the latter work, which is why, for the purposes of this study, corroboration is consistently provided from the *Fīhi mā fīh* for teachings cited from *The Masnavi*. The central importance of Friendship with God in both, and indeed all of Rumi's works, has facilitated this task considerably. Although many teachings about this topic are also attributed to Rumi in his later biographical tradition, in view of the tendency for such traditions to project later viewpoints back to their subjects, the method used in this study is to focus on the teachings in his own words.[14] Biographical stories are used here only for illustration purposes.

Rumi's *Masnavi* and *Fīhi mā fīh* represent his "practical" instruction rather than "theoretical" accounts of Sufism.[15] Teachings on any particular topic are typically scattered among the transcripts of his teaching sessions and the component books of his voluminous *Masnavi.* In consequence, there has been a tendency to resort to interpreting them on the basis of an external frame of reference, especially the influential tenth- and eleventh-century "theoretical" manuals of Sufism.[16] These works have proven to be among the most widely read prose works on Sufism ever written. This is largely because they are accessible introductions, which, at the same time, stress Sufism's compatibility with the juridico-theological Islamic system that was consolidating its dominance at the time they were written. As that religious system's dominance remained an important consideration through the centuries, these works continued to serve an important purpose. In recognition of their popularity and influence, they were among the first Sufi writings to be edited and translated by modern academicians. This has arguably made their influence on the academic understanding of Sufism disproportionate, and so it has not been inconsequential that three of the four major theoretical manuals of this period were either edited or translated by scholars who also edited, translated, and commented on Rumi's *Masnavi* and *Fīhi mā fīh,* works of entirely different genres.[17]

This study aims to interpret Rumi's distinctive teachings on Friendship with God on their own terms, and then to consider the broader significance and implications of the notion of Friendship with God in general for a more nuanced understanding of mysticism among Muslims. The first task is made possible by the consistency and mutual reinforcement evident between his *Masnavi* and *Fīhi mā fīh,* which present extensive teachings by Rumi about this topic. In order to fully appreciate the significance of his teachings, it is necessary to contextualize them, especially since the question of the relationship of Rumi, and Sufism in general, to the wider Islamic tradition has been the subject of debate. To this end, the theoretical Sufi manuals are also considered in detail, because they grapple specifically with this relationship, while Rumi had little interest in doing so, having opted not to compose any theoretical works. Since as noted, they were written during the critical tenth and eleventh centuries C.E., the development of their theories on Friendship with God sheds light on how much this doctrine was harmonized with the Islamic religious system that was then taking shape. Significantly, they debate a range of viewpoints among their contemporary Sufis about Friendship with God, including both those acceptable and those not acceptable to them at the time, and the issues and controversies that they raised. This makes it possible to use their writings in order to gain insight into the relationship between mystical and scholastic Islam more broadly. Even though their preferred theoretical resolutions do not necessarily coincide with those of Rumi and other Sufis living centuries later, these manuals remained popular because of the continued appreciation of their irenic efforts to present Sufism as compatible with scholastic Islam. An important fact to keep in mind is that works of this genre served this irenic purpose because of the circumstances when they were originally written, and are useful for this study specifically for insight into that process; they have to be treated historically themselves, and not normatively.

The existence of older monograph mystical treatises on Friendship with God from the ninth century C.E., which are also examined in this study, is significant because they enable the tracing of the development of theories about Friendship with God from more than a century before the first irenic manuals. These older treatises also have irenic aims, meaning that in combination with the manuals they can offer invaluable insights into both a wide range of theories about Friendship with God and their relationship to the emerging Islamic religious system over two centuries. It should also be mentioned that the ongoing, dynamic debate about issues related to Friendship with God at that critical time provides an indication of the kind of "practical" teachings that were current then among Sufis, since these Sufi authors were responding to them as well as external pressure from juridico-theological scholars.

To this end, this book consists of five chapters. Chapter 1 provides background information on the authors and texts that are discussed in subsequent chapters. Since Rumi's teachings are the main focus of this study and his didactic writings have received relatively little critical attention so far, his works are discussed at more length than the others. In particular, the relatively extensive analysis of his *Fīhi mā fīh* provides fresh insight into the teaching context in which Rumi's practical didactic writings were produced. The other works and their authors have already been the subject of academic studies, which I draw on in order to provide background summaries here that the reader can conveniently refer to.

Chapters 2 through 5 focus in turn on a key aspect of Friendship with God that is discussed in Rumi's teachings. These aspects are the relationship between Friendship with God and Prophethood, the divine communication that Friends of God receive, the relevance of the Shariah for Friends of God, and the significance of their miracles. As referred to above, each of these thematic chapters begins with an analysis of Rumi's teachings in his two didactic works, in order to interpret them on their own terms. This is followed by an examination of the treatment in the theoretical writings of the period between the ninth and eleventh centuries C.E. Background information is also provided, as required, for issues such as Prophethood in the Qur'an and in Islamic theology. Each chapter concludes with an evaluation of the general significance and implications of Rumi's teachings in light of the challenges encountered by those who took on the task of harmonizing mystical theories with religious scholarship.

This project began in the fall of 2006, during a sabbatical awarded to me by the School of Arts and Sciences at Rutgers, the State University of New Jersey, and has been completed after a second sabbatical in 2010. I am very grateful for the support given to me by the administration at my home institution, as well as from my colleagues in the Department of Religion. During this period, I have benefited from exchanges on the topics covered in this book with many colleagues at other institutions as well. Ahmet Karamustafa, William C. Chittick, Christopher Melchert, and Andrew Rippin read drafts of chapters at various stages of preparation and provided helpful feedback. I have also learned much from conversations with Michael Cook, G. R. Hawting, Yaseen Noorani, Omid Safi, and Abd al-Karim Sorush about issues related to this project. While I have benefited tremendously from their comments and criticism, not to mention their own scholarship and that of others I have not had the pleasure of meeting, I alone am responsible for the contents of this book.

Nearly thirteen years after his passing, I still gratefully reap the benefits of the doctoral training I received under Norman Calder in the analysis of medieval Islamic texts. Azar Ashraf, up to her retirement in June 2010, was always a warm, welcoming presence at the Firestone Library of Princeton University, where she is now sorely missed, and helped me trace vital books and periodicals on several occasions. Last, but certainly not least, I would like to thank my family for their patience with me as my preoccupation with writings about closeness to God often kept me apart from them for long hours.

1

The Sources

IN THIS STUDY Rumi's teachings are interpreted from his own didactic writings, not indirectly through later attributions or interpretations. In order to appreciate their significance, it is important to compare them with the treatment of Friendship with God in the major theoretical writings before Rumi's time. This will not only highlight distinctions between the different genres and historical contexts, but will also clarify the juridico-theological implications of Friendship with God, because those theoretical writings attempt to address them. The oldest of the theoretical writings are in fact treatises devoted exclusively to the topic, while the others are Sufi manuals that contain at least one chapter devoted to the theory of Friendship with God and its implications.[1] For ease of reference, background information is provided in this chapter on all of the works that will be repeatedly referred to in the course of this study.

Rumi is more widely known than the authors of the other works considered here. However, they have been the subjects of academic inquiry to a sufficient degree for background information to be drawn from such studies. Rumi's own didactic works have in fact received relatively little attention from scholars when one considers the amount of translations and popular writings that have been published. The important issue of the relationship between his two didactic works, *The Masnavi* and the *Fīhi mā fīh*, has been particularly neglected. Therefore, a more extensive discussion of them based on primary sources is required for the purposes of this study.

After the Prophet Muhammad, Rumi is probably the most well-known of all premodern Muslims globally. His life-story therefore is familiar to most readers, as well as the fact that virtually all of his writings are believed to have been written in the last three decades of his life, after his life-changing encounter with Shams-i Tabrīzī.[2] In fact, Shams-i Tabrīzī disappeared within a couple of years of their first encounter in Konya, and it did not take much longer for Rumi to lose hope of a reunion. From that time, he was left to focus on guiding his disciples, and it is from this period that his didactic writings originate.

Rumi's writings are predominantly in verse, an extraordinary amount (up to sixty thousand verses in total) of which was produced only during the last three decades of his life (even when taking into account that he may well have started writing poetry before meeting Shams-i Tabrīzī).[3] *The Masnavi,* which accounts for a large proportion of his poetry, is a didactic poem of approximately twenty-six thousand verses. It therefore constitutes the most substantial source for Rumi's teachings. This poem is believed to have been written in the last decade or so of his life, for the express purpose of serving as a learning resource for his disciples. The very idea of producing *The Masnavi* to fulfill such a purpose is arguably an indication that, although Rumi devoted much time to producing this learning resource, he preferred to take a less hands-on approach to actually guiding his disciples.

After the disappearance of Shams-i Tabrīzī, Rumi still took his place sometimes in front of his disciples in a traditional teaching-circle. This is known from notes taken by those present at such occasions, which were compiled within a century of his death to form the relatively modest-sized prose work known as the *Fīhi mā fīh.* Even though it does not make any reference to the existence of *The Masnavi,* the teachings attributed to him in this work correspond with those in *The Masnavi* with a very high degree of consistency; the same homilies and teaching stories are often found in the two works.[4] As a result, one can confidently attribute surviving written teachings to Rumi, both in his own verse (*The Masnavi*) as well as a smaller quantity in prose (*Fīhi mā fīh*), though neither were actually written down by his own hand, and the latter was edited without his input. Since these two works constitute the main sources for Rumi's teachings used in this book,[5] it is necessary to understand the contexts in which they were produced and their relationship to each other before any analysis of their content.

The Fīhi mā fīh

Rumi has left the world thousands of verses of poetry to enjoy, the bulk of which is represented by one of the largest divans of poems and one of the longest *mathnawī* poems ever written in Persian. This prolific literary output may be the reason for the contrasting shortness of the *Fīhi mā fīh,* which purports to represent his teaching sessions. That is to say, the wealth of poetry that he made available to his students could have made him feel comfortable about spending a relatively small amount of time teaching them in person.

The tradition of recording the oral teachings of a Sufi master had arguably been the main source of Sufi literature before Rumi's time, as it had been also for religious scholarship during the period. The process would involve gathering together the notes taken by one or more students who had attended the circle, and then compiling them, often as "the book" of the teacher. This relatively loose process could sometimes result in an incoherent book when neither the teacher nor any other single editor had overall control of the contents, and was often prone to interpolation and organic growth. The same set of notes could also be compiled into various genres, such as the manual or biographical dictionary genres. For example, virtually all of the books attributed to ᶜAbd Allāh Anṣārī (d. 481/1089), commonly known as "The Sufi Master of Herat" (*Pīr-i Harāt*), were produced in this way. Moreover, his *Ṭabaqāt al-Ṣūfiyya* ("Generations of Sufis"), though finally redacted into the biographical dictionary format as its title implies, also includes thematic chapters alien to that genre and more appropriate for a Sufi manual.[6]

The *Fīhi mā fīh*, however, does not seem to have suffered from much tampering, and corresponds so closely to Rumi's teachings in his *Masnavi* that it should be judged as authentic. Nonetheless, it does have a slightly problematic history of its own that is instructive. This is because the oldest manuscript of the work, which dates from 716/1317, contains only about two-thirds of the material found in the second oldest as well as all subsequent manuscripts and the edited text familiar today. Although this oldest manuscript only presents forty-two chapters, all of which are among the first forty-five of the seventy-one chapters found in later manuscripts and editions, it nonetheless provides the title for the work;[7] the second oldest manuscript, dating from 751/1350, provides all seventy-one chapters, but it uses the alternative title of *al-Asrār al-Jalāliyya*.[8] This is not a major problem because the content missing from the first manuscript but included in the others consists of additional chapters that appear equally authentic. However, it does make it difficult to accept that this work could have been written up by a single disciple who went over it all with Rumi himself, as has been claimed.[9]

The shorter, oldest manuscript mentions in the margin toward the end that it was compared to the original (*qubilat bi'l-aṣl*),[10] while the longer, second-oldest manuscript's colophon mentions that it was written "at the holy shrine" (*fi'l-turba al-muqaddasa*),[11] which makes it more than likely that it was similarly authoritative for its own time. There seem to be two possible explanations for why they still ended up being so different in length. The copyist of the oldest surviving manuscript may have opted not to copy the entire work at his disposal, instead going only as far as a desired length of text. This might not have been considered problematic seeing as it is not a work with a clear structure that would necessitate a complete rendering. Alternatively, one may view this as an example of a situation where further material worthy of inclusion was discovered over the years. This would mean that between the dates of the two manuscripts, already at least forty-four years after the passing of Rumi, a decision was made to add further material that was either newly found—perhaps from the notebooks of former students who had traveled away or died—or newly classified (such as chapters in Arabic) from among a larger pool of material representing Rumi's school. The second possibility seems more likely, especially since some of the additional chapters are not found after the end of the older manuscript, but instead in between earlier chapters with which they share thematic associations.[12]

If the possibility that this work may have been open to extension decades after the passing of Rumi seems surprising, one should remember that it is "a miscellaneous collection of disparate pieces."[13] Moreover, Sufi schools tended to collect the various short writings of their teachers together with transcripts of their oral teachings, sometimes in a box, compiling these materials into books only later, by which time further material that was previously still in use as personal notebooks may have accumulated.[14] One need only look at the contents of the *Maᶜārif* of Rumi's father, Bahā Walad, or the *Maqālāt* of Shams-i Tabrīzī,[15] to witness that such practices were also prevalent in Rumi's immediate circle, and are not exclusive to the *Fīhi mā fīh*. For present purposes, it is important to recognize that the *Fīhi mā fīh* represents an expanded version of Rumi's teaching sessions, rather than an abridged one; or to put it another way, this work of seventy-one chapters, a few of which are merely a few lines long while others read more like private correspondence, constitutes the totality that was compiled despite an extended effort.

Not only did just a limited amount of material accumulate after such an extended effort at compiling Rumi's teaching-session transcripts, but they include much repetition. These repetitions include the use of the same imagery,[16] joke,[17] and homily.[18] Even though Rumi himself refers to his deliberate use of repetition when students have not understood the first time around, this range of repetitions is unlikely to represent separate instances in every case.[19] They point to the likelihood that variant notes on the same oral delivery have been incorporated.

The fact that the *Fīhi mā fīh* contains only a modest amount of material in total, although it must represent at least a few years of Rumi's teaching activity, fits in with the traditional view that he withdrew into a more reclusive lifestyle after the disappearance of Shams-i Tabrīzī in around 644/1248, and wrote *The Masnavi* for the benefit of his disciples in preference to more hands-on training. Otherwise, one would expect a far greater amount of material of this kind to have been produced. There are also suggestions in the transcripts of the teaching sessions in the *Fīhi mā fīh* that access to Rumi could have been limited. For instance, chapter 9 begins with the report that someone had come to see Rumi but his wish was unfulfilled.[20] This becomes the basis of a homily through the interpretation that the individual was veiled from seeing Rumi by his own desire to see him, but nonetheless it at least presupposes that access to him could not be taken for granted. Another relevant homily in this regard is found toward the beginning of chapter 3, where Rumi explains, after apologizing for not getting up or speaking to a guest, that it is more worthy to remain in one's absorption in God than to acknowledge visitors.[21]

It is therefore perhaps no coincidence that the *Fīhi mā fīh* contains a large number of chapters that refer to the presence of a visiting dignitary. In fact, these references are fairly conspicuous because they usually occur at the beginning of the chapter, as if they may often have been demarcated, from the collected notes that were drawn upon, at the point where an individual's name is mentioned. Although this feature can be witnessed throughout the work, the frequency is higher among the first forty-five chapters representing the oldest manuscript, fifteen of which begin with the mention of an individual's name, including ten out of the first twenty chapters. Moreover, since most of the individuals named are dignitaries, it is surely no coincidence that this mostly esoteric book begins famously with a hadith about the more worldly issue of scholars and princes visiting each other.[22]

In confirmation of the significance of these visits, in chapter 11 one of Rumi's disciples comments that " when the Amir Parvane comes, Rumi gives magnificent speeches."[23] Interestingly, this is followed by a comparison with trees, which bear fruit and leaves only in season. It is argued that, like Rumi, they are active even during the winter when they do not show any outward signs of it. This would have been an unlikely comparison if Rumi gave speeches on a regular basis. It would be reasonable to conclude that Rumi's teaching sessions were not a common occurrence based on a regular schedule when visitors could be certain of gaining access; they were either such treasured occasions that dignitaries would often make the effort to attend, or were perhaps even prompted by the visits of such individuals.[24]

It should not be overlooked that, despite containing only seventy-one chapters at a stretch (some of which are less than twenty lines in length), the *Fīhi mā fīh* is not limited to teaching-sessions held at his *madrasa*,[25] but is also made up of transcripts of meetings held elsewhere, as well as material that appears to have been part of written correspondence. Individual chapters usually do not specify where the session is taking place, but one cannot simply assume that they all took place at Rumi's *madrasa* when the work alludes occasionally to sessions at other locations. For instance, chapter 23 refers to a past visit to Anatolia, where Rumi's speech moved Greek-speaking Christians who could not even understand the language in which he was speaking.[26] In addition to this reference to sessions held while he was traveling to other towns, one of the chapters begins with the expression of gratitude from an individual that Rumi has graced with his presence.[27] There is a similar allusion at the beginning of chapter 12, where Rumi exchanges pleasantries and compliments that take the form of an affected debate regarding who should be visiting whom, Rumi or the dignitary, with the implication that both alternatives were feasible.[28]

In addition to the names of specific individuals, the *Fīhi mā fīh* reveals much about the audience of Rumi's teaching sessions through its content. That is to say, it provides a profile of his students through the manner in which he chooses to teach them. It also contains the following direct comment by Rumi at the beginning of chapter 42, about the reputation of his own teaching sessions:

> "Those people who have studied or are currently students reckon that if they frequent here, they will forget their scholarship and abandon it, but, on the contrary, when they come here all their scholarship will gain a soul the same way that a body gains a soul."[29]

Although Rumi makes this comment a platform for a discourse about the nature of knowledge, for it to have been effective it must have been credible. That is to say, his teaching-circle must have been seen in some way as a potential threat to one's pursuit of traditional scholarship, with the potential to lead one to abandon such scholarship altogether. It is also worth noting that, although he offers reassurance here, he does not in any way imply that such students are the ideal people for his circle, or praise their knowledge, restricting himself to the correction that he would bring their knowledge alive through an inner dimension or soul, rather than cause them to abandon it altogether. Therefore, the notion that religious scholarship was a necessary prerequisite before undertaking the Sufi path is not supported by this comment, or indeed elsewhere in Rumi's writings, even though he is believed to have had such an education himself. Overall, this passage suggests that, although he did not wish potential disciples with this kind of profile to keep away, he did not seek them out as his preference. On the contrary, he seems to have done the opposite: his first deputy, Ṣalāḥ al-Dīn the goldsmith, was not respected by his own disciples, whom he had inherited from his father, because he did not have a similar background in scholarship, and it is well known that Shams-i Tabrīzī was considered too unconventional and uncouth by those same students.[30]

Rumi defers neither to religious nor to rationalist scholarship, criticizing both tendencies equally. In the instances found in the *Fīhi mā fīh* where Rumi refutes a rationalist conjecture or claim, invariably he not only dismisses their reasoning and premises, but he also directs insults at those who would hold such a viewpoint. For example, in chapter 59, he refutes the following statement by an astrologer:

> "That astrologer says, "Other than the heavens and Planet Earth which I can see, you claim that something beyond them exists, though in my view nothing else exists. But if it does really exist, show me where it is."[31]

Rumi dismisses the astrologer's claim on the grounds that what he is referring to, namely the spiritual world, is beyond space and locations, and challenges the astrologer to identify where his own objection to Rumi's belief is located. But he also continues his discussion in the following manner: "Since you are incapable of knowing about your own condition, how do you expect to know something about your own Creator? Only someone whose sister-in-law is a whore says that God is not in heaven. You dog, how would you know that He is not?"[32]

Rumi's critique of different kinds of religious scholarship is not part of a sectarian polemic, but rather an epistemological one. For instance, in chapter 52 he tells his audience that verbal teachings (*lafaẓ, ʿibārat*) about mystical knowledge can only inspire them to start seeking it, but not actually lead them all the way to attaining it, for which efforts at annihilating the self are required.[33] However, his clearest statement about these epistemological differences occurs in the sixty-fourth chapter, which begins:

> Every form of knowledge that can be acquired through study in this world is the knowledge of bodies (*abdān*), while that knowledge which is acquired after death is the knowledge of faiths (*adyān*): Knowing the theory of "I am God! (*anā'l-Ḥaqq*)" is the knowledge of bodies, while actualizing "I am God! (*anā'l-Ḥaqq*)" is the knowledge of faiths; seeing the light of a lamp and the flame is knowledge of bodies, while burning in the flame or the light of the lamp is knowledge of faiths. Whatever is experienced is the knowledge of faiths, while whatever is simply studied is the knowledge of bodies.[34]

Rumi hereby asserts the superiority of gaining knowledge through experience on the Sufi path over studying Sufism and understanding its theory. He also makes this point in chapter 11, where he underlines its importance for him by arguing for the superiority of the mystic (*ᶜārif*) and his mystical type of knowledge over the scholar (*ᶜālim*) and his theoretical type of knowledge, in spite of the fact that God is known by the name "*al-ᶜAlīm.*" Rumi argues that God can never be described as "*ᶜārif*" since that connotes acquiring knowledge one previously lacked.[35] Despite volunteering all of this, Rumi asserts that the *ᶜārif* is nonetheless superior to the *ᶜālim* because "what he knows is beyond logical reasoning, and he has perceived the world through direct witnessing (*mushāhada*) and direct vision (*muᶜāyana*)."[36]

It is from this position and level of authority, as an *ᶜārif* himself, that Rumi speaks to his students.[37] His sessions are therefore not occasions of debate, but rather mostly a monologue. It is probably telling that the little interaction found in the *Fīhi mā fīh* is between Rumi and dignitary guests. Nonetheless, Rumi makes concerted efforts to present his inspired and incontestable teachings in an accessible form for his students as much as he can. His distinctive method, as with his *Masnavi,* is to use analogies from folklore and everyday life experience, or citations from well-known religious traditions and texts that were accessible or familiar already to his audience. Through his teaching method, which stresses accessibility and common experience, much corroboration is found for the view that he did not require a high level of prior education from his students, neither the religious nor the rationalist kind.

The *Fīhi mā fīh* provides a more detailed picture of the *Sitz im Leben* in which it was compiled than most of the other writings of Rumi, primarily through the identification of people and places. However, it does not provide specific dates for the period during which Rumi delivered the teachings presented therein. Nonetheless, by examining the contents, a reliable estimate can be made. The use of a couplet from the second book of *The Masnavi* could point to a terminus that overlaps with the composition of *The Masnavi.*[38] This is because the second book of *The Masnavi* gives the composition date of 662/1263.[39] However, it is also important to note that the *Fīhi mā fīh* contains many prose variants of the same stories and homilies found in *The Masnavi,* in addition to this instance of the same specific couplet.[40] This single instance should therefore be interpreted carefully, without the temptation to assume from its appearance that *The Masnavi* as far as its second book had already been composed by the time it was cited in a teaching session by Rumi. It could rather turn out to be the exception that proves the rule, because no mention is made of *The Masnavi* in the *Fīhi mā fīh,* not even where this couplet in question is used, despite the fact that *The Masnavi* assumes a place of high importance in the depictions of Rumi's teaching circle found in the biographical tradition.[41] Furthermore, the heavy use of variants in prose of stories and homilies found in *The Masnavi*, mostly from the very first book, could be interpreted as demonstrating that that poem had not actually been composed yet: if it had already been composed, surely more verses from it would have been cited, and longer passages would have been used instead of the less powerful prose variants one finds.

The Masnavi draws on many of the prose works that constitute the literary heritage of Rumi's school, including the *Maʿārif* attributed to his father (eg., see pp. 89–90 below), and so it would be more than reasonable to expect it to also draw on Rumi's own prior teachings. When composing *The Masnavi*, a didactic work designed to be used for the instruction of students in his own school, what more appropriate resource to draw on than his own repertoire of teaching stories and homilies, especially if he was then unaware that after his death they would be compiled as the *Fīhi mā fīh*? From this perspective, the nature of the overlap between the two works leads to the conclusion that teaching sessions represented in the *Fīhi mā fīh* probably took place before *The Masnavi* started to be compiled in earnest, and naturally fed into the didactic poem.

One should also point out here that dating *The Masnavi* is not much easier than dating the *Fīhi mā fīh*, even with the provision of the above mentioned date in its second book. Although the composition of *The Masnavi* can be placed broadly within the 1260s, one cannot necessarily assume that no verses of *The Masnavi* were ever composed out of turn. After all, even the hagiographical tradition reports that Rumi had already completed the first eighteen couplets before being urged to write a *mathnawī* poem.[42] Though the function of that anecdote is Rumi's glorification rather than to provide an accurate history, it nonetheless reminds one of the likelihood that a poet as prolific and experimental as Rumi could have already produced some couplets in the *mathnawī* form. This would explain the occurrence of a single couplet of it in the *Fīhi mā fīh* without any reference to *The Masnavi* itself.

The dates of the lives of the individuals named (or not mentioned) support the dating of the *Fīhi mā fīh* to the mid- to late 1250s.[43] By then several years had already passed since the disappearance of Shams-i Tabrīzī, which is taken for granted consistently by the content. This dating would also precede the tenure of Ḥusām al-Dīn as Rumi's deputy, which began by 657/1259, as is appropriate since he is never mentioned in this work. Ṣalāḥ al-Dīn, who served as Rumi's deputy before him, is mentioned twice in the *Fīhi mā fīh*, however.[44] Another reason why it seems likely that the teaching sessions represented by this work took place before Ḥusām al-Dīn's tenure as deputy is that he was more of a scholar than the goldsmith Ṣalāḥ al-Dīn, famously serving as scribe and editorial assistant to Rumi in the composition of *The Masnavi*. He would therefore have been more likely to take on the preservation and compilation of these transcripts of the teaching sessions himself, had they taken place at all during his tenure.

The Masnavi

Like the *Fīhi mā fīh*, Rumi's *Masnavi* also belongs to an established genre of Sufi literature, but in this case it is one of the longest examples of it ever produced. In fact, it has also come to be widely regarded as the greatest Sufi poem ever written, and is even referred to commonly as "the Qur'an in Persian."[45] Rumi begins this poem with a prose introduction that refers to it as "*The Couplets [Book]*" (*kitāb al-mathnawī*). This title is simply the name of the form of poetry adopted for it, the '*mathnawī*' form, and so some have preferred to distinguish it by adding its most common epithet and referring to it instead as "The Couplets of Inner Meaning" (*mathnawī-yi maᶜnawī*). The discrepancy is not due to a different manuscript, most manuscripts of this work, which Rumi himself is traditionally believed to have edited originally, actually being relatively similar.[46] It has arisen because of Rumi's seeming lack of concern about the title of his poem in the *mathnawī* form, as indeed about the titles of his other works.

Before Rumi, a number of Sufis had already made use of the *mathnawī* form to compose mystical poems.[47] In common with other forms of classical Persian poetry, each half-line, or hemistich, of a *mathnawī* poem follows the same meter,[48] but what distinguishes this form from the others is the rhyme, which changes in successive couplets according to the pattern *aa bb cc dd* and so on. This enables poets to compose long works consisting of thousands of verses useful for didactic purposes. According to tradition, it was the popularity of existing mystical *mathnawī* poems among Rumi's disciples that prompted Ḥusām al-Dīn, Rumi's deputy at the time, to ask him to compose his own. This indirectly highlights an important factor, namely that such didactic poems were invariably intended for a readership beyond the immediate teaching circle, in contrast to what is discussed in teaching sessions. The high degree of consistency between *The Masnavi* and the *Fīhi mā fīh* is therefore all the more remarkable.

Ḥusām al-Dīn also served as Rumi's scribe in a process of text production that is described with echoes of the production of the Qur'an in the hagiographical tradition and is also alluted to in *The Masnavi* itself (e.g., Bk. 1, v. 2947).[49] Rumi is believed to have edited the work with Ḥusām's assistance after the latter had recorded in writing his recitations,[50] while, in contrast, Muhammad is traditionally distanced from the editing of the Qur'an by the dating of that process after his death.[51]

Rumi's *Masnavi* belongs to the group of works written in this verse form that do not employ a frame narrative. In this way, it contrasts with the more cohesively structured examples, such as the *Manṭiq al-ṭayr* ("*Conference of the Birds*") by Farīd al-Dīn ᶜAṭṭār.[52] It is also much longer than that work, which is roughly the same length as just one of the six component books of *The Masnavi.* One could, however, make a fruitful comparison between such a *mathnawī* poem with a frame narrative and any of the multisection stories that combine to make up the books of Rumi's *Masnavi.* This is because the frame narrative of each of *The Masnavi*'s multisection stories defines the beginning and end of the series of sections concerned, as well as their main teaching, and is built up episodically in the same way as the frame narrative of an entire poem. In a similar way to the interruptions of the frame narrative of poems such as the *Manṭiq al-ṭayr,* the main narrative of such a story in *The Masnavi* is interrupted repeatedly by illustrative stories, and also homilies and lyrical flights, in such a way that they enrich many times over its main teachings. Gustav Richter has pointed out these literary characteristics by focusing on the aesthetic qualities of the multisection story about the old harpist, which is found in the first book of *The Masnavi,* and Hamid Dabashi has articulated the clear logic of the sequence of sections in his exploration of the ethical teachings in the multisection story about the vizier of a bigoted Jewish king.[53]

Sections of *The Masnavi* are demarcated by their own headings. Occasionally, the headings appear to have been positioned inappropriately, such as in the middle of continuous speech, which might be interpreted as a sign that they were inserted only after the text had been prepared, and sometimes sloppily or on the basis of just the first few lines. One should not be altogether surprised at this possibility, since many such works of this genre are demarcated inconsistently and sometimes with the generic one-word heading of "section" (*faṣl*) or "story" (*ḥikāyat*). The length of the headings in *The Masnavi* is remarkably variable, with some actually longer than the passages they precede, and serving to explain and contextualize them thoroughly. It is as if, on rereading the text, further explanation was added in the form of an expanded heading. The fact that long explanatory section headings predominate in the last two books of *The Masnavi* may then be interpreted as an indication that Rumi or Ḥusām al-Dīn opted during the editing process to lengthen the headings rather than add more verses to his poem. This could have been due to time constraints, or perhaps other factors, such as the reluctance to extend the length of each component book beyond a specified limit.[54] It is also possible that section headings may have been added by more than one person, if Rumi had as little interest in them as he did in the titles of his writings.

Breaks in the flow of narratives in *The Masnavi* are actually much more frequent than the section headings demarcating commentary and secondary stories indicate. These give *The Masnavi* a distinctively multilayered and dynamic nature, which can leave the impression that he was brimming with ideas and symbolic images that would overflow when prompted by the subtlest of associations. Recently, Ahmet Karamustafa has shown that Rumi may have emulated the Qur'an's multivocality, deliberately producing the effect of engaging the reader in a highly interactive way.[55] The frequency of breaks could also be accounted for by heavy editing of an initial draft of a poem. The results of either process could potentially create an impediment to understanding the poem at the same time as they enrich each story many times more than would be possible if commentary had been restricted to a position after the conclusion of the entirety of the main narrative. However, it is evident, not least from the much-celebrated lengthy sequences of analogies that Rumi often provides to reinforce a single point, that he has striven to communicate his message as effectively as possible rather than to write obscurely and force the reader to struggle to understand him. One could argue that the only significant area where *The Masnavi* is less accessible than the *Fīhi mā fīh* is in its analogical mode of discourse, which is the convention for poems of the mystical *mathnawī* genre.

Seyed Ghahreman Safavi and Simon Weightman have recently published an innovative study that has the virtue of emphasizing the active role of Rumi as the author of *The Masnavi,* in contrast to the traditional emphasis on his passive receipt of divine inspiration. It usefully illustrates the benefit of analyzing how larger units in *The Masnavi,* such as multi-section stories, have been assembled together in a more logical order than may at first appear. In their co-written study *Rumi's Mystical Design,* which originated as Safavi's doctoral thesis written under Weightman's guidance, they go further by claiming to have made the discovery of a secret organizational plan of *The Masnavi* through this method, according to which the section headings were the starting point for the poem, before any verse was composed. Sections often positioned opposite each other are said to represent a chiasmic scheme by virtue of mutual associations, with the purpose of pointing to the need to read them synoptically in order to decipher the text's deepest level of meaning.[56] Although this approach raises the hope of uncovering the mystery of some surprising digressions in the middle of stories, the associations between sections that Safavi and Weightman have identified to support their claim are often disappointingly loose; transferable associations in a poem known for the diverse contents in each section, due to its idiosyncratically frequent digressions, are likely to be found short of compelling. It may even perhaps imply that Rumi made a poor job of it or that ring-structure was then commonplace, rather than that he reserved the deepest teachings for the select few who could decode it.[57] Moreover the fruits of this kind of synoptic reading of *The Masnavi* are said to rest to a large extent on a numerology that the coauthors never actually substantiate (and Rumi himself never hints at). Therefore, the overall impression this study gives of the composer of such a work contrasts strongly with that of Rumi the poet and teacher as he appears in all his other writings, as well as any straightforward reading of *The Masnavi* itself.[58]

It is also evident that the hidden code apparently deciphered by Safavi and Weightman does not disclose any mystical teachings that are deeper or more appropriate for secrecy than what Rumi himself conveys plainly in *The Masnavi,* as they themselves acknowledge.[59] Rumi does see a role for forms, albeit very much secondary to content, and the Safavi-Weightman approach may realistically be considered a worthy stab at mapping the broad outlines of the Sufi teachings that Rumi decided to cover in *The Masnavi,* once it is applied to the whole work. However, in the end one need only refer to Rumi's comments about the inadequacy of trying to learn Sufism from books, such as the ones from the *Fīhi mā fīh* quoted earlier in this chapter, to appreciate the extent to which an overemphasis of the significance of the teachings in books (let alone the forms of those books) would misrepresent Rumi's approach to Sufism.

This most recent attempt to make sense of the overall structure of Rumi's *Masnavi* also highlights how difficult a task that is. More significantly for present purposes, their argument for a synoptic reading highlights the fact that Rumi returns to the same topic in different component books, as well as in sections of the same book of his poem. Consequently, even if a specific theme may be dominant in one book, he does not reserve discussions on particular themes strictly for separate books of his voluminous poem. While there may be a greater focus on a particular theme in one book of the poem than in the others, this does not mean that any particular book has priority when examining Rumi's teachings about that theme. For instance, book 1 has been seen by Safavi and Weightman (following Julian Baldick)[60] to contain many teachings about the lower soul (*nafs [-i ammāra]*), but one can find plenty of homilies about it in the other books as well. Moreover, while Book 2 has a greater emphasis on the importance of association with a Sufi master, the most frequently-cited passages about this theme are actually in Book 1. Thus *The Masnavi* as a whole needs to be studied in order to represent Rumi's teachings on any particular topic, such as Friendship with God in this study, rather than a restricted portion of the poem. The process of carrying this out here will also shed light on the consistency of his teachings in different portions of this poem, which took more than a decade to complete, in addition to its consistency with his preserved oral teachings in the *Fīhi mā fīh*.

Kharrāz and His al-Kashf wa'l-Bayān

Abū Sa^cīd Aḥmad b. ^cĪsā al-Kharrāz (d. ca. 286/899) was a much celebrated early representative of the Sufi tradition in Baghdad and has left behind a number of short works. Nonetheless, little is known about the actual events of his life. The one important exception is that he lived for a while in Mecca, possibly because he had been expelled from Baghdad in the wake of the Hanbalite Ghulām Khalīl's accusations against Sufis in 264/878. As one would expect for someone considered a major figure among the early Sufis, he later becomes associated with the other major mystics of his time across a wide geographical expanse, as well as teachers in the traditional religious sciences. The writings of the prominent leader of the next generation of Sufis in Baghdad, Abū al-Qāsim al-Junayd (d. 297/910), through their focus on annihilation and subsistence in God (*fanā wa-baqā*) using terminology found in Kharrāz's writings, support the traditional identification of the latter as one of his teachers.[61]

Nada A. Saab, who has traced all such associations and provided background information on them in her unpublished doctoral dissertation,[62] has also importantly pointed out that Kharrāz has been the subject of rehabilitation in his biographical tradition. By way of illustration, she cites his saying "*kull ẓāhir yukhālifuh bāṭin fa-huwa bāṭil*" ("Any outer [reality] contradicted by the inner [reality] is false"), which has been used as the basis for attributing to Kharrāz the view that Sufis must follow the Shariah for their spirituality to be legitimate.[63] As Saab points out, the original statement does not inherently privilege the outer over the inner reality in the process of stressing the need for harmony, and in any case Kharrāz's writings, far from supporting an interpretation that stresses the Shariah, tend to contradict it.[64] As he explains in his *Kitāb al-ṣidq*, the most important priority for the Sufi is to maintain truthfulness (*ṣidq*) and sincerity (*ikhlāṣ*) in his actions, and not simply to follow juristic formulations.[65] This is a view shared by others in his generation of Sufis, including Ḥakīm Tirmidhī, who is introduced below.

Kharrāz's *Kitāb al-Kashf wa'l-Bayān* ("The Book of Unveiling and Elucidation") is a short treatise (seven pages in the printed edition) found among other similarly short writings in a manuscript housed in Kastamonu (no. 2713).[66] Its title seems to refer to Kharrāz's expressed aim to "lift the veil" over the discernment of a group of Sufis who consider Friendship with God a higher rank than Prophethood, and to elucidate the actual relationship.[67] Sāmarrā'ī, the editor of this work, has rather shortsightedly suggested that it was written to refute the theory of Kharrāz's contemporary Ḥakīm Tirmidhī,[68] but Paul Nwyia and Nada A. Saab have both pointed out that the argument does not stand up to a comparison with the contents of the latter's work.[69]

Ḥakīm Tirmidhī and His Sīrat al-awliyā'

Kharrāz's contemporary Abū ᶜAbd Allāh Muḥammad b. ᶜAlī al-Ḥakīm al-Tirmidhī (d. ca. between 295/905 and 300/910) was the most prolific mystic author before the eleventh century, which is what makes straightforward the dismissal of Sāmarrā'ī's misidentification of him as Kharrāz's target. He is usually referred to using the title "*ḥakīm,*" which was the term used for mystics in his native Transoxiana before "*ṣūfī*" eventually replaced it. However, it is important to recognize that the main reason not to call him a Sufi is to avoid anachronism, especially in view of the fact that Sufis in tenth-century Baghdad excluded him from their number for polemical reasons. Sufi authors of this school also omitted references to his dozen or so major works, even when they had been inspired by them.[70]

The academic world is indebted to the German scholar Bernd Radtke for a career devoted to the study of Tirmidhī's oeuvre. Among the latter's minor works is an autobiography, which has already been published in English translation by Radtke together with John O'Kane.[71] This short work confirms what is evident from Tirmidhī's other writings regarding his background, namely that he was well educated in the religious sciences, and traveled as a young man westward toward Mecca. His visit to Mecca proved a turning point in his life, leading him toward mysticism, and on his return to Tirmidh, he guided others and partook in practices such as *dhikr* (remembrance), which he may have learned during a sojourn in Basra en route. Tirmidhī eventually became the center of controversy back in his hometown because of his mystical teachings. Among the false accusations to which he refers in his autobiography is that he claimed to be a Prophet. Helped no doubt by his educational background and obvious intellectual prowess, he managed to defend himself robustly in the face of accusations by religious scholars, who probably represented the kind of intellectuals with whom he himself used to associate before his mystical turn.

Tirmidhī's *Sīrat al-awliyā'* (also known as *Khatm al-walāya*) is the only major systematic treatise on the subject of Friendship with God to be written before the thirteenth century.[72] It was not written as part of a polemic, but alludes to controversies in the background by the reassurance it repeatedly gives the interlocutor that Friends of God as a category are not being elevated to the same level as Prophets, let alone higher than them. Since his contemporary Kharrāz in Baghdad wrote a polemical treatise about precisely this debate, one gains the impression that this had become a major controversy at the time, and was not specified by Tirmidhī precisely because of the accusation made against him. Tirmidhī's work could therefore be considered a less blunt as well as considerably more sophisticated and detailed attempt to fulfill the same urgent need of mystics as Kharrāz's *al-Kashf wa'l-bayān* aimed to do. Tirmidhī was evidently very confident in his own learning and intellectual prowess; he neither shies away from controversial topics nor desists from criticizing religious scholars. The latter tendency, which extends to mockery, can explain why he seems to be almost completely ignored by Sufi authors in the next couple of centuries: their main concern at that time was to assert Sufism's compatibility with the systematized Islam of the religious scholars.

*Sarrāj and His Kitāb al-Luma*ᶜ *fī al-taṣawwuf*

Very little is known about the life of Abū Naṣr ᶜAbd Allāh b. ᶜAlī al-Sarrāj (d. 378/988) other than that he was the author of the *Kitāb al-Luma*ᶜ *fī al-taṣawwuf* ("The Book of Shafts of Light on Sufism"), which is the oldest manual of Sufism. It is representative of works of the Sufi manual genre through its irenic efforts at asserting a compatibility between Sufism and scholastic Islam.[73] As Ahmet Karamustafa has already pointed out, Sarrāj claims that he wrote his work due to an upsurge in engagement with and writing about Sufism that had produced only very inadequate and misleading works.[74] His own work represents an extensive introduction to Sufism by including chapters on the Sufis' doctrines, customs, methods of worship, and ecstatic experiences, as well as samples of their writings and discussions of their relationship to other religious groups.

The fact that Sarrāj was writing in a polemical context is evident by his inclusion of a large section in his *Luma*ᶜ about "errors" circulating among Sufis. Here one finds the chapters of the *Luma*ᶜ that represent the main foci of discussion in this study, including one specifically about those who consider Friendship with God superior to Prophethood. In addition to the relatively evenhanded way that he treats these "errors," rationalizing for instance why they may have developed in the first place and presenting reasoned refutations, his inclusion of controversial material elsewhere in the *Luma*ᶜ further reveals that he had a relatively broad and accommodating understanding of Sufism.[75] It was nonetheless one that regarded Sufis as following a simplified form of the approach of religious scholars, and adding to that basis a preoccupation with purifying their souls and striving for proximity to God. That is to say, Sarrāj articulates a vision of how Sufism can be compatible with juristic Islam by requiring Sufis to abide at least by its absolute requirements in addition to their own exclusive endeavors on the mystical path.

Kalābādhī and His al-Taᶜarruf li-madhhab ahl al-taṣawwuf

Sarrāj's contemporary in Bukhara, Abū Bakr Muḥammad b. Ibrāhīm al-Kalābādhī (d. 380s/990s), similarly remains an obscure individual. Unlike Sarrāj, however, he does not seem to have been primarily interested in Sufism, having composed a Hadith commentary in addition to his frugally succinct introduction to Sufism, the *al-Taᶜarruf li-madhhab ahl al-taṣawwuf* ("Introduction to the Path of the Sufis"). The most distinctive aspect of his *Taᶜarruf* is its first major section, where he presents the Sufis' theological doctrines about matters such as God's attributes and names. It is in this section that one finds a chapter about "the miracles of the Friends of God," which actually discusses more aspects of Friendship with God than its title suggests. This section is preceded by four introductory chapters listing Sufis and writings about Sufism, and it is followed by chapters on specifically mystical topics, such as states and stations and the technical terminology used to describe them. As Karamustafa has already pointed out, Kalābādhī identifies Sufism's expertise to be about the soul, and refers to this science as "wisdom" (*ḥikma*), thereby helping to introduce the tradition in a familiar form to his readers in Transoxania, where the indigenous mystical tradition was already known by this term.[76]

Karamustafa has also surmised that Kalābādhī had little more than an "academic" interest in Sufis, though he did presumably believe that they had been the target of false accusations, since he volunteers that the aim of his *Taᶜarruf* is to repair this situation.[77] The way that Kalābādhī does this is by emphasizing the importance of juristic Islam for Sufis, by asserting that they adopt the most demanding interpretations of it, and by giving a conservatively reductionist account of any controversial viewpoints that he cannot avoid including.

Qushayrī and His al-Risāla fī ᶜilm al-taṣawwuf

Abū 'l-Qāsim ᶜAbd al-Karīm b. Hawāzin al-Qushayrī's (d. 465/1072) *al-Risāla fī ᶜilm al-taṣawwuf* ("Treatise on the Science of Sufism") has been the most widely-read prose introduction to Sufism ever written, and has also generated commentaries and translations into various languages. The author is not only mentioned in Sufi sources but also in the following chronicles, of the cities of Baghdad and Nishapur respectively: al-Khaṭīb al-Baghdādī's (d. 463/1071) *Taʾrīkh Bāghdād* and ʿAbd al-Ghāfir al-Fārisī's (d. 529/1134) *al-Siyāq li-Taʾrīkh Naysābūr.* However, it is not as a scholar of Sufism that he is primarily remembered there, despite the success of his *Risāla,* which was composed in 438/1046. He is included in the former work because of a report that he visited in 448/1055, and became known there as a hadith transmitter and a scholar of Ash'arite theology and Shafi'ite jurisprudence, without any mention of his *Risāla* or Sufism in general.[78] In the latter work, which is about the city where Qushayrī himself spent his adult life, al-Fārisī (d.529/1134) specifies that he was a disciple of Abū ʿAlī 'l-Daqqāq (d. 406/1016 or 412/1021), whom Qushayrī himself frequently cites as a Sufi authority. Al-Fārisī also mentions his scholastic credentials, which are further substantiated by Qushayrī's non-Sufi writings about Ash'arite theology in particular.[79] It should therefore be no surprise for someone with such a background to write an irenic work about the compatibility of Sufism with Ash'arite theology and Shafi'ite jurisprudence so successfully.

The *Risāla* consists of four sections that are clearly demarcated by the author himself.[80] The shortest section by far is the first section, on "the doctrine of this sect in theological issues (*masāʾil al-uṣūl*)," which presents Ash'arism as the theological school of the Sufis and contains little relevant directly to mysticism. The second section is a collection of biographies of past mystics, while the thematic third and fourth sections, in combination, constitute the equivalent of a Sufi manual. It is in these two final sections, which are presented by the author as being devoted to terminology and states and stations, respectively, that one finds most of the material relevant for this study, including a chapter on Friendship with God, and another on the miracles of the Friends of God, which happens to be the longest in the entire work. The *Risāla* also has an appendix entitled "Advice to disciples" (*al-waṣiyya lil-murīdīn*), which will be referred to in this study.

Qushayrī makes his agenda clear not only with his initial theological section, but also in the introduction of the work (quoted on pp. 131–2 below), where he claims to be restoring Sufism to its original Shariah-abiding form at a time when most practitioners are astray. In addition, his omissions are also telling, such as that of al-Ḥusayn ibn Manṣūr al-Ḥallāj (d. 309/922) from his biographical section,[81] not to mention his explanation that the Sufis' adoption of their own terminology serves the purpose of obscuring the meaning of Sufi discourse from outsiders (*li-takūn maʿānī alfāẓihim mustabhama ʿalā 'l-ajānib*).[82] It would therefore be naïve to consider his work at face value as simply articulating a compatibility between Sufism and scholastic Islam that was already a reality.

Hujwīrī and His Kashf al-maḥjūb

The Persian counterpart of Qushayrī's *Risāla* in terms of longevity of popularity is the *Kashf al-maḥjūb* ("Revealing of the veiled"), which was written by his contemporary Abū 'l-Ḥasan ᶜAlī b. ᶜUthmān Hujwīrī (d. ca. 467/1075). This is the sole surviving work and main source about its author, who was born in Ghazna and relocated to Lahore before writing it. This work indicates that he was first and foremost a Sufi, but had also studied the religious sciences; although a Hanafite rather than a Shafi'ite, he was well qualified to write this kind of book with a similar agenda to his contemporary Qushayrī's *Risāla.*

Like the *Risāla,* the *Kashf al-maḥjūb* has thematic and biographical parts. However, Hujwīrī includes most of his discussions of Friendship with God in the biographical part. This is because he has reserved the final section of this part for contentious topics, by presenting each of them as the doctrines of one of the Sufi "groups" (*girūhhā*) of his day, the "accepted" ones among which are named after illustrious subjects of his biographies.[83] While the attributions often correspond appropriately to the individuals concerned, when there are extant writings of theirs available for reference, the historical existence in Hujwīrī's time of such groups is unattested elsewhere. Friendship with God is thus presented in his account of a Sufi group that he names as the "Ḥakīmīyān" and identifies as the followers of Ḥakīm Tirmidhī. This is in fact the longest treatment of any Sufi group by Hujwīrī, and is divided into several chapters, covering Friendship with God, miracles, the relationship with Prophethood, and debates related to these issues.

Hujwīrī bemoans the state of Sufism in his own day in a similar way to that of his contemporary Qushayrī before him in the introduction to his *Risāla,* which he had read and was influenced by. In the process of articulating compatibility between Sufism and scholastic Islam, rather than omission, his favored strategy is to include controversial topics and offer a qualified approval, thereby distancing himself from elements he found unacceptable. For instance, he expresses his admiration for Ḥallāj in the lengthy biography that he devotes to him, but expresses doubt as to whether his approach is a wise one for others to follow, and blames his bad reputation on the false attribution to him by later mystics of their own "heretical" beliefs.[84]

2

Friendship with God in Relation to Prophethood

> One day that sultan of the spiritual world was sitting by the entrance of the caravanserai when Rumi came out of the school at the Cotton-sellers market, mounted a swift mule, and crossed that entrance with all the students and scholars following him next to his stirrups. At that moment Shams stood up and ran to him, taking a firm hold of the bridle, to ask: "O money-changer for the spiritual world and its currency who knows the divine names, tell me which one was greater: Muhammad or Bāyazīd?"[1]

Even if the names of the characters in the narrative had not been mentioned, most readers would have been able to identify it as a version of the story about the first encounter between Rumi and Shams in Konya. It is after all the best-known story by far in Rumi's biography, and the event it describes is considered the turning point in his life: the Rumi millions across the world know and love is believed to have emerged as a result of this encounter.

As one would expect for an event of monumental importance to biographers, there are many variant accounts. What they share is the outcome, namely that Rumi and Shams bond and start to spend a great deal of time in private, a process that transforms Rumi into the ecstatic Sufi poet we recognize today. The several versions of this story can be divided into two sets, distinguished by the different ways in which the powerful effect of meeting Shams is manifested: whether through his performance of miracles or, as in the above example, his posing of a question to Rumi. One simple example of the other group of variants, which is compiled by ʿAbd al-Raḥmān Jāmī (d. 898/1492) in his *Nafaḥāt al-uns,* relates the following:

> It has been reported that when Shams arrived in Konya and entered Rumi's teaching session, the latter was sitting next to a courtyard pool with a few books in front of him. Shams asked, "What are these books?" Rumi said, "These are called discourse (*qīl wa-qāl*); what are they to you?" Shams stretched out his hand and threw all the books in the water. Rumi, in utter despair, said, "Hey dervish, what have you done? Some of these were the good works of my father which cannot be found elsewhere!" Shams put his hand in the water and took out the books one by one—water had not caused any damage to them, nor left a trace. Rumi said, "What secret is this?" Shams said, "This is direct taste and mystical state (*dhawq wa-ḥāl*). What clue do you have about it?" After this, they started their close association.[2]

This version exemplifies the way that the miracles recounted in its group of variants serve to highlight the limitations of intellectual knowledge in relation to mystical knowledge of the unseen, since they all involve displays of power over books. It remained a common factor presumably because biographers felt it was too important to change in their variant miracle stories. In light of what this encounter signals for Rumi the scholar, according to his biography, it is not difficult to see why.

Similar to the way that each member of this category of stories about their first meeting in Konya maintains the allusion to scholarly knowledge, in the first category, those variants in which the power of Shams' presence manifests itself through the question he poses to Rumi, the specific question posed is maintained consistently. As in the version related at the beginning of this chapter, it is about the Sufi Friend of God Bāyazīd Basṭāmī (d. 234/848, or 261/875), who is invariably in these versions compared with the Prophet Muhammad. Therefore, this very question must have had a special significance that prevented it from being substituted by an alternative; in its own way, it must have been regarded as irreplaceable as the comparison between book knowledge and mystical knowledge.

On the face of it, the question asked in the above version would not seem difficult to answer for anyone in thirteenth-century Konya. After all, it does not take a great deal of knowledge about Islamic theology to realize that it was far from conventional to consider the Prophet Muhammad as being anything but superior to a later Muslim mystic. It therefore begs the question why biographers should have reported that Shams caused Rumi to react in the following way:

> Rumi replied: "No way [can they be compared]! Muhammad is the chief and leader of all the Prophets and all the Friends of God, so greatness belongs to him in truth!"

Shams responded: "Explain then why Muhammad would pray, 'Glory be to You! We have not known You to the true extent that You should be known,' while Bāyazīd said, 'Glory be to me! How tremendous is my rank! I am the sultan of sultans!'"

Rumi immediately dismounted from the mule, screamed due to the awesomeness of that question, and fainted. He remained unconscious for one hour, and all the people gathered around. When he woke up, having returned from the world of unconsciousness, he took Shams by the hand and led him on foot to his school. They went into a chamber, and did not let anyone else inside until forty days had passed. Some say they did not leave the chamber themselves for three months.

It is reported that one day Rumi said: "When Shams asked me that question, I saw a small window open on the crown of my head and smoke rise from it to the top of the Magnificent Throne in heaven."

Now, having abandoned teaching at the school, preaching from the pulpit and taking up seats of honour, they became preoccupied with studying the secrets of the Heavenly Tablets of the spirits.[3]

The version I have cited here is the one provided in Shams al-Dīn Aflākī's (d. 761/1360) biography of Rumi in his *Manāqib al-ʿĀrifīn*. It does not clarify whether or not Rumi's answer to the question was correct, as the dialogue ends with Shams's unanswered challenge. Another variant in the same work, which appears more developed and probably later in origin, presents Rumi as providing the same answer at the conclusion of the story, after Shams has quoted the contrasting transmissions about Muhammad and Bāyazīd. It thus implies that Rumi passed a kind of test by answering correctly a trick question, although it nonetheless incorporates seamlessly the separate comment by Rumi in the above example about the dramatic inner reaction caused by the question from Shams.[4] Putting aside questions of historicity, what deserves to be examined is why this question about the Prophet Muhammad and Bāyazīd has been viewed by his biographers as having so much significance for Rumi that it could not be easily substituted. It was presumably regarded as a vital aspect of his mystical perspective, and it would therefore seem worthwhile to examine what Rumi had to teach about the relationship between God's Prophets, like Muhammad, and God's Friends, like Bāyazīd, in his own didactic writings.

Rumi on the Relationship between God's Friends and His Prophets

Rumi usually mentions God's Prophets and His Friends together as a pair of categories (*anbiyāʾ wa-awliyāʾ*) so as to distinguish them from other people, next to whom they are compared with "the heart in relation to the body."[5] Rumi makes this particular analogy work by stating that our hearts make any journey before our limbs do, and that Prophets and God's Friends travel to the spiritual world, then come back to urge us to follow them there and to abandon this temporary ruin. He makes a similar point in the fifteenth chapter of the *Fīhi mā fīh,* where he describes the following distinct levels of humanity: unbelievers, believers, and finally Prophets and God's friends:

> Prophets, God's Friends, and other people, with their good and bad qualities in accordance with their levels (*marātib*) and essences (*jawāhir*), are like slaves brought from the realm of infidels to that of Muslims, to be sold here. Some are brought at five years of age, some at ten years of age, and some at fifteen. When a small child is brought across, then raised over many years among Muslims and grows old there, he completely forgets the conditions of that previous realm, and has no memory of it whatsoever. Others who were brought when a bit older remember a little, while those brought when much older remember much more. Similarly, all spirits were previously in that world in the presence of God, at the time of *"Am I not your lord?" They said, "Oh yes!"* (Qur'an 7/172). Then, their food and nourishment was God's Speech without words or sounds. When those who were brought as small children hear that Speech, they do not recognize it and consider themselves alien to it. This group is veiled, having sunk completely into unbelief and error. Another group remember a little and so the fervor and passion of that previous realm reemerges in them—these are the believers (*muʾminān*). For others, on hearing that speech, the past state appears to their vision exactly as it was and the veils are completely lifted, so that they are united with it again—these are the Prophets and God's Friends.[6]

This extended analogy is representative of the numerous instances where God's Friends are grouped together with Prophets by Rumi without distinction, even though a distinction is made between them and ordinary believers. Therefore, if there were any distinction at all between Friends of God and Prophets in his eyes, it must have been much less than that between ordinary believers and them, or between believers and unbelievers in this example. Moreover, it is worth noting that God's Friends together with Prophets are elevated in this analogy on the basis of their greater sensitivity to the spiritual world, illustrated here through their degree of response to communications from there.[7]

In addition to pairing the terms *anbiyāʾ* and *awliyāʾ* frequently and classifying Prophets and God's Friends together like this, it should be clarified that Rumi emphasizes their likeness both synchronically and diachronically. That is to say, in Rumi's view God's Friends may be either successors to Prophets or their contemporary associates. For instance, in the following passage from the first book of *The Masnavī*, he quotes the Prophet Muhammad himself as asserting that some of his contemporaries are the same as him inwardly:

> Remove then your own attributes to view
> Such a pure essence which belongs to you!
> Within your heart you'll find the Prophets' knowledge
> Without a book or teachers at a college.
> The Prophet said, "There are some in my nation
> Who share my essence and my aspiration;
> Their souls are viewing me by that same light
> With which I also keep them in my sight."[8]

The Prophet's comment presented here by Rumi asserts that some of his own nation shared his mystical qualities and abilities (*gawhar, himmat*), and Rumi uses this to argue that his own contemporary readers have the potential to find eventually within their hearts the Prophetic kinds of knowledge (*ʿulūm-i anbiyāʾ*).[9] This final point is significant because, despite presenting God's Friends as being, like Prophets, on a different level to ordinary people, Rumi also stresses the possibility for his audience to share their qualities by eventually reaching their status.

Rumi's view that people still carry that mystical potential and that the divine realm is not only the source of all spirits but also remains so close to all humanity, if people would only learn to see properly by completing the mystical path, is well known to be recurrent in his poetry. It is also worth noting that he frequently stresses this aspect of his teaching in his discourses, using the most explicit and unambiguous language possible, including in the following passage:

> With hands, feet, ears, mind, eyes and mouth, you are a human being like the Prophets and God's Friends who attained fortunes and reached the goal. [You should ask] "They were also humans, like me with ears, brain, tongue, hands and feet, so why was the path given to them and the door opened for them but not for me!" One should box one's ears and wage war day and night against oneself, asking, "What have you done, and what action has emerged from you that you will not be accepted?" so as to become yourself *the sword of God* and *the tongue of the Truth!*[10]

Therefore, while Rumi presents Friends of God alongside Prophets at a very high level of humanity, for him any hierarchy is fluid and dynamic, such that aspiring mystics can rise to the same level as these highest categories.[11] It is worth noting that the basis of his appeal is that human beings usually fail to fulfill their lofty potential, rather than aim too high. For Rumi, there is a huge gulf between the common human condition and their mystical potential as realized by Friends of God, yet it is a gulf that can be bridged.

In view of Rumi's frequent pairing of Prophets and God's Friends without making any distinctions, it should come as little surprise that he occasionally uses the term for the category usually considered by his time to be higher, that of the Prophet (*nabī*), to refer to those one would have then assumed to be of a lower status. For instance, in the fifth book of the *Masnavī,* he describes the Sufi master in the following way:

> When you give your hand to the master's hand,
> A knowing, wise one who can understand,
> Who is the Prophet of his time, O student,
> Such that in him the Prophet's light's apparent.[12]

The Sufi master (*pīr*) is described here by Rumi as "the Prophet of his time," and this is related to the fact that he manifests "the light of the Prophet" (*k'ū nabī-yi waqt-i khwīsh-ast ay murīd/tā az ū nūr-i nabī āyad padīd*). The second hemistich makes it difficult to argue that Rumi means only by analogy that he is representing a Prophet, as in the saying "the shaikh among his students is like the Prophet among his companions."[13] Rather, the way that Rumi introduces the light of the Prophet here indicates that the Sufi master is identified as "the Prophet of his time" because of this intrinsic quality. In the context where this description is found, this is identified as what qualifies him as the only person one should pledge to follow: with such light, he can deliver others from their commanding selves, vain fancies, and intellect, and this is why such individuals must always exist in Rumi's view.

The continuous accessibility of the divine light, the source of the knowledge of the Prophets, is repeatedly underlined by Rumi, as demonstrated by the following passage in the first book of *The Masnavi*:

> God taught the names to Adam, and this then
> Was passed through Adam to all other men;
> God's light from Adam or Himself you can
> Acquire, as from the cup or flask, good man,
> For with the flask the cup has a close link,

So potent—blessed be that fine cup's drink!
The Prophet said: "*Blessed are they who've seen me,*
And those who've seen them are blessed equally":
When lamps reflect a candle, men of course
See it as well, because that is the source;
Through hundreds of lamps though it should be passed,
The source is met by those who see the last—
Either through that last flame gain strength and influence
Or the soul's candle, for there is no difference.[14]

This passage ends with the assertion that there is no difference whatsoever (*hīch farqī nīst*) between the later lamp's flame and the original candle of light. With this most emphatic climax Rumi aims to assert the continuity of such divine knowledge without any dilution whatsoever.[15] This is a conviction that he repeatedly expresses in his writings, and it fits well with his overall message about the close proximity of the divine and human realms.[16]

Having already highlighted the frequency with which he mentions together and interchangeably the "*walī*" and the "*nabī*," it is worth looking closely at the rare instances when Rumi does make distinctions of some kind between them. In the following passage from the fifteenth chapter of the *Fīhi mā fīh*, Rumi compares Muhammad with Khiḍr and Moses:

> God occupied Moses with the people, though he acted by the command of God and was also completely occupied with God. However, He made one side of him become occupied with the people for their welfare.
>
> God occupied Khiḍr completely with Himself.
>
> God at first occupied Muhammad completely with Himself. Afterwards, He commanded that he call people to faith, counsel them, and reform them. Muhammad moaned abjectly, "O Lord, what sin have I committed for You to drive me from Your presence. I don't want the people!" God said, "Muhammad, don't grieve, for I won't leave you to become occupied with the people! At the same time as that, you will be occupied with Me. When you are occupied with the people, the intensity of your occupation with Me will not become reduced by one iota from what it is right now: whatever activity you engage in, you will remain in complete union (*ʿayn-i wiṣāl*) with Me."[17]

This passage suggests differences between Khiḍr and the Prophets Moses and Muhammad. Khiḍr is occupied completely with God and nothing else, while the other two are also at the same time occupied with their community. This implies that a difference of the Prophets is that they must also be occupied with the "welfare" of their community, whom they "call to religion, counsel, and reform," even though the assumption throughout this discourse by Rumi is that being occupied exclusively with God is the more desirable condition.

In this regard, the comparison between Moses and Muhammad, which represents the main focus of Rumi's discourse here, is worth noting. Muhammad is told most emphatically that, while carrying out his role in his community, he will remain in complete union with God just as he had been before he was occupied with anything else. On the other hand, Moses has one side of him occupied with people while at the same time being "completely occupied with God." Though slightly ambiguous, one would assume their situation is similar, but that Muhammad's initial protest serves to highlight the wonder of his dual perception without any reduction in his all-important and more cherished total preoccupation with God.

In the forty-sixth chapter of the *Fīhi mā fīh*, Rumi describes Prophets in a way that may explain why he considered their occupation with God much more highly than their occupation with their communities:

> Divine favour (*ʿināyat*) and self-exertion (*ijtihād*) are very far apart. It was not through self-exertion that the Prophets attained the station of Prophethood (*maqām-i nubuwwat*); rather they attained that fortune through divine favour. However, the custom is that whoever attains that will then lead his life according to self-exertion and uprightness, which is for the benefit of the ordinary people (*ʿawwām*)—so that they will consider their opinions reliable. This is because the ordinary people cannot perceive the inward dimension (*bāṭin*) and only see the outward appearance (*ẓāhir*).[18]

The context in which this characterization is presented is an appreciation of the value of divine favor. This is achieved by crediting divine favor with the attainment of the station of Prophethood. In contrast, the more mundane task of helping ordinary people is what self-exertion can achieve. In addition to providing an explanation for Rumi's preference for preoccupation with God rather than people, it also relegates self-exertion for outward acts to a matter necessitated simply by the limitations of the masses, rather than one having any intrinsic mystical value. This passage could also be interpreted as hinting that there are different expectations of the behavior of Friends of God, seeing as they do not have a responsibility to address ordinary people as Prophets do.

One thing that is not at all ambiguous in the comparison of the conditions of Moses, Khiḍr, and Muhammad cited above is Rumi's assertion that Khiḍr was completely occupied with God and nothing else. Rumi's general aim for the comparison seems therefore to be to reassure his audience that the Prophet Muhammad, due to special Divine Grace, is spared from falling short of the Friends of God like Khiḍr in preoccupation with God despite his additional burden of dealing with the masses (much to his own happy surprise).[19] Muhammad's protest to God here emphasizes that no virtue was seen by Rumi in becoming preoccupied with one's community as compared to being preoccupied with God.

Muhammad is frequently described as the first among the Prophets by Rumi whose preferred interpretation of the title "Seal of the Prophets," which is given to him in Qur'an 33/40,[20] is that he surpassed the other Prophets:

> He was the seal (*khatm*): his generosity (*jūd*)
> Had not been matched, nor will it ever be.
> When one excels his peers in what they do
> Don't you say: "this craft's seal (*khatm*) belongs to you!"[21]

Further passages in the *Fīhi mā fīh* provide reinforcement of the view that Muhammad was the greatest of the Prophets. For instance, in chapter 25 Rumi alludes to the "*law lā-ka*" ("If not for you . . .") sacred tradition (*ḥadīth qudsī*):[22]

> "It is well-known that Muhammad was the origin, for God said: '*If not for you, I would not have created the heavens!*' All nobility, humility, and authority and high stations are bestowed by him and are his shadow, since they appeared from him, in the same way that whatever this hand of mine does comes from the shadow of my mind."[23]

This passage might be interpreted as suggesting that Rumi followed the doctrine of the primordial Muhammadan light (*nūr Muḥammad*) being the first thing created out of God's light and from which everything else was created.[24] That is certainly a notion to which Rumi alludes occasionally. However, it should be pointed out that he also frequently refers to Adam as the first of creation, including not only in the passage from *The Masnavi* cited above, but also earlier in the very same chapter of the *Fīhi mā fīh* as this passage under discussion.[25] Therefore, the notion that Muhammad somehow preceded the rest of creation seems to be a concept which interested Rumi enough for him to make use of it for his own purposes, but not a doctrine to which he adhered absolutely.

This passage comes at the start of a discourse on the power of the mind of the mystic, and is soon followed by Rumi's declaration that there is always an individual who, in relation to the rest of his contemporaries, is like the mind in relation to the limbs. It could therefore be argued that his primary interest here is the contemporary situation rather than origins, and the description of Muhammad serves in this context to buttress his assertion of the continuity between Prophets and Friends of God. If Rumi's audience already accepted that Muhammad fulfilled this function for all humanity through time, then he could use that as a precedent for arguing that the leading Friend of God of any generation plays a similar role in relation to his own contemporaries.

In the sixty-third chapter of the *Fīhi mā fīh*, Rumi expresses similar views in response to someone who makes the claim that he has reached an experience beyond even the Prophet Muhammad himself and the angels closest to God:

> Someone said, "I have a mystical state (*ḥālat*) in which there is no room left even for Muhammad or the cherubim!"[26] . . . It is strange for you to have a spiritual moment (*waqt*) in which there is no room left even for Muhammad, seeing as Muhammad does not have a state which has no room left for a stinking wretch like you! When all things are considered, you have attained this level of spiritual state only through his blessing (*barakat*) and influence. This is because all gifts are poured down on him first of all, and it is only afterwards that, through him, they are distributed among others. The custom is like this: God said: "*Peace be upon you and God's mercy and blessings, O Prophet!* We have poured all the gifts on you." [The Prophet] then added, "*And on God's upright servants.*"[27]
>
> The path to God is very frightening, blocked up, and full of snow. [Muhammad] was the first one who risked his life, drove his horse on, and cleared the path. Whoever now follows this path benefits from his guidance and favour, since he made the path manifest first of all and put up signs everywhere with wooden posts, saying: "Don't go in this or that direction!" If you do go in that direction, you will perish like the ʿĀd and the Thamūd,[28] but if you go in the other direction, you will find salvation like those who believe in God. All of the Qur'an expounds this, for "*In it are clear signs,*"[29] which means "We have given signs on this path, and if anyone should aim to break any of these wooden posts, all will go after him, saying 'Why are you destroying our path? Do you want to make us perish? Are you a highway-robber?'"
>
> You should know that Muhammad is the leader: unless one first comes to Muhammad, one will not reach us, in the same way that, if

> you wish to go somewhere, first your intellect leads, saying: "You must go to such-and-such a place. This is in your best interests." Afterwards, your eyes lead, and following that your limbs start to move, in this order, even though the limbs may know nothing of the eyes and the eyes know nothing of the intellect.[30]

In this passage Rumi uses three different ways to illustrate Muhammad's superiority over all others. He is the first to receive God's gifts, which reach others only thanks to him. Second, he cleared the path "through the snow" and put up signposts, in this way making it possible for others also to complete that path. Third, he determines our own endeavors as the mind controls the rest of the body. It is perhaps instructive that Rumi opts not to respond to the conceited claimant by saying that the opposite of his claim is true, namely that Muhammad is actually the one who has states far beyond his reach. Moreover, the image of clearing a path through the snow implies that others can follow the path taken by Muhammad all the way to its completion thanks to his signposts, though they cannot surpass it. The first two of the three images could therefore be interpreted as meaning that those who follow the path after Muhammad can reach the same limit, or attain up to as many "gifts" as him, though he clearly has the distinction and honor of being the first to complete the path to its furthest extent, and to receive the gifts. He would therefore serve to represent the upper limit of mystical possibility. Rumi's choice of analogies indicates that he did not encourage a retrospective focus on the Prophet at the expense of contemporary representatives.

The third image, however, seems to be more philosophical, giving precedence to Muhammad in a chain of causation. As referred to above, Rumi uses comparable imagery also for the Friend of God in the twenty-fifth chapter of the *Fīhi mā fīh*, where, after having commented on Muhammad's special role as the subject of the "*If not for you*" sacred tradition, he insists that there is always a "vicegerent of the time like the Universal Intellect, next to whom the intellects of people are his limbs, with whatever they do emerging from his shadow" (*khalīfa-yi waqt ū hamchun ᶜaql-i kull-ast ᶜuqūl-i mardum hamchun aᶜḍā-yi way-and harchi kunand az sāyi-yi ū bāshad*).[31]

It is surely not inconsequential for Rumi to volunteer that it makes no difference whether those further down the chain (eyes and limbs) recognize which cause, or causes, directed them to act. That is to say, according to this view, the role fulfilled by Muhammad does not depend on it being acknowledged by later mystics. It was only thanks to Muhammad that the false claimant achieved what had made him so dismissive of the Prophet in his ignorance. In the same discourse, the reader finds what might clarify why it is that Rumi implies that later mystics may not even acknowledge who has directed their own endeavors at various steps removed:

> "A Prophet is not that form; his form is what the Prophet rides on. The Prophet is that love (*ʿishq*) and affection (*maḥabbat*), and that is everlasting. These are as distinct as Ṣāliḥ and his she-camel, which represents his form. The Prophet is that love and affection, and that is forever."[32]

This passage serves as a reminder that when Rumi refers to a Prophet, or Friend of God for that matter, he is not primarily interested in the historical personality he names, but rather what that Prophet represents, and in particular his role in the mystic's relationship with God.[33] The historical personality of the Prophet Muhammad is like Ṣāliḥ's she-camel, while "love" and "affection," which ride it, represent Rumi's intended meaning when referring to the Prophet.

To recapitulate, if Rumi saw any differences between Prophets and Friends of God, he viewed them as too negligible to bother highlighting them. This can be seen where he refers to categories of worshippers of God, with Prophets and Friends of God being paired together, his interchangeable use of the terms for these types of devotees, and his emphatic assertion that there is a necessary continuity of mystical guidance from the beginning of Creation until the end of time, in which no dilution or weakening of intensity occurs. One difference he refers to is the necessity of Prophets to be occupied with the people to whom they have been sent as well as with God, whereas the Friend of God is occupied solely with God. In relation to this point, Rumi makes an effort to argue that the Prophet Muhammad's occupation with God remains just as intense. This appears to be in order to preempt any suggestion that he may in consequence be mystically inferior to a Friend of God, in the way that Moses has been viewed in relation to Khiḍr.[34] For Rumi, Muhammad is not only mystically at least the equal of all Friends of God, but he holds a supreme rank representing the upper limit of mystical attainment.

In most instances, such descriptions of Muhammad, who can be assumed to have been perceived in this way already by Rumi's students, serve to support his assertions about the comparable loftiness of contemporary Friends of God, and especially the leading Friend of God of every era. Rumi does not show any real interest in an elaborate hierarchy of Friends of God, and frequently stresses the importance of valuing even the most modest examples, who always have the potential to ascend to the highest level in any case. His combined emphasis on "the Friend of God of the age" and on appreciating the Friend of God whom you happen to follow suggests that his primary concern was his exhortation of the contemporary Sufi aspirant rather than theological doctrine about people in the past. The priority of this concern for Rumi would also account for his emphasis on the shared potential of all people to reach the lofty level reached by Prophets and Friends of God, if they fulfill their mystical potential.

The importance Rumi places on there always being a Prophet, or Prophet-like representative with negligible difference, among Mankind is perhaps expressed most emphatically in his story about the man who claimed to be a Prophet after Muhammad. In this story, which is found in the fifth book of *The Masnavi* (vv. 1121–1243), a man causes outrage among his community by his claim to be a Prophet and the greatest of them all (*ān yakī mīguft man payghambar-am/az hama payghambarān fāḍiltar-am*). He will not be talked out of it even when his conciliatory king, in response to the community's fiery complaints, attempts to persuade him to renounce his claim. And yet, what will surprise any conservative Muslim reader of *The Masnavi* is that it is the disbelief of the community that Rumi condemns, while giving a robust defense of the claim to Prophethood in his conclusion to this story: in addition to pointing out that even a bee is said in the Qur'an to receive divine communication (*waḥy*), he asserts that all representatives of the divine have the nature of the Prophet Muhammad in them: "Whoever you see flushed with *Kawthar*, he/Has Muhammad's nature—keep his company!" (*har ki-rā dīdī zi kawthar surkh-rū/ū muḥammad-khū-st bā ū gīr khū*).[35]

While readers familiar directly with Rumi's didactic writings should not be too surprised by these observations and the high degree of consistency of Rumi's message, those who depend on the existing secondary literature, either as a substitute or as the means by which to interpret Rumi's writings, could be forgiven for being taken aback slightly here. In the specific case of Rumi's perception of Friends of God in relation to Prophets, one can for instance refer to the chapter on prophetology in Annemarie Schimmel's influential *The Triumphal Sun*, where she asserts that Prophets exclusively represent for Rumi the highest point of spiritual development. Although it is understandable in the context of a chapter on Prophetology, without referring to Friends of God here at all she may give the reader the impression that Rumi privileged the Prophets over them.[36] Schimmel's chapter is taken up mostly with the importance of the Prophet Muhammad in Rumi's worldview, elevating him far above all others. What she does not point out is that in virtually every one of her own citations, the Prophet represents for Rumi the mystical leader and not a historical personality from the seventh century C.E. One might wish to consider the fact that Rumi took the innovative step of omitting formal praise of the Prophet Muhammad from the start of his poem of the mystical *mathnawī* genre, contrary to the established conventions. Such a decision would have been virtually unthinkable if Schimmel's characterizations were accurate; they overlook the fact that Rumi's predilection was to emphasize the closeness of all humanity to the divine, even if that was best achieved by doing without the eulogies customary at the beginning of a poem of this genre.[37] This is not to suggest that he lacked reverence for the Prophet Muhammad, but that his message of Sufism was one that contrasts strongly with those manifestations of the tradition where devotion to the Prophet is placed emphatically at the heart of their practice.

John Renard has already corrected a number of Schimmel's oversights in the course of completing his *All the King's Falcons*, which is based on a dissertation he completed under her supervision in 1978. He includes an afterword in which he comments perceptively with regard to Rumi's stories about Prophets: "what Rumi is really selling is a vision of the relationship of the divine to the human and of a way homeward. Prophets and their deeds thus become metaphorical guideposts."[38] In the course of compiling this helpful anthology, Renard had noticed that Rumi's treatment of Prophets and Friends of God cannot be assumed to fit in with mainstream theological dogmas, and he observes with regard to his belief in the continuity of divine communication that "Rumi then proceeds to the logical but technically untenable conclusion that anyone can become a Friend of God or Prophet."[39]

In his *The Sufi Path of Love*, William C. Chittick had already started to correct Schimmel's oversights a decade before Renard. He also underlines how Prophets and Friends of God are paired together in Rumi's worldview, though it is the importance of the latter which he appropriately focuses on. In his discussion of "Prophets and Saints," he stresses the distinction that Prophets are sent to the whole community and bring formal teachings as well as mystical ones.[40] As shown above, for Rumi the mystical is far superior to the formal, and a clarification of this point would have been invaluable in view of depictions such as Schimmel's. That is to say, the distinction may be an additional quality, but was not considered a loftier one, as shown above by Rumi's account of Muhammad's reluctance to bear such a burden and the reassurance from God that his more important inner relationship would not be jeopardized by it, not to mention his comments about the added burden on Prophets to deal with ordinary people.[41] Being primarily a study of Rumi's biographical tradition, Franklin Lewis's more recent *Rumi: Past and Present, East and West* offers a synthesis of earlier studies of Rumi's actual teachings. It is therefore simply symptomatic of the field that Lewis begins his section on the Friends of God with the assertion, "The power of the Friends of God are of an order just below those of the Prophets, and they speak as in a veil with the voice of God."[42]

The best explanation for the tendency to read into Rumi's writings is the weight of the dogma in Islam that Muhammad is the last of the Prophets and can never be surpassed. Like all dogmas, this came to be formulated in a historical process, and has been interpreted in a number of ways. The next section of this chapter provides an overview of the historical origins of this dogma, and this in turn will be followed by an exploration of how the earliest Sufi authors discussed the relationship between Friendship with God and Prophethood.

Prophethood in Early Islam

At the beginning of this chapter, I suggested that the question of who is superior between Muhammad and Bāyazīd would have been something of a "no-brainer" for anyone present then with even a rudimentary knowledge of Islam. While this observation is perfectly valid, it is worth remembering that theological positions among Muslims, just as among members of any other religion, took time to become formulated, and that they became consolidated only after much discussion and debate. In order to be able to see Rumi's viewpoint in perspective and to situate him and his fellow mystics with some degree of accuracy among Muslims, it will be useful to consider the viewpoints of his predecessors, beginning with a reminder of the establishment of theological positions relating to Prophethood before Rumi's time.

It is well known that Muhammad is the founding Prophet of the religion of Islam, but it is often overlooked that, as a fundamental article of faith, Muslims believe that Muhammad was a member of a very long line of Prophets (124,000 is frequently given as the total number of them, but even this has been considered too limiting by some).[43] Far from a unique intervention in human history by God, Muhammad's mission came to be regarded as the last one in a cyclic process that began as far back as creation. When Prophets are considered necessary intermediaries between God and Mankind, it should not be surprising that Adam is considered the first Prophet,[44] and that "all communities" are believed to have been sent at least one Prophet from among the hundreds of thousands dispatched by God.[45]

However, there is a unique gap in this process, according to the Muslim dogma that asserts the finality of Muhammad's Prophetic mission. Resting on a single verse in the Qur'an (33/40) and a specific interpretation of its use of the title "Seal of the Prophets" among those actually ventured by early Muslims themselves,[46] this dogma has the effect of giving a special universal significance to the mission of Muhammad until the end of time. Thus, according to the worldview shared by all Muslims, God remains in continuous communication with Mankind, through Prophets, at least from the beginning of time until the death of Muhammad, and then briefly again at the end of time, when Muslims believe Jesus will reappear at that critical juncture for their relationship with the Deity. This leaves the period from the death of Muhammad to the reappearance of Jesus as the irregular period in which the relationship between God and Mankind must take a different form, and it is over the precise form this takes that differences of opinion among Muslims are most pronounced.

As Yohanan Friedmann has shown through his extensive research into the relevant early Islamic sources, the belief that "Seal of the Prophets" (*Khātim* [or *Khātam*] *al-nabiyīn*) means that Muhammad was the final Prophet took as long as three centuries to become widely established in all its dimensions, being notably absent from discussions of his Prophethood in early major creeds (*ʿaqāʾid*), while also contradicted by certain preserved Qur'an commentaries and hadiths.[47] Nonetheless, it had indeed become widely established already long before Rumi's time, so for present purposes what is important to understand are the factors behind such a theory of finality, which seems ostensibly to be going against the grain of so many aspects of the Qur'anic worldview,[48] and in particular the mystical emphasis on continual communication between God and humanity.

Friedmann has underlined that the closure of Prophethood is hardly a new idea in near eastern religions. While the emergence of Christianity may have been the reason for its eventual adoption in Judaism as a "shield to protect the established religious system,"[49] for the Islamic tradition, Friedmann points to the upsurge of Prophetic claims among the opponents of Muhammad's first political successor, Abū Bakr, during the Wars of Apostasy (*ḥurūb al-ridda*).[50] That is to say, while in Judaism the arrival of later Prophets was for long not perceived as being a threat, a similar semi-extension of all dimensions of Prophethood did not gain much currency among early Muslims due to the immediate crisis of succession in 10/632. This leads Friedman to remark that "it stands to reason that especially the upsurge of prophetic claims during the *ridda* period served as an impetus for the development of the dogma under discussion."[51] However, then there could have hardly been a "religious system" to shield.

A very early development in relation to leadership of the Muslim community would certainly make sense, and is perhaps supported by the use of alternative titles to "Prophet" for Muhammad's successors by competing schools, regardless of their political or religious perspectives. At the same time, however, one cannot assume that these titles were always understood as representing subordinate ranks to Prophets.[52] Moreover, the evidence Friedmann himself has provided to show that the theological dogma did not become universally established for at least two centuries points to a later determination of the full implications of the interpretation of "Seal of the Prophets," beyond the role of Muhammad as leader of the Muslim community.

Besides leadership of the Muslim community, in the Islamic tradition the most significant qualities of a Prophet have become understood to be the receipt of divine communication and the establishment of laws. It would therefore not be unreasonable to propose that the doctrine of the "Sealing" of these particular aspects of Prophethood should have become established and written about as late as the third/ninth century, once a religious system based on the authority of his divine communication had become established. It is, after all, difficult to see what notions could have existed at all about the finality of the religious law or the closure of divine communication before that process. This could explain why religious genres such as creeds and Qur'anic exegesis do not engage until then with this issue, which may therefore have been seen up to that point as being restricted to leadership.[53] Friedmann suggests that Muhammad was seen as unsurpassably great long before he was regarded as the last Prophet, and points out that being last was then hardly seen as a virtue. However, this could have served an important purpose in reaction to claims of Prophethood that were combined with rebellions against Muhammad's political successor. Therefore, contrary to his suggestion, the argument could be made that the belief that Muhammad was the last Prophet may well have predated the belief that he was unsurpassably great. After all, being unsurpassable would only have had a function in regard to serving as a "shield to protect the established religious system," by which one would presumably refer to that constructed by the religious scholars in subsequent centuries. The dogma would have become theologically relevant only at this later date when Muhammad's routinized charisma served as the basis of their authority. For instance, it was only during this century that Muhammad's normative example (*sunna*) came to be regarded as second only to the Qur'an in importance as a source for Islamic law (largely through the efforts of Muhammad b. Idrīs al-Shāfiʿī, d. 188/820).[54] To be precise, the Prophet's *sunna* came to be classified, along with the Qur'an, as divine communication (*waḥy*), though distinguished from the Qur'an as a theologically lesser kind that is not recited in prayers (*ghayr matlūʾ*).[55]

The unsurpassability of Muhammad's Prophethood together with divine communication of the Qur'an's exclusive category served as basic ingredients in the process of making immutable his law (*sharīʿa*), as interpreted by religious scholars. The eventual theological sealing would have both relegated the legal opinions of Muhammad's successors to a subordinate level of authority and at the same time eliminated the possibility of a subsequent individual abrogating his shariah by means of further divine communication (*waḥy*). One can therefore argue that, since the Prophet's charisma came to be routinized under the control of the religious scholars by the early third/ninth century, their own authority as its interpreters was what was in reality becoming "sealed," or "shielded."

At the same time, one cannot help but agree with Friedmann that this closure of Prophethood contrasts jarringly with the emphasis in the Qur'an on Prophethood being a virtually indispensable cyclic process, a message that qualifies it as arguably the most universalist of the holy scriptures of the Abrahamic religions. And since, in mystical interpretations of Qur'anic theology, God's attention and communication with humanity must continue at all times, it should come as little surprise that, among the various theories proposed by Muslim mystics to account for the irregular "Prophetless" era (between the death of Muhammad and the return of Jesus), one finds those that assert that the situation prior to his death remained the norm to a large degree—that is to say, it has not altered as drastically after his death as one might have expected, because most of the Prophet's functions are still carried out in this gap period by variously defined substitutes.

As outlined above, the understanding of Prophethood developed by early Muslim theologians asserts that there are no more Prophets among Mankind between the death of Muhammad and the reappearance of Jesus. While it goes without saying that this doctrine has the inherent advantage, for the religious scholars who established it, of preventing any abrogation of the mission of the Prophet Muhammad which they claim to interpret most authoritatively, it was also perceived by Muslims themselves as having disadvantages. Their concern manifested itself through hadith reports in which followers of Muhammad express their deep anxiety on hearing that there would be no further Prophets after his passing. The most significant loss that this would bring was perceived in such hadiths to be the halting of divine guidance through a Prophet and his ability to receive communication from God. Without a living Prophet in their midst, the followers feared the loss of the close level of access to God that he provided. The consoling response that Muhammad offers in these hadiths to worried followers is that there would still be true dreams (*mubashshirāt, ruʾyā*) from a divine source after the end of his Prophethood.[56]

Among Muslim traditions, the Shi'is as well as the Sufis share a distinctive emphasis on the necessity for communication between God and humanity through intermediaries, which would be incompatible with the view that this could ever have a break in continuity.[57] The Shi'is began first to develop such a doctrine possibly as early as the lifetime of the sixth Imam Jaʿfar al-Ṣādiq (d.765), since both Twelver Imami and ("Sevener") Ismaili schools proposed that specific members of Muhammad's family in a line of succession would serve as the intermediary through whom God maintains His communication with creation and nurtures it during the uniquely Prophetless era.[58] For the Shiʿis, a solution for the succession to the Prophet as well as the break in continuity of Prophethood was thus provided by God, through "the Imams."[59] It should therefore be little surprise to learn that Sufis adopted a doctrine that stressed the continuity of the Prophet's functions as a mystical guide, through Friends of God.

Friendship with God and Prophethood in Kharrāz's (d. ca. 286/899) al-Kashf wa'l-bayān and Tirmidhī's (d. between 295–300/905–910) Sīrat al-awliyāʾ

The oldest surviving mystical treatises that discuss this issue were written during the latter part of the third/ninth century, and therefore might prove a valuable test for the hypothesis that the "Sealing of Prophethood" in all its religious aspects came to be established close to that time. Even though they are the oldest surviving mystical writings on this topic, the *al-Kashf wa'l-bayān* of Abū Saʿīd al-Kharrāz (d. ca. 286/899) and the *Sīrat al-awliyāʾ* of Ḥakīm al-Tirmidhī (d. between 295–300/905–910)[60] indicate that the relationship between Friendship with God and Prophethood had already been developed and argued over with some degree of sophistication. This is because, far from implying that they might represent the first statement on the subject, they actually refer to a major existing controversy.

The *al-Kashf wa'l-bayān* was written by Kharrāz specifically as a refutation of an existing view that the Friends of God can be superior to the Prophets. Kharrāz confirms at the very start of his treatise that this was an ongoing debate among Sufis themselves: he identifies those who "elevate the station of the Friends of God higher than that of the Prophets" as a group of Sufis who were in error (*faʾinna qawman min ahl al-taṣawwuf ghaliṭū al-tamyīz bayna maqām al-anbiyāʾ wa'l-awliyāʾ fa-jaʿalū maqām al-awliyāʾ arfaʿ min maqām al-anbiyāʾ*).[61] He concludes with an appeal for his argument to be heeded, so that "the bane of excessive claims" (*āfat al-daʿwā*) will be removed from them and they may be rid of "the peril of accusation and suspicion" (*mahlakat al-tuhma wa'l-ẓinna*).[62] This comment indicates that his motive for resolving this issue was primarily an effort to improve relations with non-mystics.

For Kharrāz, the Friends of God have a rank that is so close to that of the Prophets that it has been misunderstood as being in fact superior. Kharrāz argues that both Friends of God and Prophets have been specially created by God to fulfill specific purposes in a similar way to the angels,[63] and that "both Prophets and Friends of God are immersed in the ocean of God's will."[64] However, by virtue of being intercessors for the rest of humanity, Prophets should be regarded as superior.[65]

Since Kharrāz's main concern is to refute the view that Friendship with God is a loftier station than Prophethood, one would expect his arguments to shed light, at least indirectly, on the arguments of his opponents. No texts have survived arguing the opposite viewpoint, making his treatise invaluable as a source from which such arguments might potentially be extrapolated. In this regard, Kharrāz's comment volunteering that "the allusion of the Friends of God is more tender than the literal expression of the Prophets" (*ishārat al-awliyāʾ araqq min ʿibārat al-anbiyāʾ*) may be instructive.[66] He explains that this is due to the fact that, unlike Prophets, they are not required to exhort others to act appropriately, which presumably required less lofty, literal expressions, a viewpoint echoed above in Rumi's writings. They are thus free from the Prophets' extra trial (*miḥna*) of giving such commands. Though Kharrāz can insist that these trials that Prophets must endure actually qualify them as superior, the concession to Friends of God that he makes in the course of this argument does not serve his stated purposes in any way. The fact that he goes to the trouble to explain why the Prophets' expressions are not as "tender" suggests therefore that this may have represented what he perceived to be an irrefutable aspect of the view which he was arguing against.

Kharrāz chooses to refer to the story of Khiḍr and Moses in the Qur'an,[67] identifying the interpretation of this story as a source of the error of those who consider Friendship with God superior.[68] In that story, in response to his appeal to be guided to someone with greater knowledge, Moses is led by God to "one of Our servants, whom We gave mercy, and whom We taught knowledge from Our presence (*ladunnā*)" (Qur'an 18/65).[69] This individual, known as Khiḍr in the exegetical tradition and usually considered not to be a Prophet himself, initially refuses to allow Moses to stay and learn from him, with the argument that he does not have the capacity to follow him, but finally relents on the condition that Moses does not question any of his actions. However, Moses fails in this challenge three times, and, just in case the reader has any doubt, before taking his leave Khiḍr explains to him how his own seemingly bizarre and unlawful actions were on God's command and not his own.[70] Kharrāz's argument against a plain reading of the story is that by accompanying a Prophet, the Friend of God, like Khiḍr, always adds to that Prophet's honour (*sharaf*).[71] This enables him to describe the companionship (*ṣuḥba*) of the Friend of God as awakening that Prophet, imparting wisdom to him, and teaching him to act appropriately, as the Moses and Khiḍr story exemplifies, and yet maintain that it serves simply to increase the credit of the Prophet concerned, even if that seems counterintuitive at first.[72] As Nada A. Saab has pointed out, the editor of this work, Qāsim al-Sāmarrā'ī, finds this point difficult to reconcile, and looks to textual transmission errors for an explanation, even though Kharrāz's point is not without its own logic.[73] For instance, if one considers the Prophet Moses as the main character in the story, he remains the most important one, even if he ends up overwhelmed and turned away. The argument seems to be that the whole purpose of the encounter was for the sake of Moses, as in all Prophet/Friend of God encounters, so it should be interpreted as a sign of his importance even if Khiḍr takes on a seemingly superior role.

What is most significant about his discussion therefore is that it implies that the Moses and Khiḍr paradigm, together with the greater tenderness of the sayings of the Friends of God, probably represented two formidable elements of the arguments of his opponents, those who argued for the superiority of the Friends of God over Prophets. Kharrāz chose to respond to them in some imaginative way, rather than ignore or circumvent them. But his argument concerning the interaction of Friends of God and Prophets on the model of Moses's experience with Khiḍr in the Qur'anic story, and his concession that the Prophets' expressions are less tender arguably only weaken his case.

The biggest clue of all that Kharrāz found it a struggle to argue convincingly in favor of the status of Prophethood is his assertion that Prophets were Friends of God before they received their Prophethood, making the latter a bonus honor (*ziyāda*) in addition to the Friendship with God they already possessed.[74] He makes no effort to provide an explanation or rationale for this combination of Prophethood and Friendship with God in one person, but simply states it here as an obvious sign of the Prophets' superiority, suggesting that its purpose here is solely to make this case; it is remarkable that he seemingly accepts thereby that Prophethood struggles to compete on its own against Friendship with God.[75]

It is surely no coincidence that Kharrāz's contemporary Ḥakīm Tirmidhī, the author of the first systematic account of Friendship with God, aims polemical retorts in the course of his *Sīrat al-Awliyā'* to "exoteric scholars" (*ʿulamā al-ẓāhir*) and "hypocritical ascetics" (*qurrā'*).[76] This reinforces the view that, rather than being part of a purely internal debate among mystics, he formulated his theory in response to disagreements directly with opponents among religious scholars and renunciants. Both Kharrāz and Tirmidhī are reported to have become the target for such opponents, and in the latter case this is confirmed in his own autobiography.[77]

The *Sīrat al-Awliyā'* is a fairly systematic treatise on Friendship with God by Tirmidhī, who includes the occasional involvement of an interlocutor as a foil, thereby implying that it was to some degree a responsa work. The interlocutor voices concern whenever Tirmidhī makes a remark that might imply the superiority of the Friend of God over the Prophet. On a general level, the treatise asserts that after the mission of Muhammad there continue to be individuals who are closer to God than the rest of humanity and receive communications from Him as well as miraculous powers. While Tirmidhī gives these mystical successors of Muhammad titles different to Prophet, indicating different categories of holy person after the end of the cycle of Prophethood, he nonetheless argues that Muhammad's title "Seal of the Prophets" does not mean the final Prophet.[78] Instead, he interprets "Seal of the Prophets" to mean that Muhammad's Prophethood had the unique distinction of having been both perfected by God and "sealed" by Him from the interference of the self (*nafs*) and Satan.[79] This distinctive interpretation of "Seal of the Prophets" seems to be designed for the purposes of his own innovative theory of "the Seal of Friendship with God" (*khātam al-walāya*). That is to say, it facilitates his argument that the possessor of this newly identified rank has attained the most perfect level of Friendship with God possible, one sealed by God from the interference of the self or Satan.[80] His interpretation of "Seal of the Prophets" may also have been related to his argument that some "portions of Prophethood" (*ajzā' al-nubuwwa*) continue among those with the rank of Friend of God.[81]

In addition to his innovative identification of the rank of "the Seal of Friendship with God," it is important to point out that Tirmidhī divides the remaining Friends of God into two broad categories, that of the still aspiring *walī Ḥaqq Allāh*, or "Lesser Friend of God,"[82] and that of the *walī Allāh* or "Friend of God." In combination, they would arguably embrace all mystic seekers of proximity to God, because the Lesser Friend of God strives through struggle against his self (*nafs*), whereas the Friend of God is an elite type who is drawn up (*majdhūb*) by God to His presence without need any longer for the same struggle. It is possible for the Lesser Friend of God to become drawn up by God eventually, and on that basis also become a fully fledged Friend of God according to this scheme, but Tirmidhī implies that this is rare.[83] All of Tirmidhī's comparisons with Prophets are restricted to the elite Friend of God, so this might explain the purpose of the distinction he aims to introduce: it enables him to reserve the loftiest characteristics for an exclusive group among those who are said to be Friends of God, and thereby avoid attributing them too liberally.[84] His contemporary Abū al-Qāsim al-Junayd (d. 298/910), who was the most widely accepted Sufi leader of the period in the eyes of posterity, has been shown to restrict to an elect group some mystical experiences that others considered more universal, suggesting the possibility that this was not then such a rare strategy for discussing topics that may not have been readily accepted otherwise.[85]

The general challenge Tirmidhī strives to meet appears to have been the same as Kharrāz's, namely how to argue for the acceptance of the lofty station of the Friend of God while reassuring opponents that this figure cannot surpass the Prophet, the specific issue that always alarms the interlocutor in his treatise. Tirmidhī uses as his proofs Qur'anic verses and hadiths, which reveal his own strong background in religious scholarship, despite some unusual selections and interpretations. For instance, he refers to Ibn ʿAbbās's alternative reading of Qur'an 22/52, which includes "and one with whom God communicates (*muḥaddath*)" alongside Apostle (*rasūl*) and Prophet (*nabī*), as categories of individuals sent by God. By identifying the *muḥaddath* in this alternative reading as the Friend of God, and referring to another instance where the Qur'an (17/5) states that God sent servants, he uses scriptural authority to argue that the Friend of God is also among those sent by God (*mursalīn*).[86]

The interlocutor's uneasiness at this point necessitates some kind of distinction between the categories, which Tirmidhī duly provides. Tirmidhī distinguishes the Apostle (*rasūl*) from the other two categories but does not compare the Prophet (*nabī*) and Friend of God (*walī*) directly with each other. Only the Apostle is sent on a mission to a specific community.[87] The others follow or teach others what the Apostle brings. Therefore, his strategy here seems to be to use a distinction between the Apostle and the regular Prophet in order to maintain the highest status for the Apostle, while at the same time reducing the difference between the regular Prophet and the Friend of God.

Another statement of Tirmidhī's in this regard is the following comment, where he describes the different ranks of the Friend of God: "Some of them have received a third of Prophethood while others have been given a half, and others still more, as far as the one to whom the greatest share of that has been given, the one who possesses the Seal of Friendship with God" (*fa-minhum man uʿṭiya thulth al-nubuwwa wa-minhum man uʿṭiya nisfuhā wa-minhum man lahu ziyāda ḥattā yakūn awfarahum ḥaẓẓan min dhālika man lahu khatm al-walāya*).[88] The above statement's omission of the maximum portion possible for the Friends of God to acquire leaves the relationship between them and Prophets ambiguous. In the same context, Tirmidhī remarks that the highest-ranking Friends of God approach the location of Prophets. Since, according to him, the Prophets other than Muhammad possess less than 100 percent of the parts of Prophethood,[89] the precise level of difference between the highest ranking Friend of God, especially the Seal of Friendship with God, and a Prophet other than Muhammad arguably becomes negligible. Tirmidhī's understanding of the "parts of Prophethood" could lead potentially to the view that some of the Friends of God are at a higher level than certain Prophets other than Muhammad, since they may have more of these "parts."

As Radtke has highlighted already, it is not the only instance where Tirmidhī refers to the Friend of God possessing portions, or parts (pl. *ajzāʾ*), of Prophethood.[90] In the two other instances, we discover that he means the qualities of a Prophet, such as receiving divine communication, which high-ranking Friends of God also receive, thereby possessing that "part" of Prophethood, and reaching "close to the Prophets."[91]

In the previously cited examples, Tirmidhī certainly downplays the difference between the Friend of God and the Prophet. When it comes to discrediting his opponents, he cites the following three hadiths transmitted by them, which cause his interlocutor uneasiness one more time, because they lend themselves to the interpretation that Friends of God are superior to Prophets.[92]

> "God has some servants who are neither Prophets (*nabiyūn*) nor martyrs, and the Prophets and martyrs envy them because of their closeness (*qurb*) and their place (*makān*) before God."
>
> "Twelve Prophets shall wish they belonged to my community of followers."
>
> "I could safely swear an oath that only ten individuals will enter paradise ahead of the advanced members of my community, among them being Abraham, Ishmael, Isaac, Jacob, and Mary."[93]

It is important to note that Tirmidhī cites these hadiths in the context of his criticism of hypocritical ascetics.[94] He chides them for denying the possibility that elite Friends of God can receive divine communication, even though they themselves transmit such provocative hadiths as these three examples. However, none of these hadiths actually refers to divine communication. Rather, they all lend themselves to the interpretation that Friends of God can be superior to at least some of the Prophets. This suggests that Tirmidhī did not intend himself to assert the superiority of Friends of God, attributing that view instead to his opponents as a means of showing that they would go as far as to transmit these hadiths, while they stubbornly refuse to accept his more modest assertion. He does not present these hadiths in order to develop directly his own argument about the Friend of God in any way. Nonetheless, by mentioning them at all, he has provided material which can encourage opponents to accuse him of claiming that Friends of God are a superior category to Prophets.[95] At the same time, he thereby reveals that the claim of superiority over Prophethood was recognized as a very serious charge to make against anyone.

In summary, contrary to what had been frequently assumed before the works of Radtke made Tirmidhī's writings widely accessible, nowhere in his *Sīrat al-awliyāʾ* does he argue that Friends of God as a category are at a level higher than Prophets. This is highlighted by his descriptions of the individual who ranks highest among the Friends of God in his system, as having "the Seal of Friendship with God." He himself is subordinate to the Seal of the Prophets, Muhammad. Though he is second only to the latter when it comes to sovereignty (*mulk*), he is said to have "almost joined the Prophets" (*dhālika min al-anbiyāʾ qarīb yukādu yulḥiquhum*), and interchanges between the heavenly treasuries used by Prophets and those used by the other Friends of God, making him a kind of honorary Prophet.[96] This strikes one as the best way to make someone the equivalent of a Prophet without articulating it in such terms.

The prominence among the earliest mystical writings of these two independently written treatises on Friendship with God may be interpreted as part of an ongoing response to a need felt by mystics at that time to accommodate the "Sealing of Prophethood" dogma. This seems to be confirmed by the efforts of these two ninth-century authors to find ways to reassure the reader that Friendship with God is not superior to Prophethood. It suggests that there had not previously been a strong concern to give deference to the rank of Prophet, which enabled the prior adoption of the view that Friends of God could actually be superior. However, they both seem to have been prompted to find a way to refute such notions by a more recent development seriously affecting the members of the mystical community. The consolidation of the dogma of the Sealing of Prophethood in all its religious aspects, including mystical supremacy, would be a strong contender for that external development which prompted Kharrāz and Tirmidhī's writings. Moreover, the difficulty that Kharrāz encountered shows that he was not engaged simply in correcting a marginal viewpoint, or a viewpoint that he necessarily disagreed completely with himself, while Tirmidhī reveals a reluctance to concede totally to the view that Prophethood both ended with Muhammad and was an altogether higher rank. After all, while he repeatedly reassures the interlocutor in his *Sīrat al-awliyāʾ* of the superiority of Prophethood over Friendship with

God, and assumes this as the basis of all his discussions, he nonetheless opts to stress Muhammad's distinctly higher rank in order to facilitate doing the same for a rank among the Friends of God; the bearer of this rank is in all aspects subordinate to Muhammad, but not necessarily to all the other Prophets.[97] While it may sound controversial from a later perspective, a similar assumption of virtual equivalence between Prophets and Friends of God has been seen in the writings of their influential contemporary in Baghdad Abū al-Qāsim al-Junayd (d. 297/910), who is normally portrayed as taking care to avoid being labeled a heretic.[98]

The key characteristics of Friends of God that emerge from this debate are the ability to receive divine communication, to be directed by God rather than the religious law, and to perform miracles. The influence of these early writings can be measured by the prominence in subsequent writings on Friendship with God of these same key characteristics, each of which forms the focus of an independent chapter in this book.

Friendship with God and Prophethood in Sarrāj's (d. 378/988) Kitāb al-Luma^c and Kalābādhī's (d. 380s/990s) Kitāb al-Ta^carruf

Although the treatises by Tirmidhī and Kharrāz are the major sources available for the ninth century, they may still leave a concern that they could represent relatively marginal positions for their time. It is important to consider other sources by way of comparison and to note that a contemporary as influential as Abū 'l-Qāsim al-Junayd makes negligible distinctions between Friends of God and Prophets, if any at all,[99] while the most influential Sufi of Basra at the time, Sahl al-Dīn al-Tustarī (d. 283/896), sees hardly any difference between the two categories either.[100]

A century had passed since the writings of Kharrāz and Tirmidhī before the oldest surviving Sufi manuals dealing with this topic were written. When it comes to the issue of *walāya*, the earliest Sufi manuals, namely Abū Naṣr al-Sarrāj's *Kitāb al-Luma^c fī al-taṣawwuf* and Abū Bakr al-Kalābādhī's *Kitāb al-Ta^carruf li-madhhab al-taṣawwuf*, treat the subject using contrasting methods, but both reveal that the same challenges were being faced at the time of writing.[101]

Sarrāj's method is to include within a series of chapters on those whom he considers to have erred (*man ghaliṭa*) among the Sufis a chapter on "those who err regarding Prophethood and Friendship with God." This is introduced as a refutation of those who consider Friendship with God as excelling Prophethood *(tafḍīl al-walāya ͨalā al-nubuwwa)*, and so he tackles the same concern Kharrāz had confronted a century earlier. This further confirms that holding such a view was not some passing fancy held by a fringe minority. Sarrāj ends this chapter by stating that "Friendship with God, including the holiest kind,[102] is illumined by the lights of Prophethood and never reaches that, let alone excels it" (*al-walāya wa'l-ṣiddīqiyya munawwara bi-anwār al-nubuwwa fa-lā tulḥiqu al-nubuwwa abadan fa-kayfa tufaḍḍilu ͨalayhā*).[103]

In the course of this chapter Sarrāj attempts a similar strategy to that of Kharrāz, in that he identifies the Moses and Khiḍr narrative in the Qur'an as being the cause of this doctrine. However, he attempts to tackle it in his own way: He instead opts to neutralize its effects by stating that God may choose to bless whomsoever He pleases with special qualities in a specific area or at a specific time, without them being consequently considered to have a superior status categorically. On the basis of the examples he refers to, such as Adam receiving prostrations from the angels, Muhammad splitting the moon and producing water from his fingers, and Mary receiving dates when in need of food, one would presume he means in this context that, seeing as Khiḍr is described as "one of Our servants, whom We gave mercy, and whom We taught knowledge from Our presence (*ladunnā*)" (Qur'an 18/65, quoted by Sarrāj here),[104] his superiority in the encounter with Moses was in this specific area of divine knowledge. Sarrāj's point would then be that, although this specific Qur'anic story portays Khiḍr as having superior knowledge in this encounter, this on its own does not mean that Friendship with God is superior to Prophethood in general. In fact, later in the same chapter, while discussing the issue of divine communication, he even asserts, "Had an iota of the lights of Moses appeared to Khiḍr, he would have become obliterated, but God veiled him from that as a restriction and to maintain a bonus for Moses, so understand that, God willing!"[105]

As shown above, Kharrāz had already attempted to subvert the more obvious interpretation of this Qur'anic story. Sarrāj's argument is perhaps more convincing than that of his predecessor, though he gives no support for his later assertion that the divine communication of Moses was so superior that it would have been too much for Khiḍr to bear. The obvious question it raises is where was that divine communication during his encounter with Khiḍr? As it stands, it remains simply a dogmatic declaration that is arguably contradicted by the famous Qur'anic story, where Khiḍr's divinely comunicated knowledge is beyond Moses's grasp, even if he argues that this should be regarded as a blip.

After Kharrāz's efforts, which Sarrāj presumably found too unconvincing to repeat, the wisdom of his attempt to tackle the same Qur'anic story head-on, albeit in a different manner, is questionable. The weaknesses in his own attempt can explain why later Sufi authors influenced heavily by his *al-Lumaͨ* opted not to follow him closely in this particular regard. However, one should not overlook a significant merit to Sarrāj's approach: he enables the possibility of attributing to Friends of God, like Khiḍr, Mary, Āṣaf, and others, instances of extreme closeness to God comparable with that of Prophets, all without this necessitating the view that Friends of God must be superior, or even the equals of Prophets. In light of this, it is worth pointing out that Sarrāj refers to Friendship with God repeatedly in the introduction of his *Lumaʿ*. He calls Sufis "*awliyāʾ*," mentions that they have received "the crown of Friendship with God," and calls the Prophet Muhammad "the sun of the Friends of God."[106] It is in the same introduction that he defines Sufi epistemology as consisting of "what is in the book of God, what has been transmitted about the Apostle of God, and what has been revealed in the hearts of God's Friends."[107] All of this confirms the central importance of Friendship with God for his understanding of Sufism, and helps clarify why he opted for an argument that does not limit the extent of temporary experiences of Friends of God, even as it gives reassurance that Friends of God cannot reach the status of Prophets.

In his *Kitāb al-Taʿarruf*, Abū Bakr al-Kalābādhī (d. ca. 380/990) does not devote an independent chapter to opinions about the relationship between *walāya* and *nubuwwa*, but instead comments on this issue within two separate chapters, on "the angels and the apostles (*rusul*)" and "the miracles (*karāmāt*) of the Friends of God," respectively. In the first of these chapters, after mentioning that there has been some debate between the relative ranks of angels and apostles or Prophets (using *nabī* and *rasūl* interchangeably), and concluding that Prophets are superior, he then adds:

> "They are completely unanimous that the Prophets are the most excellent (*afḍal*) among Mankind, and that there is no one who can be the equal of the Prophets in excellence, whether a holy person (*ṣiddīq*), a Friend of God (*walī*), or anyone else, however glorious his power or mighty his importance."[108]

By including this assertion in a chapter ostensibly about the relationship between angels and apostles, and acknowledging directly the existence of a debate only about that latter relationship, Kalābādhī spares himself from having to discuss the issue of Friendship with God's relationship to Prophethood with any depth and consistency. At the same time, he takes the opportunity to assert, as an aside, a reassuring viewpoint concerning it.

The subject of the second of these chapters is the opinion of Sufis about the miracles of the Friends of God (*qawluhum fī karāmāt al-awliyāʾ*). After affirming the ability of the Friends of God to perform miracles, albeit to a lesser degree than Prophets in the main,[109] he opens a discussion of Friends of God in general by mentioning the debate about whether or not they can be aware of their status. Kalābādhī at first offers two definitions of "*walāya*" by stating that "*walī*" can simply mean "friend" as opposed to "foe," as well as meaning someone who has "a *walāya* of exclusivity, election and choice, which a man must know about and realize" (*walāyat ikhtiṣāṣ wa-iṣṭifāʾ wa-iṣṭināʿ wa-hādhā tūjibu maʿrifatahā wa'l-taḥaqquq bihā*).[110] The purpose of his initial assertion that there is, in addition, a general and relatively mundane kind of *walāya*, making all believers Friends of God in some capacity, is perhaps in order to make the term seem less strange and suspicious, rather than for any polemical reasons, since it is all-embracing. Whatever the reason, it lends itself to serving as reassurance that the status and title should be accepted without undue concern.

The only direct comparison he makes between Prophets and the Friends of God is that the Prophet is immune to sin (*maʿṣūm*), but the Friend of God is "preserved" *(maḥfūẓ)* from regarding his carnal soul (*al-naẓar ilā nafsih*) as well as the bad traits of his human nature (*āfāt al-bashariyya*).[111] His concluding comment in this chapter is that only God knows the spiritual reality of the Friends of God:

> "The signs of Friendship with God are not simply external ornaments and their manifestation of extraordinary wonders, but rather its signs are in one's innermost depths, consisting of what God communicates there, which are things that only God and the person experiencing them in his innermost depths can know about."[112]

Overall, one could argue that Kalābādhī's aim seems to be to increase the acceptability of *walāya*. This is seen in his efforts to support the belief in the miracles of the Friends of God, and his preference to insist that one can only know the real meaning of a Friend of God if one is experiencing it as a Friend of God already. Rather than attempt a detailed comparison of their status with that of Prophets, Kalābādhī avoids engaging in the debate, or even elaborating on the reasoning behind his own affirmation of the superiority of Prophethood over Friendship with God. In contrast, Sarrāj takes on the challenge by dismissing as ill-founded the comparison of the different ranks on the basis of specific qualities attributed to Friends of God at a particular instance, including in the Qur'anic stories about Khiḍr, Mary, and Āṣaf. This strategy effectively preserves the superiority of Prophets while also enabling the attribution of the loftiest possible experiences in temporary form to the Friends of God. His observation that a follower cannot be superior to the one whom he is following furthermore guarantees that Muhammad could never be excelled by the Friends of God who come after him, even if they have comparable experiences.[113]

While it must be acknowledged that Sarrāj and Kalābādhī's works were introductions to Sufism, an entirely different genre to the monograph treatises by Kharrāz and Tirmidhī, they were nonetheless still confronting the same issues as their predecessors, making a comparison instructive. Their works are representative of their time, as even the traditionalist Sufi Abū Ṭālib al-Makkī (d. 386/996) emphasizes the affinity between Friends of God and Prophets, commenting in his *Qūt al-qulūb*: "[the Friends of God] are [Muhammad]'s brothers, because their hearts are in accord with the hearts of the Prophets" (*kānū ikhwānuh li-anna qulūbahum ʿalā qulūb al-anbiyāʾ*).[114] Clearly it was still a controversial subject, and also one they both considered too fundamental for Sufism simply to ignore in their introductory works. This can also be witnessed by the efforts of both of them to increase the acceptance of Friendship with God and some of the lofty experiences and abilities of those who possess this rank, rather than to deny or devalue them significantly. Such experiences and abilities of the Friends of God could reach even the level of Prophets for fleeting moments according to the less reticent Sarrāj, and Kalābādhī's ambiguous conclusion to his discussion leaves open many possibilities that are "things that only God and the person experiencing them in his innermost depths can know about."

Friendship with God and Prophethood in Qushayrī's (d. 465/1072) Risāla and Hujwīrī's (d. ca. 467/1075) Kashf al-Maḥjūb

Among his influential *Risāla*'s thematic chapters, Abū'l-Qāsim al-Qushayrī[115] includes one on Friendship with God (*walāya*), and a separate one on the miracles of the Friends of God (*karāmāt al-awliyāʾ*) that is by far the longest chapter in his entire work. He avoids confronting directly the question of the superiority of Prophets or Friends of God in the first of these chapters,[116] but at one point in the second of these chapters, which is actually about four times as long as any other chapter in the *Risāla,* he asks rhetorically:

> "How can it be allowed for these miracles [of the Friends of God] to be made manifest when they surpass those of the apostles (*muʿjizāt al-rusul*) in significance? Is it permissible to consider the Friends of God as superior to the Prophets (*hal yajūz tafḍīl al-awliyāʾ ʿalā al-anbiyāʾ*)?"[117]

Echoing Sarrāj's general observation about followers of a Prophet, Qushayrī answers this question in the negative by asserting that the miracles of the Friends of God are dependent on the Prophet whom they follow, and concludes that "the rank of the Friends of God does not reach that of the Prophets according to unanimous agreement on that" (*fa-ammā rutbat al-awliyā᾿ fa-lā tablugh rutbat al-anbiyā᾿ ᶜalayhim al-salām lil-ijmāᶜ al-munᶜaqid ᶜalā dhālik*).[118] This emphatic assertion notwithstanding, Qushayrī nonetheless chooses to argue for the possibility that the miracles of the Friends of God may be greater than those of the Prophets.[119] He also discusses whether or not a Friend of God can know that he is one and feel reassured about his final outcome. Like Kalābādhī before him, Qushayrī accepts that this is possible (see further chapter 4).

The importance of Friendship with God for Qushayrī's contemporary ᶜAlī Hujwīrī's[120] understanding of Sufism is obvious from the amount of attention he devotes to it in his *Kashf al-maḥjūb*. He discusses issues related to Friendship with God and Prophethood, including their relationship to each other, as part of his chapter on the Sufis who follow the teachings of Ḥakīm Tirmidhī, the so-called "Ḥakīmiyān." This chapter is five times as long as his other chapters devoted to Sufi groups, and one of the longest in the entire work. Hujwīrī credits Tirmidhī with being the first ever to use the term "*walāya*" for Friendship with God, and expresses his enthusiasm for this predecessor's theory, remarking: "Understand that the foundation of the Sufi path and gnosis (*qāᶜida wa-asās-i ṭarīqat-i taṣawwuf wa-maᶜrifat*) is entirely based on Friendship with God and its affirmation."[121]

Hujwīrī tackles the relationship between Friendship with God and Prophethood head-on, in the section of this chapter entitled "the discourse concerning the superiority of Prophets over Friends of God" (*al-kalām fī tafḍīl al-anbiyā᾿ ᶜalā al-awliyā᾿*). However, unlike Kharrāz and Sarrāj before him, he does not mention the story of Moses and Khiḍr at all in this discussion, which he begins with the following statement:

> In accordance with the agreement of all leaders on this path, in all moments and states the Friends of God are followers (*mutābiᶜān*) of the Prophets and confirmers (*muṣaddiqān*) of their mission. Moreover, Prophets are superior to Friends of God, seeing as the endpoint of Friendship with God is the start of Prophethood.[122]

In addition to this declaration that "the endpoint of Friendship with God is the start of Prophethood" (*nihāyat-i walāyat bidāyat-i nubuwwat buwad*), Hujwīrī consistently compares the relationship between Prophets and Friends of God in ways that assert the superiority of the Prophets but stop short of attributing to them a level that is completely unattainable by Friends of God. Thus when favoring the viewpoint that miracles are performed while in an intoxicated state, he asserts that Prophets are continually in such a state while Friends of God are only temporarily so, being like ordinary people for the rest of the time. He concludes this argument by asserting:

> "The station of sobriety (*ṣaḥw*) of the Friends of God is the level of the ordinary people (*ʿawwām*), while the station of their intoxication (*sukr*) is the level of the Prophets."[123]

Similarly, Hujwīrī comments that while Friendship with God has a beginning and an end Prophethood does not. The end of Friendship with God is union (*jamʿ*), and Prophethood is always in union (*jamʿ*), with the Prophets having been part of God's knowledge and will before they came to exist.[124] This could be interpreted as regarding Friends of God as having the potential to reach eventually the same station that Prophets hold eternally. That is to say, it opens the possibility to interpret his repeated declaration that "the endpoint of Friendship with God is the start of Prophethood" as meaning that a Friend of God can eventually reach an overlapping level with the Prophets, albeit one that is temporary in contrast to their permanent enjoyment of that level. This may well have been influenced by Sarrāj's earlier argument that Friends of God have the same level of experiences as Prophets (or even higher), but only fleetingly, seeing as much of the *Kashf al-maḥjūb* is influenced by the *Lumaʿ*.

This pair of highly influential Sufi manuals from the eleventh century reveal in their own distinctive ways that the possibility for Friendship with God to surpass Prophethood remained a viewpoint requiring an articulated refutation by their irenic authors. While Qushayrī opts to refer only briefly to the debate in direct terms, preferring instead to focus on the less threatening topic of miracles, Hujwīrī presents, as a refutation of that viewpoint, a distinction which still accommodates Friends of God at the same level of Prophets, albeit temporarily. Nonetheless, by opting to present his argument as one that affirms the superiority of Prophethood over Friendship with God, Hujwīrī indicates in his own distinctive way the undesirability of being identified with a viewpoint that elevates Friends of God threateningly high, which is all too clear from Qushayrī's strategy. It should also be noted that, although Hujwīrī expresses his admiration for Tirmidhī at the beginning of his discussion of this topic, and even locates it in the context of a discussion of the latter's followers, he does not present fundamental aspects of his viewpoints. There is no mention of the Seal of Friendship with God (although Hujwīrī does present his own more elaborate hierarchy), nor the continuation of "parts of Prophethood."[125]

Conclusions

The importance of appreciating the different historical contexts for writings about the relationship between Prophets and Friends of God is perhaps highlighted most strongly by the analysis of those works that preceded the Sufi manuals: they reveal that the earliest debate among mystics was whether or not the Friends of God were actually superior to the Prophets. Kharrāz offers a fairly unconvincing critique of such a position, which includes some concessions to superior characteristics among Friends of God, while Tirmidhī repeatedly reassures his interlocutor that he is not placing the Friends of God above Prophets, in the course of recounting a theory that sees them as being virtually at the same level. This debate continues to be brought up even in the manuals of Qushayrī and Hujwīrī two centuries later, despite the fact that these two works were preoccupied with integrating Sufism with the religious system of the theologians and jurists.

Sarrāj and Hujwīrī among the authors of Sufi manuals in the tenth and eleventh centuries continued to address this debate directly. An argument for the superiority of Prophets is set forth by Sarrāj, which nonetheless concedes that Friends of God can have the same level of experience as Prophets at least fleetingly, and this position is reiterated to a large extent by Hujwīrī in his *Kashf al-maḥjūb*. To their credit, none of the irenic authors actually shies away from emphasizing how important they regard Friendship with God, although it is only Sarrāj and Hujwīrī among them who go as far as to leave open the possibility that the Friends of God can reach the same level as Prophets. The fact that this pair did not simply settle for a more deferential view is in itself a sign that their works are much more multidimensional than mere apologetics.[126]

If there is one thing that the exploration of the treatment of this topic in these works has revealed, it is that the debate about the relative status of Prophets and Friends of God was never a simple one to answer for mystics. The difficulty is due to the challenge of affirming that Prophets are superior without at the same time downgrading the status of the Friend of God, which they considered to be the very basis of their mystical tradition. The effect on Rumi when he was asked the question "Was Abū Yazīd greater or Muhammad?" according to that biographical story dramatizes the dilemma involved. When the question is left without elaboration like this, the dramatization works on the assumption that Rumi too considered Friendship with God the basis of his mysticism, as represented here by Abū Yazīd, who after all was in his view the very greatest of the past Friends of God.[127] At the same time, however, he did not wish to acclaim anyone as being greater than the Prophet Muhammad.

Toward the beginning of this chapter I suggested that the question "Was Abū Yazīd greater or Muhammad?" would not have seemed a challenging one to most people in thirteenth-century Konya. This chapter demonstrates that, as a Sufi, Rumi belonged to the tradition that would have seen the difference between a Prophet and a Friend of God as being as negligible as possible. This can explain why such a question could have been regarded by biographers as the kind capable of making him swoon. More significantly, Rumi's didactic writings also confirm that he considered any differences between them too negligible to articulate, other than in the context of rebuking a contemporary for self-glorification.

Rumi stands apart in particular for considering Friendship with God to be flexible and dynamic, with aspirants being capable of partaking in it while aiming to become fully fledged Friends of God. The attempt by Tirmidhī to divide Friends of God into different categories may be an indication that the earliest mystics had also defined them very accommodatingly, especially since his contemporary Kharrāz uses the term for his readers collectively. "Friend of God" (*walī Allāh*) may well have been an earlier designation of Muslim mystics than "Sufi," which is already conceded by the tradition to be one that was adopted at a relatively late stage.[128] One possible reason for adopting a new designation may well have been the fact that the rank of "*walī Allāh*" had become the subject of controversy, but this can be no more than conjecture because of the limited material available.

In the course of this exploration, it has also become apparent that, even though it is very far from the level which is reached in later Sufism, Rumi exceptionalizes Muhammad from the other Prophets to a greater degree than most of the authors of the formative texts do. Only Tirmidhī veers to any degree in this direction, and that is for the specific needs of his theory of the Seal of Friendship with God. Therefore, it would appear that, by the thirteenth century, it had become more customary to attribute to Muhammad a distinctly higher status than the other Prophets and the Friends of God. The exceptionalization of the Prophet Muhammad facilitates the argument for increased parity between Friends of God and other Prophets, without leading to claims that the former are superior as a category to the latter. As Gerald Elmore has put it in reference to Ibn ʿArabī and his followers, who argue that Friends of God after Muhammad can even be superior to the Prophets who came before him (i.e., all Prophets except him), "[I]n lifting up their super-prophet, in reality the Sufis were simply crowning their own apotheosis."[129]

Since the different historical context in which Rumi lived has been specified, it would be instructive to have a contemporary point of comparison close to his locale. His predecessor in Anatolia, Najm al-Dīn "Dāya" Rāzī (d. 654/1256), who was also of Persian origin, gives some comparable teachings to Rumi. His exceptionalization of the Prophet Muhammad is expressed emphatically in the chapter of his *Mirṣād al-ʿIbād* on "The Abrogation of Religions and the Sealing of Prophethood by Muhammad," which begins with a citation of the Seal of the Prophets verse in the Qur'an (33/40) and Muhammad's saying, "I excel the other Prophets in six ways *(faḍḍaltu ʿalā al-anbiyāʾ bi-sitta)*."[130] While exceptionalizing Muhammad, Rāzī is able to assert the superiority of Khiḍr in his encounter with Moses and to take the position that Moses was not only sent to him in order to learn divine knowledge (*ʿilm-i ladunnī*), but also that he had previously heard the speech (*kalām*) of God only by means of intermediaries, such as the burning bush or a voice, even if it had appeared to be direct like Khiḍr's (and Muhammad's) knowledge.[131]

It is surely no coincidence that Rāzī's favorable comparison of Khiḍr with Moses is given in his chapter on "the station, conditions and attributes of the Sufi master," for which their relationship serves as the Qur'anic paradigm. The master-disciple relationship would also explain Rumi's disinclination to suggest that Friends of God after the Prophets are deficient in terms of knowledge and closeness to God, as well as the general tendency among Sufis from the medieval period onward of "crowning their own apotheosis." It is supported especially by his aforementioned story in the fifth book of *The Masnavi* about the man who claimed to be a Prophet after Muhammad: His comments reveal that the aim of this story is to exhort his contemporaries to have as strong a faith as possible in the Friends of God among them, and not be so quick to reject the possibility that they may have just as lofty characteristics as the Prophets. What seemed to have been Rumi's priority is for mystic aspirants to follow their masters absolutely, avoiding even the temptation to defer to scriptures or images of past Prophets instead. This is because it was believed to be the most effective way of overcoming the self and completing the Sufi path.[132] The theoretical formulations structured for the benefit of religious dogma would necessarily take second place in such practical mystical instruction.

3

Divine Communication

> Mawlana's mystic book *The Masnavi*
> Is the Qur'an in Persian poetry.
> How to describe that man of lofty station?
> Though not a Prophet, he brought revelation.
>
> (Anon)

It is common in the Persian-speaking world to hear Rumi's *Masnavi* being referred to as "The Qur'an in Persian," which has been articulated in the poem cited above as "*qur'ān dar zabān-i pahlawī.*" For most people, this serves simply as an appropriate way of expressing the highest possible praise for a poem with religious content. Some have also pointed to the fact that *The Masnavi* contains an extraordinarily high number of Qur'anic citations as the reason for this particular epithet.[1] This feature of *The Masnavi* has even prompted, since at least as early as half a century after Rumi's passing, the identification of it as a form of commentary on the Qur'an, but that was disapproved as too modest for such a poem in a saying attributed to Rumi himself (see p. 87).

The above-quoted verses themselves have uncertain origins, the earliest written record having been identified as a nineteenth-century Indian commentary on *The Masnavi.*[2] However, this is of less consequence than one might assume, since the first comparison of Rumi's poem with the Qur'an is as old and authentic as it could possibly be because it is found in *The Masnavi* itself.[3]

The second couplet cited above expands on the first couplet because the Qur'an is considered by Muslims to be one of the divinely communicated books of revelation (*kitāb*, pl. *kutub*), which are sent down by God exclusively through His Prophets.[4] Therefore, the poet who calls *The Masnavi* a divinely communicated book of revelation must wonder what that makes Rumi when Islamic dogma accepts no Prophets after Muhammad. At a popular level, the enigma about *The Masnavi* expressed in these verses playfully points to it having a divine quality that defies logic and expectation. At a mystical level, however, it could be argued that this enigma neatly encapsulates the belief among Sufis in the continuity of divine communication.[5] It is therefore surely no coincidence that Rumi's biographical tradition from its early stages presented his poetry emphatically as the product of divine communication, one which Rumi recited while his deputy Ḥusām al-Dīn Chalabī recorded it in writing, in a manner echoing the revelation of the Qur'an to the Prophet Muhammad.[6] This process is also alluded to in *The Masnavi* itself, which includes the following verse: Ḥusām al-Dīn, please fetch a scrap or two/And write about the guide what I tell you![7]

The question to be explored in this chapter is the position that Rumi himself takes in relation to the early Sufi theorists concerning the nature of the divine communication received by Friends of God after the mission of the Prophet Muhammad, and, as an extension of that, his comparison of his own *Masnavi* with the Qur'an.

Rumi's Teachings on the Friend of God's Divine Communication

It would not be considered a surprising choice by most readers of Rumi's poetry if one were to suggest that the most distinctive characteristic of his mysticism is his celebration of the continual communication of God with His creation. As one of his most famous lyrical poems expresses it:

> Each breath from all sides comes love's voice's sound.
> We're going to the heavens! Who'd like to look around?[8]

The notion that divine communication is ubiquitous and not limited to the Qur'an is a viewpoint Rumi expresses very frequently, including in the following passage in the *Fīhi mā fīh*, where he refers to one of the Qur'an's own verses for corroboration. It appears immediately after a critique of a Qur'an-reciter who knows only its form and rejects anything else, including its true meaning:

> *Say: "If the ocean were ink for the words (kalimāt) of my Lord, the entire ocean would be used up before my Lord's words would be"* (Qur'an 18/109). Now, with just 50 drams of ink one can write out the Qur'an, so this

is just a symbol of God's knowledge, and not the entirety of it. An apothecary has put a small amount of medicine in a paper wrapper, and you say that his whole shop is here—that is idiotic! In the eras of Moses and Jesus and others, the Qur'an existed: God's speech (*kalām-i khudā*) was there, but it was not in Arabic.[9]

What is significant about this passage is Rumi's assertion that God's speech (*kalām-i khudā*) is not limited to the Qur'an revealed in Arabic to Muhammad, but rather it is possible for it to be received at other times and in other languages. Although here he only identifies the earlier Prophets, Moses and Jesus, whom all Muslims regard as Prophets and bearers of holy books of divine communication, Rumi's underlying message is that God's knowledge cannot be limited. In this way, it is in harmony with his stress elsewhere that divine communication is by nature continual and unrestricted.

An instance where Rumi names a specific individual in receipt of the same kind of divine communication as Prophets after the revelation of the Qur'an to Muhammad can be found in the fourth book of *The Masnavi*. Here, Rumi presents a miracle story in which Bāyazīd Basṭāmī (d. 234/848, or 261/875) predicts the future birth of Abu'l-Ḥasan Kharaqānī (d. 425/1033) at a particular location, by means of a scent he perceives there. Rumi compares this specifically with the miracle story of the Prophet Muhammad perceiving a scent from Yemen, where Uways al-Qaranī had become a devoted follower of his without having ever met him. This miracle story is important not only because Rumi makes no distinction between the miracle of Bāyazīd and that of Muhammad,[10] but, more significantly for the present context, because he describes the Friend of God's knowledge in the following terms:

The Tablet that's Preserved was his director—
From what is that "preserved"? From any error.
Not through stars, magic, or one's dreams at night,
But *waḥy-i ḥaqq*, and He knows best what's right!
Sufis may call it mere "heart-inspiration,"
To hide it from the general population.
It's "inspiration of the heart," since He
Is manifest there—it's thus error-free.
Believer, *through God's light* you now can see;
From error you have full immunity![11]

The above passage identifies the source of the ninth-century Sufi Bāyazīd's knowledge as the Qur'anic "Preserved Tablet" (*lawḥ-i maḥfūẓ*, based on 85/22), the heavenly tablet considered in Islamic theology to be the origin of the books of revelation brought by Prophets.[12] In addition, Rumi refers to the use of two alternative terms for the divine communication received by Sufi Friends of God like Bāyazīd: "communication from God" (*waḥy-i ḥaqq*) and "inspiration (or communication) from the heart" (*waḥy-i dil*). He considers the first term accurate and associates it with the divine communication of the Prophets, as the term "*waḥy*" on its own like this and unqualified had already been considered in earlier Muslim theological discussions (including among Sufis).[13] However, Rumi asserts that even when the term "*waḥy-i dil*" is used instead for Friends of God like Bāyazīd, this is simply as a disguise, to avoid controversy among the general population (*az pay-i rū-pūsh-i ʿāmma*). Presumably this term would be more acceptable to them because it implies something less directly from God, the Truth (*ḥaqq*), than *waḥy-i ḥaqq*. Nonetheless, Rumi argues that the use of the less controversial term can also be considered accurate because, according to a sacred hadith, God disclosed to Muhammad that the heart is where He reveals himself.[14] That is to say, the meaning of *waḥy-i dil* is effectively the same as *waḥy-i ḥaqq* because God is in the heart of the Friend of God.[15] Rumi hereby declares that the difference is simply a matter of semantics.

It is worth noting that, although he asserts that the divine communication received by Bāyazīd is the same kind in reality as that received by the Prophet, even if a different term is used for it, Rumi alludes implicitly to an important distinction between the divine communication received by Muhammad and that received by a Friend of God: By stating that Sufis use a different term in order to hide the truth from ordinary people, he not only acknowledges that it was controversial to say that theirs was the same as that of the Prophets but he also reveals that the Friend of God's divine communication is not something that all Muslims need to be persuaded to accept. While the divine origins of the Qur'an must be accepted according to the religion's theological dogmas, the divine communication and authority of the Friends of God did not require the same universal allegiance—Rumi implies that fellow mystics alone need to understand that their divine communication is at the same level, and that mystics were not interested in the allegiance of the masses.

Rumi expressed this view about the continuity of the highest form of divine communication even after the passing of the Prophet Muhammad, and the end of the cycle of Prophethood this had signaled according to Islamic dogma established long before his time, not only in poetry about Bāyazīd but also orally during his teaching sessions with his disciples. In the thirty-first chapter of the *Fīhi mā fīh* he emphasizes, even more emphatically than seen above, his opinion that the divine communication of the Friends of God is the same as that of the Prophets, even if it is conventionally called something different:

> When it is stated that, after Muhammad and the other Prophets, *waḥy* is not sent down to other people, that is not the case. It is simply not called "*waḥy.*" But this is what was meant when the Prophet said, "The believer sees by the light of God." When one sees by God's light, one sees everything: the first, the last, the absent, and the present, since nothing is veiled from God's light. Thus, what is meant is *waḥy* even though it is not called "*waḥy*" (*pas maʿnī waḥy hast agarchi ān-rā waḥy nakhwānand*).[16]

This passage is found immediately after an anecdote about Bāyazīd explaining that God wanted to perfect him by enabling him to attain total union (*waṣl-i kullī*). It is therefore probably no coincidence that this mention of Rumi's favorite Sufi Friend of God from the past is followed by a reiteration of his conviction in the ongoing nature of divine communication, which stresses again that there is no difference between that of the Prophet and that of the Friend of God in spite of the use of different terms. Moreover, in this example he cites once more the saying of the Prophet Muhammad "The believer sees by the light of God," which had been commonly used by Sufis as confirmation of their miraculous knowledge.[17] Thus on the authority of the final Prophet himself, Rumi argues that there can be no substantial distinction between different levels of divine communication when the means of perception is the light of God, from which nothing can remain hidden.

From Rumi's assertion that his favorite Sufi hero Bāyazīd received the same divine communication as the Prophets, one would be justified in wondering whether Rumi might have expressed similar thoughts in relation to himself and *The Masnavi*, especially in view of the emphasis in the hagiographical tradition on the divine communication behind it. In fact, Rumi refers to his much celebrated magnum opus in such terms on several occasions, and not only in the introduction of the work, where it is a convention in the *mathnawī* form of poetry to include hyperbolic praise. His longest and most systematic argument for the divinely communicated nature of *The Masnavi* is found in a passage toward the end of the third book. This sixty-four verse passage is divided into six short sections,[18] the first of which is presented under the rubric "Mention of the malicious thought of those who lack understanding." The "malicious thought" referred to here is criticism of his *Masnavi* and mockery of the poem as a trivial collection of fables, which appears to be the prompt for his discussion of *The Masnavī* and its loftiness in comparison with the Qur'an. Rumi begins by taking solace in the observation by his predecessor Sanāʾī (d. 525/1131) that even the Qur'an was criticized in this way by contemporaries of the Prophet who did not have the capacity to see beyond its outer form. This initial discussion of criticism directed against *The Masnavi* is resumed in the last of the six sections that make up this passage, which rounds it off with a reference, in its very last verse, back to the specific piece of advice from Sanāʾī (see below).

The second section in this passage is a commentary on the Prophet Muhammad's statement that the Qur'an has an inner aspect as well as an outer form, and that this inner aspect has seven further levels. This is therefore an expansion on the theme of failing to appreciate the worth of a text due to inability to see beyond its outward form, which was initiated by the reference to the critic of his own poem. Rumi illustrates his argument with the Qur'anic example of Satan (2/30–34): Unable to perceive Adam's spiritual rank, he is blamed for showing dismissive condescension toward him on the basis of his outer form.

The third and fourth sections of this passage focus on Prophets and Friends of God. In the third section, Rumi argues that when Prophets and Friends of God retreat it is not because they feel any need to hide from people. Like the Qur'an and *The Masnavi*, these holy men should not be judged merely on the basis of their modest outward appearance, for they are inwardly loftier than the heavens. The fourth section compares Friends of God with the rod of Moses and the incantations of Jesus; though they may seem like just another stick or everyday words, they are both in reality miraculously powerful because they are directed by God.

These initial four sections can be seen as preparing the ground for the final and most important two sections of this passage, in that they demonstrate the importance of perceiving the inner value of both holy texts and holy men even if they should appear modest outwardly. The fifth section is presented under the rubric "the exegesis of the Qur'anic verse: 'O hills and birds, repeat his praise!'" What this verse represents in the Qur'an is God's command to the hills and birds to repeat David's Psalms in harmony with him. David's Psalms (*zabūr*) are of course one of the four Muslim "books of revelation" (*kutub*), and so what Rumi is pointing out is that even birds and hills can receive a book of revelation from God by His command. Because of its key role in this passage, I have translated this section below in its entirety:

> Glory made David's face appear so bright;
> Hills in devotion wept at such a sight.
> The hill joined Prophet David when he'd sing,

Both minstrels, drunk with deep love for their king;
When the command "*Repeat his praise!*" first came
The two became one voice, their song the same.
God told him, "Separation you have known,
Cut off from good friends for my sake alone,
A stranger with no close associate,
In whose heart flames of longing have been lit;
You seek companions, minstrels, singers too—
Eternal God presents these hills to you."
He makes them singers who can sing so well;
He makes these hills fall drunken in a spell,
So you'll know God can make a mere hill sing
And God's Friends too experience such a thing—
Through God's creation melodies each hears:
Their sound each moment reaches God's Friend's ears,
Unheard by men in the vicinity—
He who has faith in him lives joyfully!
Inside his soul he hears inspired words too,
Although those sitting near him have no clue!
Questions and answers at a rapid pace
Enter your heart from realms beyond all space;
Though you can hear them, others cannot hear,
Even if they should bring their own ears near.
Deaf man, I know your ears do not perceive;
You've seen the outward signs—why not believe?[19]

We have already seen that Rumi considers the main obstacle to accepting that Friends of God can receive the same kind of divine communication as Prophets to be their unassuming outward appearance, an issue of considerable importance to him throughout his writings. By pointing out that mere hills can be inspired by God to sing the Psalms, as the Qur'an itself affirms, Rumi argues that there should be no surprise that our contemporaries who have reached proximity to God can also receive the same order of divine communication as Prophets. This section therefore serves to affirm that divine communication Prophets receive can also be received by Friends of God, should God choose to bestow it on them.

As mentioned previously, Rumi refers back to Sanāʾī in the final section of this passage, which follows immediately after this exegesis. Presented under the rubric "the answer to the one who criticized *The Masnavi* due to deficient understanding," this final section is translated below:

Deriding dog! You're barking. Sense you lack!
You're mocking the Qur'an behind its back!
This is no lion from which you can flee
And save your faith from its ferocity.
Till Resurrection the Qur'an declares:
"You slaves of ignorance once had such airs,
Reckoning me a fable none should heed,
Sowing your unbelief and mocking's seed—
What you were scoffing at you now can view:
The transient, worthless fairy tale is you!
I am God's Speech, subsisting through His Essence,
The purest gem, food for the soul's transcendence!
I am the sun's light shining on you now,
Though I've not parted that sun anyhow."
The Water of Life's spring is here, behold!
I free the mystic lovers from death's hold.
If your vile greed had not caused such a smell,
God would have poured drops on your grave as well.
No, I'll heed the advice from Sanā'ī—
I won't let critics' comments bother me.[20]

Rumi begins this final section in an extraordinary manner. He insults the skeptic who had rudely criticized his *Masnavi*, and accuses this "dog" of effectively criticizing the Qur'an behind its back (*ay sag-i ṭā'in tu aw-aw mīkunī/ naqd-i qur'ān-rā birūn-shaw mīkunī*). But how can criticizing *The Masnavi* be the same as criticizing the Qur'an behind its back? In view of the section that immediately precedes it, this seems to be Rumi's way of stressing memorably the point that his poem is also a product of divine communication, and therefore shares the same origins as the Qur'an. This is a significant development from the first section of the passage, where they were described as simply sharing the same fate of being criticized by superficial readers. It has been made possible by the precision with which Rumi has constructed his argument through the six successive sections of this passage, so as to reveal the folly of skepticism on the basis of appearances, in particular with regard to the possibility that Friends of God have the ability to receive the same divine communication as Prophets.

The last three couplets in this passage have caused editors much difficulty. Since there is no punctuation in medieval Persian texts, editors must themselves choose where to insert it. A common additional difficulty in *The Masnavi* is identifying the point where one character's speech ends and another's (or Rumi's own reflection) begins.[21] Often it is not very consequential, but in this case there is much at stake. In the above translation, I have followed the punctuation provided in the edition prepared by Mohammad Estelami.[22] The reference to mystic lovers (*ʿāshiqān*) would certainly lead most readers to agree with his decision, let alone the transition signaled by "*nak man-am*" at the start of verse 4292. Moreover, there is another compelling reason why his punctuation is correct, and that is the use of the Qur'anic term "*yanbūʿ*" (spring) in that same couplet. This is an unusual word that occurs only once in the Qur'an in this singular form; significantly, the context in which it is found is where those who refuse to believe that the Qur'an recited by Muhammad originates with God are described as follows: "And they say, 'We will not believe you unless you make a spring (*yanbūʿ*) gush forth from the earth for us" (Qur'an 17/90).

The use of this unusual term taken from this particular verse in the Qur'an is of course wholly appropriate for this context in *The Masnavi*, where Rumi is discussing skeptics. It even echoes the comparison of the Friend of God with Moses's rod and Jesus's spells in an earlier section of this carefully constructed passage. He compares himself, as a Friend of God to whom *The Masnavi* has been revealed, with the miraculous proof that the skeptical unbelievers demanded before they would believe in the Qur'an revealed to Muhammad; this is achieved by the way he miraculously releases mystic lovers from death, as if by a spring from the Water of Life. By using the term "*yanbūʿ*," Rumi implies that he himself serves as a miraculous confirmation of the divine origins of the Qur'an, because his divinely communicated poem is a miracle of the same origin.

It should be noted that Rumi also refers more specifically to the divinely communicated nature of his extemporaneous teachings in both his *Masnavi* and the *Fīhi mā fīh*. In addition to the references to the process of recording his *Masnavi* into writing mentioned above, Rumi also expresses this point during his teaching sessions. In the fifty-ninth chapter of the *Fīhi mā fīh*, he remarks:

> My speech is not under my control, and this frustrates me because I want to give my friends a homily (*mawʿiẓa*) but my speech will not comply—this is why I am frustrated. However, the fact that my speech is higher than me, and I am controlled (*maḥkūm*) by Him, makes me happy; this is because any speech which God utters brings life to wherever it reaches and has other tremendous effects: "*You did not throw when you threw, but rather God threw*" (Qur'an 8/17). An arrow that flies out of God's bow cannot be blocked by any shield or armour. This is why I am happy.[23]

Whereas his biographical tradition repeatedly stresses the divinely communicated nature of his poetry, Rumi appears to regard such divine communication to be more broad ranging. That is to say, at least his speech at his teaching-circles must be added to his divinely communicated writings. Moreover, the primary message of the above passage is that Rumi is not in control of his speech, with divinely communicated speech arriving only when it chooses to, and not necessarily when Rumi wishes it to arrive. This is in accord with the concept of divine communication in the traditional biography of the Prophet Muhammad as an involuntary process.[24]

A secondary message in the above discourse by Rumi is that the divinely communicated speech that reaches him is miraculously powerful, bringing about tremendous effects which cannot be resisted, comparable with Moses's rod and Jesus's spells. Appropriately then, the Qur'anic verse cited here (8:17: "You did not throw when you threw") is the one traditionally interpreted as referring to Muhammad's action of throwing pebbles in the direction of enemy forces before the Battle of Badr, which the Muslims subsequently won against all odds with only a fraction of the number of men of their Meccan foes. Sufis before Rumi had already begun to use this same Qur'anic verse in support of the theory of the annihilation of the Sufi in God,[25] even though it is contextualized differently within the biography of the Prophet Muhammad. The divinely communicated nature of Rumi's speech is thereby implicitly viewed as a consequence of his self-annihilation and performance of acts under compulsion by God rather than at his own choosing.

The tremendous effects of divine communication are referred to by Rumi also in his extraordinary story about the man who claimed to be a Prophet after Muhammad. In this story, which is found in the fifth book of *The Masnavi,* Rumi describes how a man tells his community that he has become a Prophet, with the implication that this is set after the mission of Muhammad because he cites the Qur'an as proof, and causes extreme outrage. The following passage from the story describes the dialogue between him and the king of his nation, who tries to resolve the crisis by talking him out of his claims:

> The king asked him, "What's *waḥy* for such a fuss?
> What's gained by Prophets that's so marvelous?"
> "What does he not achieve?" the man replied,
> "What fortune does he not gain far and wide?
> And though the Prophet's *waḥy* is not a treasure
> It's not less than the bee's by any measure:
> When '*God inspired the bee*,'[26] its home thereafter

Was filled completely with the sweetest halva.
By means of God's *waḥy*'s light, it then transformed
The world with wax and honey, which it formed.
We honored[27] Man and he soars high—so please
Don't try to claim his *waḥy*'s less than a bee's!"[28]

The outrage of the community, who had demanded the claimant's head, is what has led the king to try to talk him out of his claim by suggesting it is no great thing to be a Prophet anyway. Therefore, the most extraordinary aspect of this whole story is that Rumi takes the side of the claimant by putting in his mouth a compelling argument that the receipt of divine communication by a man should not be denied when even the humble bee is described in the Qur'an as receiving it. He also criticizes the deniers of the man's claims for being too skeptical about their contemporary's spiritual claims simply because of their own selfish nature.

It is also worth noting that in this story the only quality of Prophethood discussed is the receipt of divine communication. No suggestion is made by the claimant that he is bringing a new religion and no attempt is made by him to perform other miracles. Divine communication is therefore singled out here as the central characteristic of Prophets, the one valued the most by the claimant, and also arguably the one men can continue to receive if even a bee can receive it. This final point is supported with the authority of the Qur'an, which is thereby used to authenticate divine communication of the same category as itself (usually termed "*waḥy*") outside its own covers. Therefore, although this story lacks support from Rumi's corpus of writings for the interpretation that he believed in the continuation of Prophethood in all its aspects, one can nonetheless find plenty of corroboration for his belief in the continuity of divine communication of the highest kind, even chronologically after Muhammad's Qur'an, and this appears to be the key characteristic of Prophethood from his perspective.

In summary, the implication in Rumi's hagiographical tradition that *The Masnavi* was of divine origin finds support in the content of the poem itself. Rumi unambiguously asserts that Friends of God can receive the same level of divine communication as Prophets, and argues specifically that *The Masnavi* is from the same source as the Qur'an. Furthermore, Rumi consistently dismisses any suggestion that the divine communication received by Friends of God is of a different class to the divine communication received by Prophets. He even volunteers the explanation that different terms are used for them simply so as to avoid disturbing people with insufficient understanding. As mentioned above, this explanation in itself points implicitly to a real distinction between the two types of divine communication: The divine communication of the Prophets is for everyone to accept because the religion of Islam demands this, while that of the Friends of God is for mystics who can perceive it, and it is in fact too challenging for people outside of their circle to accept. From another perspective, by comparing his *Masnavi* with the Qur'an, he could be interpreted as implying that the latter (as well as other holy books of revelation) has been classified as exceptional for dogmatic purposes. According to Rumi, in reality the Light of God cannot be divided hierarchically as such dogmas would imply. Finally, it should be mentioned that Rumi not only dismisses distinctions between the divine communication of the Friends of God and that of the Prophets but also does not articulate a distinction between these and others kinds of divine promptings and inspirations.

One could be forgiven for finding them surprising teachings about divine communication for a Muslim mystic because of the emphasis on the closure of divine communication to Prophets after the Qur'an. This has indeed been reinforced by the marking of a distinction in early Sufi writings between the divine communication of a Prophet and that of a Friend of God, with deference being given to the former. However, there is evidence in the oldest surviving writings on this topic that Rumi's teachings were neither unprecedented nor extreme, as the next section of this chapter will demonstrate.

Divine communication in Kharrāz's (d. ca. 286/899) al-Kashf wa'l-bayān and Tirmidhī's (d. between 295–300/905–910) Sīrat al-awliyā'

The receipt of divine communication has been considered a principal characteristic of Friends of God, similarly to Prophets, not just by Rumi, but since the ninth century, when the oldest surviving mystical writings on this topic were produced. The ninth-century treatises on Friendship with God reveal that the status of the divine communication of the Friend of God in relation to that of a Prophet had become one of the most contentious issues at that time. For instance, one could argue that in the course of his effort to refute the view of "a group of Sufis" (*qawm min ahl al-taṣawwuf*) that Friendship with God is superior to Prophethood, Abū Saʿīd al-Kharrāz struggles most with the task of ranking their divine communication.[29] He identifies the Qur'anic story about Moses and Khiḍr as the basis of the overall viewpoint he aims to refute,[30] and since this story specifically portrays the Prophet Moses as seeking to gain knowledge from Khiḍr, who had received it directly from God's presence, it is not difficult to see how it could support the viewpoint that the divine communication of the Friends of God is superior to that of the Prophets.[31]

As shown in chapter 2 above, Kharrāz wishes to refute this viewpoint, and so he opts to argue for a novel interpretation of the famous Qur'anic story. What is most significant about his discussion therefore is that it implies that the Moses and Khiḍr paradigm, because of its implication that Khiḍr had superior knowledge, represented a formidable argument of his opponents. Moreover, as shown also in chapter 2 above, the other viewpoint that Kharrāz implies was a formidable one of his opponents is that "the allusion of God's Friends is more tender than the expression of the Prophets" (*ishārat al-awliyā° araqq min ʿibārat al-anbiyā°*).[32] Although Kharrāz provides an explanation for this, his mere concession of it, in combination with his struggle to reinterpret the Moses and Khiḍr story, would suggest that the divine communication of the Friend of God was the key factor in debates about superiority.[33] This is further confirmed by the fact that he cites a relatively lengthy direct comparison of the different categories of divine communication. Since his citation of the opinion of "one group of God's Friends," which is presented below, asserts that the highest form is reserved exclusively for the Prophets, it makes one wonder why he would have engaged at all with the comparison of allusions of Friends of God and expressions of Prophets, unless it had become an unavoidable issue.

> One group of God's Friends says that "God spoke to Moses directly" (Qur'an 4/164), and spoke to the Prophets with divine communication through the angels (*waḥy al-malā°ika*), and spoke to the believers with *ilhām* from Him the same way that He communicated with the Mother of Moses when he said: "We communicated (*awḥaynā*) with the Mother of Moses" (20/38). His *waḥy* to her was His command to her by means of *ilhām*: "Put him out in the basket, and she did in the river" (28/7), just as God communicated to (*alhama*) the bees, and said: "Your Lord communicated to (*awḥā*) the bees to make houses in the mountains and the trees," (16/68) and as God said, "Then God sent a raven scratching up the ground, to show him how to hide his brother's naked corpse" (5/31), so humans could do the same.
>
> God also communicated to (*alhama*) the cattle, then made them subservient to humans because of their honor before God, so who can doubt God's giving of divine communication (*ilhām*) to humans with their distinction above the rest of creation? Among the Prophets are those who do not receive divine communication through angels (*waḥy bi'l-malā°ika*), but they are communicated with (*yūḥā*) by means of *ilhām*, and visionary dreams. The elite Friends of God among the believers have inherited this.[34]

The viewpoint Kharrāz cites here is that Moses receives direct divine communication from God, while the other Prophets normally receive divine communication mediated by angels. A third type of divine communication is received by non-Prophets, the way that the mother of Moses and the bees were commanded according to the Qur'an, and some Prophets receive only this kind of divine communication and not the kind mediated by angels, with the clear implication that this "*ilhām*" is inferior to the latter. When one looks more closely at the passage, one quickly notices that, when choosing the terms for the classification, no regard has been paid to the actual vocabulary used in the Qur'an, where, for instance, the mother of Moses and bees are said to have received divine communication using verbal cognates of *waḥy*. In fact, this is what leads to the above statement: "His *waḥy* to her was His command to her by means of *ilhām*."

Kharrāz's decision not to comment on this statement suggests that he was not overly enthusiastic about it, even though it could have been used for his arguments regarding the divine communication of Friends of God. However, even if he were to have justified this classification, it would have remained problematic. This is because the divine communication received by Moses without mediation is at the top of his hierarchy, and if the highest form of divine communication is the least mediated and most direct form, one would be inclined to assume that an increasing degree of mediation becomes involved the lower one descends the hierarchy. And yet it is only the middle category, the divine communication received by Prophets via angels, that specifies any mediation. According to this scheme, the third form does not involve angels or any other intermediaries. However, even though it is described in the Qur'an with the use of cognates of *waḥy*, it is classified here using the alternative term "*ilhām*," as if to underline its distinction. One can therefore detect a certain degree of inconsistency in the rationale of the entire hierarchy presented here, unless one is to assume for an external reason that the divine communication of non-Prophets must necessarily be of an entirely lower category, regardless of the degree of mediation involved, simply because they are not Prophets.

John Wansbrough has pointed out that the "fundamental dilemma of Islamic thought: revelation as the unmediated speech of God, or revelation as the prophetical (angelic) report of God's speech"[35] is more generally applicable in Qur'anic exegesis, a reminder that it was not restricted to Kharrāz or the mystical tradition he is citing here. His discussion is based on the key Qur'anic verse for this issue, Qur'an 42/51:

> "It is not granted for any human being that God speak to him other than by means of *waḥy*, or from behind a screen *(ḥijāb)*, or that he send

an emissary who communicates (*yūḥī*) [to the human being] with His permission that which He wishes."[36]

Wansbrough points out that, in a plain reading of Qur'an 42/51, "*waḥy*" would logically signify divine communication without an intermediary or barrier, as the first of a list of three different modes of communication by God (directly, behind a screen, or through an intermediary). This suggests to him that there must have been an external reason for it not to be interpreted in that way in the first place, and instead to be conflated with the third mode listed in the verse. The reason must have existed at a very early stage, since exegetes of the second/eighth century already associated "*waḥy*" with the mediation of an angel.[37] Wansbrough identifies the external reason as polemic with the Jewish tradition over whether or not Moses was privileged with being spoken to directly by God, a remnant of which may also be detected in Qur'an 4/164 (*wa-kallama Allāh Mūsā taklīman*). Therefore, according to Wansbrough, Qur'an 42/51 had to be interpreted in a counterintuitive way if the exceptionalization of Moses was to be challenged. The result was that two of the three possible modes listed in the verse were interpreted counterintuitively as being the same, even though, this classification may have originated from a Jewish context in which a literal reading would have supported the opposite view. If he is correct, then it would imply that the problem of the Prophets' divine communication being mediated might have been a self-made one dating from before the mid- second/eighth century, and that Kharrāz is citing a viewpoint regarding divine communication that disregarded the polemic with the Jewish tradition. One could argue alternatively that the insistence by exegetes on the mediation of the Angel Gabriel might have been attractive because it could serve as a sign of authenticity, therefore a mark of the superiority of the divine communication received by Muhammad over that received by poets and other sages in the first century after his passing, rather than primarily as a means to de-exceptionalize Moses, only for this strategy to come back and haunt the theologians later.

For present purposes, what is interesting to observe is that Kharrāz does not appear to be on the firmest ground when tackling the issue of the relationship between the divine communication of the Friends of God and that of the Prophets. He cites a problematic theological position he does not comment on, and takes the trouble to explain why the expressions of Prophets are not as tender as those of Friends of God. The lack of a single honed argument suggests that the need to assert the superiority of the divine communication of the Prophets may have been only recently felt by Kharrāz.

In the *Sīrat al-awliyā'*, Ḥakīm Tirmidhī[38] responds to the interlocutor's broad question "What is the difference between Prophethood and Friendship with God?" specifically by distinguishing their forms of divine communication:

> The difference between Prophethood and Friendship with God is that Prophethood involves a speech (*kalām*) which detaches from God as divine communication (*waḥiyan*) accompanied by a spirit from God (*rūḥ min Allāh*). *Waḥy* comes to an end, and He seals it with the spirit, by means of which it gains acceptance. This is something that is obligatory to believe in; if one rejects it, that would be infidelity, because that would be rejection of God's speech (*kalām Allāh*).
>
> Friendship with God belongs to the one whose divinely communicated speech (*ḥadīth*), which comes from the heavenly treasuries, God takes charge of, and causes to reach him. He possesses divinely communicated speech, which separates from God on the tongue of that which is due (*ʿalā lisān al-ḥaqq*)[39] accompanied by a tranquility in the heart of the divinely attracted recipient (*majdhūb*), so he accepts it and is pacified with it.[40]

The fact that Tirmidhī defines the relationship between Prophethood and Friendship with God on the basis of different kinds of divine communication in itself indicates the primary significance of this quality which they share. Moreover, his decision to propose an entirely different categorization of their types of divine communication corroborates the impression gained from Kharrāz's work, namely that it had only recently become a concern for them to assert the superiority of Prophets in this regard. Tirmidhī's method of tackling this problem stands out in contrast to the descriptions by Kharrāz (as well as in later texts), by his avoidance of the term "*ilhām*" and his attribution of the exact same amount of mediation, or accompaniment, to the divine communication of the Friends of God as to that of the Prophets.

It would have been reasonable to expect Tirmidhī to describe the divinely communicated speech as reaching the Friend of God in the form of *ilhām*, to parallel his immediately preceding description of the divine communication of the Prophet being received in the form of *waḥy*, since Tirmidhī uses the actual term "*ilhām*" elsewhere in the same work, as one of the identifying signs of a Friend of God (with no mention there of "*ḥadīth*").[41] His decision not to do so at this point could well have been related to its usage during his lifetime as an unmediated form of divine communication, especially since his other idiosyncrasy here is to attribute equal levels of accompaniment; Tirmidhī has opted to create his own terminology for the divine communication received by the Friend of God, and this could explain why.[42] The actual terms he has chosen also support this view, because they implicitly favor Prophethood as being theologically superior, by comparing "*kalām Allāh*" with "*ḥadīth,*" in view of the obvious connotations of these terms since before the writing of his work. They suggest a deliberate agenda, as does Tirmidhī's opaque description of the Friend of God's divinely communicated speech reaching the Friend of God "on the tongue of that which is due" (*ʿalā lisān al-ḥaqq*), even though he usually reserves the usage of "*ḥaqq*" for the lower category "*walī ḥaqq Allāh,*" and as being accompanied by inner peace (*sakīna*) for the heart instead of a spirit from God.[43]

What is clear, however, is that Tirmidhī does not propagate in this treatise the view that the divine communication of the Friends of God is superior to that of the Prophets. Yet at the same time he avoids forcing the divine communication of the Friend of God to defer to that of the Prophet; when asked about this in the *Sīrat al-awliyāʾ*, he simply responds that God would not allow divine communication received by the Friend of God to contradict His book (*kitāb*) because He protects His Friend's heart the way that He protected the Prophet from the Satanic verses.[44] This suggests that the divine communication of the Friend of God cannot be in error, and so there is no need to worry and scrutinize the specifics of its relationship to the Qur'an, and this is made possible by Tirmidhī's method of depicting parallel experiences, which both have direct protection by God rather than acquire that through one another.

In a later paragraph of this treatise Tirmidhī refers to a further form of divine communication, which he terms "*najwā,*" or "conversation," explaining that this is of a lower level than the "*kalām*" or "*ḥadīth*" communications mentioned previously.[45] It therefore allows for the possibility that those who have not yet reached the rank of full Friendship with God may still receive some form of divine communication. The main deficiency of *najwā* is that it is not accompanied by inner peace, and Tirmidhī explains that this means that the recipient is still unsure of whether it arrives from God or from his own self. Implicitly, therefore, the mention of an accompaniment to the divine communications of Prophets and fully fledged Friends of God in the previous typology serves to indicate that those two forms both come with guarantees of divine origins.[46] Tirmidhī, through his notion of "*najwā,*" offers an early theoretical precedent for Rumi's later teaching that disciples still aspiring to become Friends of God may already receive some divine communication. Although Tirmidhī's typology may seem strange at first because it was innovative and not widely adopted, he tackles the issue with a greater deal of discrimination and sensitivity than many other commentators.

It is not so much these oldest treatises on Friendship with God that have shaped common wisdom regarding this issue in later Sufism, but instead the more widely read, and consequently influential, Sufi manuals of the tenth and eleventh centuries. It will be instructive therefore to consider in the next two sections of this chapter the strategies that these theoretical works employ to argue for the superiority of the Prophets' divine communication.

*Divine Communication in Sarrāj's (d. 378/988) Kitāb al-Luma*ᶜ *and Kalābādhī's (d. 380s/990s) Kitāb al-Ta*ᶜ*arruf*

Toward the beginning of the introduction of Abū Naṣr al-Sarrāj's *Kitāb al-Luma*ᶜ *fi'l-taṣawwuf*,[47] one finds the following statement of Sufi epistemology:

> "Nothing is known or comprehended other than what is present in the book of God, what has been transmitted about the Messenger of God and what has been revealed to the hearts of His Friends (*futiḥa ᶜalā qulūb awliyā'ih*)."[48]

Sarrāj hereby affirms that there is another source to add to the Qur'an and the transmitted Prophetic Hadith, namely knowledge received from God by the hearts of His Friends. Since this is mentioned third in a list of three sources, it is presented as being hierarchically the lowest of them in status. However, regardless of such a position, this third source is also, in theory, the only one among the three that remained open to extension after the lifetime of the Prophet Muhammad, during which both the Qur'an and the Hadith are traditionally believed to have originated. Therefore, for practical purposes and quantitatively, it was arguably the most influential of the three sources. For example, in Sarrāj's own *Luma*ᶜ one can witness how the discourse is often based on and shaped by the inspired sayings of Sufis rather than the far outnumbered citations of textual revelation.[49]

In addition to this epistemological approach, Sarrāj also discusses theologically the relationship between the divine communication of Prophets and that of Friends of God. This is found in his chapter on "Those Who Err regarding Prophethood and Friendship with God," which has already been discussed in chapter 2 above.[50] He begins this chapter by identifying, like Kharrāz, the Qur'anic story about Moses and Khiḍr as the source of the erroneous view he wishes to refute, namely that Friendship with God is superior to Prophethood (*tafḍīl al-walāya ᶜalā al-nubuwwa*). One can detect from his summary, as well as his reminder that Moses had been spoken to by God and had received the commandments as tablets, that Khiḍr had been regarded as superior by the group (*firqa*) which held this view on account of his seemingly superior knowledge in this story. As the reminder about Moses already causes one to anticipate, his method of refutation is to argue that this story is about an isolated incident from which one should not make general conclusions. While this may sound effective and logical, the consistency of his argument faces the greatest challenge in his response to the viewpoint that the divine communication of the Friends of God is superior to that of the Prophets, which is presented below:

> As for those who expressed the opinion that the Prophets receive divine communication (*yūḥā*) by means of an intermediary (*wāsiṭa*) but the Friends of God receive snatches of communication (*yatalaqqifūn*) from God without an intermediary, it is said to them: "You are mistaken, because the Prophets experience this continuously, that is to say '*ilhām*' and snatches (*talaqquf*) from God without any intermediary, but the Friends of God receive it only intermittently. Moreover the Prophets also have a mission, Prophethood, and a divine communication via the descent of Gabriel (*waḥy bi-nuzūl Jibrīl*), while the Friends of God do not."[51]

This passage is instructive in a number of ways. First of all, one can witness here that Sarrāj does not attempt to refute the view of "the erring group" that Friends of God receive divine communication without the involvement of an intermediary. Instead, he describes that by using the term "*talaqquf,*" which implies something fleeting, and equates it with the established term *ilhām* only when attributing that also to Prophets. This may be no accident, but a deliberate substitution of terms because of the established definition of "*ilhām*" as direct divine communication, which Sarrāj himself opts not to question: in this situation, his strategy is instead to assert that the Prophets receive the Friend of God's unmediated *ilhām* form of divine communication too, but in a superior "continuous" form (*ʿalā al-dawām*) rather than intermittently. This is in addition to their own mediated *waḥy* for which the Angel Gabriel descends. Therefore, the totality of the divine communication Prophets receive is greater than that of the Friends of God, even though there is nothing exclusive to Prophets that is at an entirely different degree of explicitness to the divine communication received by the latter.

However, what is perhaps most interesting of all to witness in Sarrāj's argument is that, despite wishing to argue for the superiority of Prophets, he chooses not to try the more direct method of arguing that their mediated *waḥy* is by itself superior to unmediated *ilhām*, even though Kharrāz had done that before him, admittedly somewhat halfheartedly. When one considers that he wrote his *Lumaᶜ* in part to present Sufism as being compatible with scholastic Islam, this approach shows a surprising degree of restraint and seriousness. Since it would have been easier simply to assert that the form of divine communication exclusive to Prophets is the superior kind, his alternative strategy suggests that Sarrāj either did not wish to refute the notion that *ilhām* is the superior form of divine communication, as the unmediated form, or felt unable to do so convincingly. This is highlighted further by the fact that the argument he resorts to is implicitly contradicted by the Qur'anic story about Moses and Khiḍr: If Prophets continuously receive the same highest form of divine communication the Friends of God receive only intermittently, then how could Moses have ever been in a situation in which Khiḍr had greater knowledge than him?

Kalābādhī, Sarrāj's contemporary in Bukhara,[52] does not discuss directly the divine communication of the Friend of God in his *Kitāb al-Taᶜarruf*. However, this work gives indications that the omission should not be interpreted as meaning that he did not consider this a significant attribute of theirs. For instance, he includes a very brief notice on "unveiling by means of thought" (*al-kashf ᶜan al-khawāṭir*), where he defines the unveiling of this kind that comes from God as an "alert" (*fa-alladhī min Allāh tanbīh*).[53] Then, toward the end of this short manual, he includes chapters on God communicating an alert (*tanbīh*) by means of a supernatural voice (*hātif*), clairvoyance (*firāsat*), and visions (*ruʾyā*), respectively[54] All of these forms of inspiration are illustrated with anecdotes, but no attempt is made at systematization.

Kalābādhī's decision not to engage in any theoretical discussions about the divine communication of the Friend of God, despite judging this to be a prominent attribute, puts into perspective the efforts of his contemporary Sarrāj. The most obvious explanation is Kalābādhī's consistent avoidance of controversy, whether by omitting any mention of them whatsoever, or by referring to controversial issues only indirectly.[55] He succeeds in this way to give an account of Sufism which affirms that communications from God reach His Friends without bringing the attention of the reader to anything that may be considered controversial from a scholastic religious perspective.

With neither Sarrāj nor Kalābādhī adopting the approaches of their ninth-century predecessors, and the former including a serious discussion of the topic among "the errors" associated with Sufism he debates in the *Lumaᶜ*, one is left with the impression that those earlier treatises had not succeeded in putting an end to arguments for the superiority of the divine communication of the Friends of God. Sarrāj's approach to this issue, namely to argue that

Prophets possess what the Friends of God possess (and in a superior, continuous form) in addition to their own exclusive Gabriel-mediated form of divine communication, reads like a concession to the basis of the argument of his opponents—that is to say, he acknowledges that the highest form of divine communication is the direct and unmediated kind, and so he simply argues that Prophets also possess it and receive it continuously to boot. In comparison with such theoretical arguments, Rumi's denial of any substantial difference between the two types of divine communication would seem relatively modest and uncomplicated.

Divine Communication in Qushayrī's (d. 465/1072) Risāla and Hujwīrī's (d. ca. 467/1075) Kashf al-Maḥjūb

It should perhaps be of no great surprise that Qushayrī, like Kālābādhī before him, decides not to engage directly in the discussion about divine communication. This may be partly because his *Risāla* famously begins with a section attributing Ash'arite theological beliefs to Sufis, leaving little scope for such a discussion.[56] It is worth noting, however, that toward the end of that theological section, when it comes to discussing God's dispatch of the Prophet with the mission to establish Islam, he writes the following:

> [God] is the One who causes Mankind to worship by means of "the tongue of" the Prophets in such a way that no one can censure or oppose Him. He is the One who helped our Prophet, Muhammad, by means of clear miracles (*muʿjizāt ẓāhira*) and resplendent miracles (*āyāt bāhira*)[57] which removed excuse and clarified what is certain and what is to be denied. He is the one who protected the territory of Islam after his death by means of the Rightly-Guided Caliphs, and then guarded and aided the Truth by means of the proofs of religion which He manifested on "the tongues of" His Friends.[58]

What is interesting to witness here is the way that Qushayrī explains God's preservation of Islam after the passing of the Prophet. Whereas, he protected the territory of Islam (*bayḍat al-islām*) by means of the Rightly-Guided Caliphs, it was through "the proofs of religion manifested on the tongues of His Friends" that He protected the Truth (*ḥārisa al-ḥaqq wa-nāṣarah bi-mā yūḍiḥuh min ḥujaj al-dīn ʿalā alsinat awliyāʾih*). When this comment is compared with Qushayrī's assertion that God caused Mankind to worship Him by means of "the tongue of the Prophets," one gains the impression that in his worldview Prophets were succeeded by Friends of God as religious intermediaries between God and

Mankind and as His spokesmen. Moreover, if the means by which Prophets led others to worship God is understood to be through divinely communicated oral teachings, then after Muhammad a similar role was carried out by Friends of God with regard to "the proofs" of the religion he had established.

Qushayrī affirms his conviction that Friends of God receive divine communication also in his thematic chapters in the *Risāla*. For instance, in his explanation of the technical Sufi term "*khawāṭir*" ("a speech which enters consciences": *khiṭāb yarid ʿalā al-ḍamāʾir*),[59] he presents a typology distinguishing between those that come from an angel, the self, Satan, or God.[60] While the other types experienced by Sufis require some kind of check, including the type coming from an angel (by corroboration with knowledge), the kind that comes directly from God cannot face disagreement by the recipient and is therefore absolutely authoritative. This approach would favor unmediated divine communication over the mediated kind, while also echoing Tirmidhī's argument that the Friend of God's divine communication cannot err. However, in comparison with his predecessor Sarrāj, whose *Lumaʿ* influenced many parts of his own *Risāla*, Qushayrī hardly engages at all with this particular issue.

Despite including in his *Kashf al-maḥjūb* an extensive discussion of the relationship between Prophethood and Friendship with God, Hujwīrī surprisingly does not compare the divine communication of Prophets and God's Friends in this context.[61] However, in his biography of Junayd in the same work, he includes the following utterance, which gives him occasion to discuss this topic:

> It has been related that [Junayd] said: "The speech of the Prophets is information on the basis of presence (*ḥuḍūr*) with God, while that of the Friends of God is an allusion on the basis of witnessings (*mushāhadāt*)."
>
> The soundness of information depends on direct vision, and that is why witnessings only give rise to thoughts. Information cannot be given except from direct vision, and allusions can only be by means of reference to other things. Therefore the perfection and end of the Friends of God is the beginning of the time of Prophets, and there is a clear difference between a Friend of God and a Prophet, as well as the superiority of Prophets over Friends of God, contrary to the opinion of the two heretic groups who say that Friends of God are superior to Prophets.[62]

Hujwīrī's commentary on the saying by Junayd is instructive because he bases the superiority of Prophets over Friends of God on the form of knowledge they possess and its source. Even though he makes no reference to divine communication as such, like Qushayrī, he seems to elevate the more direct kind. It is the virtue of directness that appears to tilt the balance in favor of direct visions over allusions.

The coinciding decision of the authors of the eleventh-century not to even compare the divine communication of Friends of God with that of Prophets stands out because of their contrasting approaches to the issue of the relationship between Friendship with God and Prophethood in general. Hujwīrī's decision not to deal with it directly, and mention only something tangentially related through a biographical anecdote, suggests that he may have supported the reasoning that had led to the earliest view among mystics about the superiority of the divine communication of the Friends of God; however, rather than maintain the same view, he preferred instead to discuss the alternative topic of perception of God, where the Prophets could be attributed with the more direct form of vision, rather than indirect "witnessings." Similarly, Qushayrī's related comment about the proofs of religion being manifested on "the tongues of the Friends of God" in succession to Muhammad would suggest that silence on this issue should not be taken as an indication of lack of importance. This silence comes as a surprise when considered in the light of what they do cover in their works about Friendship with God and the forms of non-verbal inspiration peculiar to it, not to mention the value they place on the sayings of past Sufis. It also stands out when compared with other writings of the time. For instance, in the discussion of the station of divine communication (*ilhām*) in ʿAbd Allāh Anṣārī's (d. 481/1089) *Manāzil al-sāʾirīn* ("The Stations of the Wayfarers"), a mnemonic instruction book for his disciples in Herat, the divine communication received by Prophets is classified as the first and lowest degree: "The first (i.e. lowest-ranking) degree is the inspiration of a Prophet: a message which comes down as Prophetic inspiration (*waḥy*) which is indisputable, and involves hearing (*samāʿ*) or may be absolute (*muṭlaqan;* i.e. without hearing?)."[63]

Silence on this particular topic may have been the best approach for Qushayrī and Hujwīrī in the context of their irenic agendas, since they would neither wish to limit the possibilities for the divine communication of the Friends of God nor run afoul of religious dogma. As a result of this approach, they avoided stifling discussions about this topic among later Sufis, including eventually Rumi.

Conclusions

The oldest surviving writings about the relationship between the divine communication received by Friends of God and that received by Prophets, which date from the ninth century, reveal that this issue was contested among Sufis themselves since the earliest stage for which we have any evidence. It seems that the understanding that *waḥy* is the highest form of divine communication was not universally accepted from the time of the first Sufi writings, with the requirement of mediation being identified as a disadvantage by proponents of the superiority of the *ilhām* of Friends of God. Differing theories to refute that view were attempted in the ninth and tenth centuries, and yet even in the late tenth century Sarrāj still decided not to argue that the *waḥy* divine communication received exclusively by Prophets is in itself superior to the *ilhām* of Friends of God, arguing instead that Prophets receive both types of divine communication. This last-resort kind of argument would suggest what the differing attempts to argue for the superiority of the divine communications exclusive to Prophets also indicate, namely that a successful argument remained elusive. Tirmidhī stands out among all of these authors, for proposing a distinction between the Prophets' divine communication and that of the Friends of God which prevented the latter from being considered superior because it was less mediated. He achieved this by creating new vocabulary, opting not to use the term "*ilhām*" when making the comparison, and attributing the same amount of mediation to both kinds. This was arguably his way of demonstrating his recognition of the inherited problems in this debate and responding to the need for an innovative solution. What is surprising therefore is that his creative and consistent scheme was not adopted by his successors, who instead struggled with the inherited difficulties or skipped over the issue altogether. As demonstrated in the previous chapter, this does not appear to be the first case in which Tirmidhī had been overlooked by his successors in the mystical tradition without obvious justification traceable in his actual writings on the topic. In comparison, the silence of Qushayrī and Hujwīrī arguably facilitated the preservation of more controversial theories than Tirmidhī's, such as that later taught by Rumi himself.

As mentioned previously, there are two main reasons why people conventionally refer to Rumi's *Masnavi* as "the Qur'an in Persian." It is usually meant as the highest form of praise for a book, but sometimes it is linked to his heavy incorporation of Qur'anic citations. As I have argued elsewhere, the suggestion that Rumi's *Masnavi* follows closely the holy text does not stand up to scrutiny, because Rumi incorporates Qur'anic verses for his own purposes rather than use the holy text as his starting point, even to the extent of appropriating some Qur'anic verses for his own speech and dismissing part of a much-quoted verse.[64] Rather, the frequency of these Qur'anic citations may be a sign of his greater intimacy with the text and his identification of his own poetry with it. Rumi's biographer Shams al-Dīn Aflākī (d. 761/1360) has preserved in his

Manāqib al-ᶜĀrifīn the following story, which appears to confirm that his disciples understood him in this way:

> It is recounted that one day Sulṭan Walad said:
>
> Among the companions, one made a complaint to my father, saying, "The scholars (*dānishmandān*) argued with me, saying, 'Why do they say that *The Masnavi* is the Qur'an?' I said, 'It is a commentary (*tafsīr*) on the Qur'an.'"
>
> My father was silent for a moment, then said, "O dog, why shouldn't it be [the Qur'an itself]? O donkey, why shouldn't it be [the Qur'an itself]? O brother of a whore, why shouldn't it be [the Qur'an itself]. Certainly, there is nothing contained in the vessels of the words of the Prophets and Friends of God apart from the lights of the divine secrets, and God's speech (*kalām Allāh*) has leapt out from their pure hearts and has flowed on the streams of their tongues."[65]

This story reveals to us the viewpoints of Rumi's early generations of followers regarding the relationship between his *Masnavi* and the Qur'an. Although it should be remembered at the same time that he would have been very unlikely to have responded in this way to anybody but a serious disciple on the mystical path, if the diplomacy evident in his *Fīhi mā fīh* is representative, the depiction of Rumi reacting in this way is consistent with his own writings about *The Masnavi* and the Friend of God's divine communication in general. Moreover, his teachings are far from unique in medieval Sufism. Aside from well-known cases of Sufis classifying their own writings as having been divinely communicated to them (e.g. Ibn ᶜArabī's *al-Futūḥāt al-Makkiyya*), in thirteenth-century Anatolia, Najm al-Dīn Rāzī also regarded the highest form of divine communication as reaching all who complete the Sufi path with their souls at peace (*mutma*ʾ*inna*), commenting in his *Mirṣād al-ᶜIbād*:

> The difference between divine communication (*ilhām-i ḥaqq*), allusion (*ishāra*), and the Speech of God (*kalām*) is as follows: divine communication is an address by God to the heart which is "tasted," or perceived intuitively (*dhawq*), but without understanding; allusion is an address which is both perceived intuitively and understood, but it is expressed implicitly, not explicitly; the Speech of God is an address which is both explicit and perceived intuitively, and it is also understood. When the soul is in the station of inspiration (*nafs-i mulhama*), it does not experience the speech of God; this appears only once

> the soul is pacified (*nafs-i muṭma'inna*), as is indicated in the verses: "O pacified soul, return to your Lord!" (Qur'an 89/27–28). That is an explicit address.[66]

What is interesting to witness here is that Rāzī considers the highest form of communication with God no less than the Speech of God like the Qur'an itself,[67] and also as being communicated to the perfected mystic—a person whose soul has become pacified—even though he makes a distinction between that and the *ilhām* form of divine communication. That is to say, someone with the opposite tendency to Rumi, who has been shown to dismiss any distinction between such forms of communication, still agrees about the continual accessibility of the highest form. Unlike earlier theorists, Rāzī clearly was not motivated to define distinctions in order to avoid encroachment on the qualities and experiences of Prophets by Friends of God, suggesting that by his day it was much less of a concern in general for Sufi authors.

It is important to note that, in contrast, Rumi dismisses hierarchical distinctions even to the point of encouraging aspirants on the Sufi path to strive to rely increasingly on some form of divine communication instead of depending on less direct knowledge until the path's completion. This is implicit in his numerous poems that urge the audience to share in his enjoyment of ubiquitous divine communications, and is also discussed in the following well-known passage from the second book of *The Masnavi:*

> The Sufi's book's not marked with words men write,
> For it's a heart like snow, one pure and white;
> The scholar's work through words he writes is known;
> By footprints is the Sufi's method shown.
> Like hunters he has hunted game instead;
> He saw deer tracks and followed where they led.
> For several steps, on tracks he has relied,
> But now the scent of musk serves as his guide.
> When he gives thanks for tracks, completes the way,
> Of course through them he'll reach his goal one day;
> To rise one stage by scent earns more for you
> Than tracks or circumambulation do![68]

In this passage, words (*ḥarf*), tracks (*āthār-i qadam*), and scent from the deer's musk gland (*bū-yi nāf*) represent the different means by which one may pursue one's goal. They correspond to the learning of a scholar, following in the footsteps of one's master ahead of you, and following more direct communication from God, as represented by the musk of the deer. The final verse may therefore be interpreted as meaning that to follow divine communication of some kind in order to complete the path is superior to following outwardly articulated instructions and examples on the Sufi path, even though they will also lead you to the goal eventually. His mention of circumambulation may be either for increased effect or as a reference back to the learning of the scholars, with the aim of underlining that guidance through direct divine communication is superior to that as well. The way that these different means succeed one another implies that it is only at the more advanced levels that one can rely on divine communication alone, though not exclusively at the final station. In contrast, the scholar's notebook has no purpose for the Sufi according to this scheme, which is consistent with Rumi's remarks elsewhere, and can help explain why scholars of all stripes were wary of associating with him to such an extent that Rumi himself acknowledges their fear.[69]

When it comes to attaining divine communication of the very highest kind, Rumi could have found his own inspiration much closer to home, namely in the spiritual diary attributed to his father, Bahā al-Dīn Walad (628/1231), which is known as the *Maʿārif*. The relevant section (the 109th in Furūzānfar's edition) begins in extraordinary fashion with Bahā Walad asking God to give him a divinely communicated book (*kitāb*) comparable to those given to Moses, David, Jesus, and Muhammad before him:

> "*The inspiration of the Book is from God*" (Qur'an 39/1): I said, "O God, since my inner being, my perceptions and my mind are just like a bunch of roses in the grasp of Your will, and it is You who gives perceptions attributes and causes them to change, I first want You to give me books of wisdom without requiring me to undergo suffering: just as You gave the Torah to Moses's inner being and the *Furqān*[70] to Muhammad's inner being, the Gospel to Jesus and the Psalms to David, give me holy books of wisdom from the unseen world."[71]

Although Bahā Walad does not use a specific technical term such as *waḥy* here to specify what kind of communication is meant, by asking for "books of wisdom" (*kitābhā-yi ḥikmat*) comparable with the books sent to the Prophets Moses, David, Jesus, and Muhammad, he is indicating no less than the Prophetic level of divine communication. Bahā Walad continues his discussion by comparing such communication with the spiritual transformations God can bring about in creation, suggesting that his appeal is for the most explicit and powerful bestowal of grace from God possible, whether that should be manifested in books of revelation or in other forms. He cites the Qur'anic verse "O hills, repeat His praise!" (34/10) as proof of the extraordinary transformations that God can bring about, since it refers to how He even caused inanimate hills to repeat along with the Prophet David the revealed holy book of the Psalms. Further examples he presents include the transformation of Moses's rod[72] and the transformation of stones held by the Prophet Muhammad, which miraculously declared the Muslim testimony of faith in response to a challenge by his enemy Abū Jahl.[73] There are enough similarities here to suggest that Rumi's argument about the status of his *Masnavi* may well have been influenced by this section of the *Maʿārif.* It is more remarkable to find these sentiments expressed in a work attributed to Rumi's father than to Rumi himself, seeing as the biographical tradition portrays the father primarily as a preacher and seminary teacher, and does not attribute to him a transformative experience comparable with his son's. The reliability of the *Maʿārif* and its attribution to Rumi's father is something that would need to be verified, especially in order to rule out the possibility that this might be part of Rumi's own corpus of writings from which he drew for his *Masnavi.* However, if accepted as the authentic work of Bahā Walad, as it is traditionally understood, it would show just how widely accepted it then was to regard divine communication of the highest kind to be continually accessible. Bahā Walad was of course not interested in receiving that in order to rival previous books of revelation, let alone abrogate the Islamic religion, but once those functions of Prophetic divine communication were safeguarded, it would seem that there was then a lot more room for the divine communication of the Friends of God than is usually assumed from the theoretical manuals. With regard to the significance of safeguards against threats to the Islamic religious system, the next chapter will investigate how Rumi and the early Sufi tradition understood the relationship between Friends of God like themselves and the juristic formulations of the religious scholars.

4

The Friend of God and the Shariah

> One day the jealous jurists, out of stubbornness and denial, asked Rumi whether wine is allowed or forbidden. What they had in mind was to deny the pure reputation of Shams al-Dīn. Rumi answered with an analogy, saying: "It depends on who drinks it, for if a flask of wine is poured into the ocean, that would not be transformed or polluted, and it would be permissible to use its water for ablutions and drinking. However, without doubt one drop would make a tiny pool of water unclean. It is likewise when whatever flows into the salty sea becomes overwhelmed by salt. The straightforward answer is that, if Shams al-Dīn drinks it, for him everything is permitted, since he has the overwhelming power of the ocean. On the other hand, for a brother of a whore like you, even barley bread is forbidden!"[1]

This anecdote presented in Aflākī's *Manāqib al-ᶜārifīn* is instructive in a number of ways. The most significant point is that Shams-i Tabrīzī was understood to drink wine—if this were not the case, the whole basis of the above anecdote would be void. The heavily negative description of the jurists (*fuqahā*ʾ) trying to catch Rumi out also reveals an animosity perceived at least a generation after his death among the latter's followers, who compiled this anecdote, which could well be an accurate portrayal of Rumi's own experiences.[2] This is because the anecdote is followed by the following verses found in the story about the Sufi master who was seen drinking wine, from the second book of his *Masnavi*:

> They're false, but even if your words were true
> What harm to a huge sea can one corpse do?
> He's more than *the two jarfuls and small pool*[3]
> That one small drop should ruin him, you fool!

Abraham's fire was not reduced one bit—
So warn the Nimrods: "Be afraid of it!"[4]

The viewpoint attributed to Rumi in the anecdote is therefore actually corroborated by these verses of his own poetry, which may have even generated it as exegesis. Regardless of the origins, what this material conveys is Rumi's teaching that, for a Sufi Friend of God like Shams al-Dīn, wine is permitted despite the legal formulations of scholars. With wine-drinking being one of only a few offenses that draw a prescribed "*ḥadd*" penalty,[5] this implies that Rumi regarded the Friend of God as not being subject to the laws and ethical codes of the Islamic religious system.

In this instance, Rumi employs the analogy of the pollution of water on the basis of the jurists' own theoretical formulations as proof for his relativist approach to religious laws: the larger the quantity the less chance of it being made impure (and therefore unsuitable for ablutions) by the same amount of pollutant. Elsewhere, Rumi often alludes to the concession in their legal system for those compelled to act in contravention of the Shariah.[6] He therefore uses arguments based on principles already established by scholars of Islamic jurisprudence, but for the purpose of denying that the authority of their legal system is absolute. As well as being particularly apt, this is one clear indication that he had studied jurisprudence himself.

Islam is popularly characterized today as a religion centered more on law than theology, with, for instance, many Muslims unaware of their theological school while in no doubt about their legal affiliation. The Qur'an certainly refers to the requirement to follow divine commands, and contains a limited number of them, so it is not altogether surprising that the institutionalized religion of Islam that developed by the tenth century became based on the discipline of jurisprudence.[7] By Rumi's time, jurisprudence was also the most prestigious scholarly discipline in the educational system. It would therefore have been extraordinary if Rumi had not been trained in this field, even if, at the same time, the status of the discipline could have given an incentive for his disciples to exaggerate his accomplishments in it.

This chapter explores in detail Rumi's didactic writings on the relationship of the Shariah to the Friend of God, and then examines the writings of the major Sufi theorists on this issue as far as the authors of the eleventh-century manuals, which have acquired a normative position in this regard over the centuries. With the benefit of an understanding of the historical development of Sufi teachings about this issue, especially during the period of consolidation by juristic scholars of the Shariah's supremely authoritative position in Islamic societies, it will then be possible to make a fully informed evaluation of Rumi's teachings and their place in Sufism.

Rumi's Teachings on the Friend of God's Relationship to the Shariah

Rumi's voluminous magnum opus, *The Masnavi*, famously begins with the much-celebrated "Song of the Reed." However, the first teaching story that follows after the remarkably short exordium of this *mathnawī* poem is less celebrated. This is no doubt because the narrative describes a murder. In brief, this story has four main characters: a king, a slave-girl, a healer sent by God, and a goldsmith. The king falls in love with the slave-girl and buys her, only to discover that she is ill. God answers his prayers by sending him a special healer, who discovers that the reason the slave-girl is ill is that she pines for her lover, a goldsmith in Samarqand. He then plots to kill the goldsmith slowly with poison after luring him to the king's court using flattery and promises of riches. All goes to plan. Although it heals the slave-girl, who had become lovesick in separation from the goldsmith and therefore benefited from the slow manner of his loss of handsomeness and demise before dying, the murder remains troubling to the reader. One might well wonder why Rumi should have chosen to begin the long sequence of teaching stories in his *Masnavi* with one that would be difficult to stomach?

Rumi himself provides us with evidence that readers would find it unpalatable, in the form of an extended justification of the murder of the goldsmith at the conclusion of this story. What is most interesting about this justification for present purposes is that it rests on the fact that the goldsmith was killed by a Friend (or Friends)[8] of God, and therefore at God's command, as the following passage demonstrates:

> The goldsmith's murder by the healer here
> Was not due to a personal wish or fear,
> Nor for the king's mere carnal gratification
> Without God's order and communication (*ilhām*).
> Think of the child whose jugular Khiḍr slit—
> Most couldn't see its hidden benefit:
> With such communication (*waḥy*) from the Lord
> One's every deed's correct, in full accord;
> He who gives life may kill; we must condone.
> His deputy's hand is just like His own.

Like Ishmael lay your neck before his blade
And smile for this brave sacrifice you've made,
So that your soul will live on joyfully
With God, like Ahmad's soul, eternally.
Each lover drinks the wine of his own soul;
When slain by his beloved that's his goal.
The king did not kill him because of lust—
Stop all your false suspicion and distrust!
You thought that he did wrong there, didn't you?
When God refines, no flaws can filter through;
The aim of holy struggle's suffering loss,
So that the furnace burns the silver's dross.
That's why for good and bad we scrutinize,
And gold is boiled so that the scum may rise.
If his deeds weren't from God's communication (*ilhām*),
He'd be a dog, not ruler of a nation!
He had been purified from lust and greed;
His deed was good, but seemed a wicked deed:
When Khiḍr destroyed that boat out in the sea
What seemed destructive was true piety;
Moses was veiled, though virtuous and with light
From God. Without wings you will not take flight![9]

In order to justify the goldsmith's murder by the healer on behalf of the king, for what may well appear as the superficial matter of enabling the latter to gratify his desires, Rumi refers repeatedly to the Qur'anic story (18/60–82) of Khiḍr and Moses.[10] The general teaching of the story with regard to acts outside of the law is that individuals very close to God, such as Khiḍr, who is usually classified by Sufis as a Friend of God, act on the basis of direct communication rather than follow any legal formulations, even if this means contravening them.

Rumi's many references to acting directly on the basis of divine communication indicate that he considered this the loftiest goal of Sufism. The clearest example is in the story about ʿAlī and the enemy knight who spat in his face, which forms the culmination of the first book of *The Masnavi*. The story centers on ʿAlī's decision to drop his sword when spat at by an enemy knight who was at his mercy, rather than slay him. The introduction to the story indicates that ʿAlī acted with pure sincerity (*ikhlāṣ*), that is to say he was purified of self-interest, as he himself explains to his astonished enemy:

A reason had emerged in that attack
For me to choose to draw my sabre back,
So "he loves for God's sake" should be my name,
"He hates for God" my sole desire and aim,
"He gives for God" my liberality,
"He clings to God" my being for all to see;
I'm mean or generous too for God alone,
I'm His possession, not what men can own.
My deeds for God are not from supposition
Or imitation (*taqlīd*), but through direct vision.
Reasoning (*ijtihād*) and calculation I have fled
To tie my sleeve to God's cloak hem instead.[11]

ʿAlī's explanation is the same as that given by Rumi in the story of the healer and the king, as well as Khiḍr in the Qur'an, namely that he acts according to direct instruction from God, rather than according to any other ethical system. In his case, this is in spite of the fact that he was perfectly justified by both law and conventional ethics to slay his opponent. The common factor is therefore the authority of communication from God, rather than committing something considered "right" or "wrong" from the perspective of the law. The fact that two technical terms from Islamic jurisprudence are used here (*ijtihād, taqlīd*) reinforces the contrast between the way a Friend of God acts and how the Muslim legal schools (*madhāhib*) require Muslims to act.

This particular teaching is repeated throughout Rumi's didactic writings, and not in his poetry alone. For instance, in the *Fīhi mā fīh* he relates the following anecdote as a means of teaching the superiority of the direct knowledge of God's decrees, which the Friend of God possesses, over the formulations of scholars of jurisprudence:

> Bāyazīd's father took him to the madrasa when he was a child, in order for him to learn jurisprudence (*fiqh*). When he was brought before the teacher, he asked "Is this the jurisprudence of God (*fiqh Allāh*)?" He was told "This is the jurisprudence of Abū Ḥanīfa." He said, "I want the jurisprudence of God."
>
> When he was taken to the grammarian, he said, "Is this the grammar of God?" He was told, "This is the grammar of Sibawayh." He said, "I don't want this."
>
> Wherever he was taken he asked such questions. His father felt unable to cope and left him. After that, in the continuation of this

quest, Bāyazīd came to Baghdad. On seeing Junayd, he cried out, "This is the jurisprudence of God!"

How should a lamb not recognize its own mother when it has suckled on her breast, and was originally born from intellect and discrimination. Abandon the external form (*ṣūrat-rā rahā kun*)![12]

The expression "jurisprudence of God" (*fiqh Allāh*) stands out here as an innovation, with the normal way of classifying Islamic jurisprudence being in relation to its formulator, as here with Abū Ḥanīfa (d. 148/767). Disregarding the fact that it would be somewhat absurd to suggest that God studies and formulates His own law in the manner of an Abū Ḥanīfa, the use of this surprising expression has the effect of highlighting the deficiency of conventional Islamic jurisprudence in relation to the actions of a Friend of God. This is because Bāyazīd Basṭāmī is depicted here as rejecting theoretical knowledge obtained indirectly from God through scholarship, for the direct knowledge which he recognized as being actualized in the Sufi Friend of God, Junayd of Baghdad. Rumi's concluding comments are significant here, because he clarifies that Bāyazīd recognized this in Junayd instinctively due to his own spiritual origins with God and not on the basis of theoretical formulations. What he therefore considers the external form (*ṣūrat*) of this direct knowledge is the theoretical knowledge of religious scholars, which he advises his audience to strive to transcend in the manner of Bāyazīd.[13]

On numerous occasions in *The Masnavi*, Rumi describes the way the Friend of God acts on the basis of God's direct command with an alternative emphasis, namely as being out of "compulsion under God" (*jabr*) in contrast to free will:

The word "compulsion" (*jabr*) spurs my heart ahead;
Those who aren't lovers feel entrapped instead.
It's not compulsion but divine communion,
Not clouds, but the full moon brought to our vision.[14]

The use of the term compulsion here highlights the involuntary nature of this experience of the Friend of God. That is to say, such an individual reaches a level where all his actions are directly inspired by God. The examples given in the above-mentioned narratives are dramatic in order to be as effective as possible, but Rumi's understanding of this condition is that it eventually applies even to the more mundane acts of Friends of God while they are in communion with Him. The following passage of *The Masnavi* follows a description of how human spirits escape their bodies during sleep and return to God until sleep ends, but that the mystics are always in this condition:

The mystic's (*ʿārif*) in this state while wide awake:
God said, "They're sleeping,"[15] so make no mistake!
Asleep to worldly things by night and day,
Just like a pen, God's hand he must obey:
Those who don't see the movement by His hand
Think that the pen moves by its own command![16]

In confirmation of the condition ʿAlī fulfilled in the previously mentioned story, the image of the pen and the hand that moves it by night and day implies that this should be perpetual. It would therefore include mundane matters as well as the more dramatic and controversial ones.

While the Friend of God's inspired performance of acts outside the law on God's direct command has an authoritative precedent in the Qur'anic story of Khiḍr and Moses, this also happens to be one of the most problematic parts of the Qur'an in the relationship between Sufis and the religious scholars (*ʿulamāʾ*). As far as the latter are concerned, though the law may be flexible in many areas, none are privileged to be able to act above their legal formulations, and mystics are not given any special concessions in this regard. It is therefore predictable that this would emerge as an area of tension and conflict, with various compromises being made through history by those with less power at the time. It should therefore be noted that Rumi is uncompromising in his teachings about this topic. He depicts a relationship between God and His Friend wherein God would feel insulted if His Friend should opt to move away from a position of intimacy and privilege to one of pious obedience:

If someone's prayer-niche faces certain vision (*ʿayn*),
Then turning round to faith (*īmān*) means degradation:
If you're now waiting on the king, you'll lose
If traveling off to trade for him you choose;
If those sat with the sultan later must
Wait at the gate, they'll feel that it's unjust.
He's brought his hands, so with your lips they'll meet;
It's now a sin (*gunāh*) to choose to kiss his feet—
Lowering your head is worship usually,
But now it's error and deficiency.
The king grows jealous if an onlooker
His perfume to his proud face should prefer.[17]

The passage above clarifies vividly Rumi's recurrent teaching that pious humility and worship is actually an error and deficiency in the worshipper who has already been privileged with close intimacy with God. This would be no better than resorting to ordinary faith (*īmān*) based on theological formulations after you have already acquired superior direct vision of God (*ᶜayn*). The same point is reinforced with further vivid examples in the following passage, which also includes the famous saying, "Consider the obedient deed of the masses as the sin of [God's] elite" (*ṭāᶜat-i ᶜāmma gunāh-i khāṣṣigān . . . dān*).

When you are swimming deep within a river
Why turn back then to check the water's colour?
To check the color if you should swim back,
You're swapping silk for a moth-bitten sack!
The common folk's good deed is God's Friend's sin;
Their "unions" would be veiled states he's put in,
For if a king should make his own vizier
A law-enforcer, this would be severe—
A big sin that vizier must have committed,
For not without a cause is this permitted.
However, if he'd been one from the start,
He might have loved this job with all his heart.[18]

Both of the above-cited passages stress Rumi's teaching that the Friends of God are at a closer level to God than ordinary believers, and that this proximity requires them to act according to different instructions, those which are communicated to them directly by God. Moreover, this is not simply an alternative, but a superior mode of devotion to God, where one is embroiled in the goal of religious devotion, or "the silk" compared with "the sack"; that is why it would be a serious error to take a step backward to a less direct relationship with God.

It is not simply a matter of contravening the law or not, but acting according to a different basis entirely, without regard for such indirect theoretical formulations. This point is important to bear in mind when considering the main teaching story in *The Masnavi* about this issue, seeing as the action at the center of this story is a Sufi shaikh's wine-drinking, which has been pointed out to one of his wavering disciples. Rumi uses incredible skill to maintain ambiguity in this story about whether or not the Sufi master is actually drinking wine. He never denies it directly, and even when the shaikh's disciple rebuts his accuser, he adds the following comments:

They're false, but even if your words were true
What harm to a huge sea can one corpse do?

He's more than the two jarfuls and small pool[19]
That one small drop could ruin him, you fool . . .
He is an ocean which is limitless—
Your corpse can't dirty it and make it less.
Unbelief's measurable, with boundaries;
He and his light have no peripheries.
Near boundless ones restricted things are naught.
"*All but God's face must perish*"[20] this truth taught.
With him no faith or unbelief can dwell
Since he's the kernel, while they are the shell.[21]

The disciple considers his shaikh to be beyond the need to be concerned about becoming corrupted, or being made impure by anything, a characteristic the shaikh himself confirms later in this story.[22] Although here the justification might not be articulated in terms of the shaikh receiving direct communication from God that may contravene the law, the implication nonetheless is that he subsists in God. He has become "the kernel," beyond "the shell" of faith, unbelief, and all other temporal things, so it would be absurd to judge him by that realm's standards.

As mentioned above, there is much ambiguity in this story because there is no attempt to deny that the shaikh may have been drinking wine. Nonetheless, whenever the disciple himself tastes what he assumes to be wine, it turns out to be honey instead. This occurs when the shaikh hands him his own wineglass to inspect, and also after the shaikh instructs him to fetch him some wine he needs to treat the pain he is suffering. On the latter occasion, the disciple willingly seeks out and tastes what he believes to be wine, but is frustrated to discover that everything in the vats has been changed to honey instead. The story ends with the hadith-based conclusion: "Though the whole world be filled with blood completely/ God's slave will drink what's lawful, if you heed me."[23] This serves as a reminder that according to the Shariah, when compelled and left with no other option it is acceptable to consume what would normally be classified as unlawful. Or to look at it another way, when their every act is under compulsion from God, then the Friends of God's heedlessness of legal formulations is perfectly legitimate even by that legal system's own provisions.

The reason for Rumi's maintenance of ambiguity throughout this story is explained in his homilies during the narrative breaks. One finds here not only his teachings about the differences between a master and a novice disciple but also those about the circumstances in which a master, or Friend of God, who has completed the Sufi path might opt not to completely disregard lower stations he has already transcended, namely for the benefit of guiding others:

> Signposts serve those still traveling, since they
> Inside the desert often lose their way.
> The eyes of those who've reached the destination
> Don't care for signposts to another station;
> If such a man refers to signs, it's so
> The scholars too can have a chance to know.
> A father for his child makes baby sounds,
> Even if his own knowledge knows no bounds;
> The teacher may have great ability,
> But still she'll start her class with ABC.
> To teach a toddler who can hardly stand
> One must use words that he can understand;
> You must use the same words as children do,
> So they can learn new knowledge then from you.
> People are like his children; out of tact
> The shaikh, while counseling, keeps in mind this fact.[24]

Rumi asserts here that Friends of God, or masters, who have completed the path take into consideration the welfare and needs of others in order to teach them how to advance from their own lower level. This is the only reason why they should ever refer to way-stations on the mystical path, since they have completed it themselves and have thereby become free from any need for them. Although the above homily refers only to examples of students and rote-learning, the narrative from which it emerges implies that some of a shaikh's disciples may also fall into their category. More specifically, this is illustrated in the previously mentioned story by the shaikh's performance of a balancing act between telling the truth about his own station, condition, and actions, while at the same time nurturing his novice disciple who had misgivings after seeing him drinking from a glass of wine.

The main teaching of this story in *The Masnavi* is further elaborated during a digression in the middle of the narrative, which serves to contrast the condition of the shaikh with that of a perpetual sinner who boasts to the Prophet Shoayb that God never punishes his sins.[25] This individual is shown to have simply not realized that he was being punished all the time, the same way that the darkening of an already blackened pot will go unnoticed, although it would be perceived immediately on a white pot. The point of this excursus from the main story about the shaikh who was seen drinking wine therefore seems to be to refute any thought of permissivism. Justification is given for the shaikh to be drinking wine, but the casual attitude of a boastful non-mystic toward violating the law of the land is mocked as being based on complete ignorance. This distinction is nonetheless consistent with the way that the shaikh's actions are justified, namely as being due to his transcendence of temporal things, including legal systems devised by religious scholars. The perpetual sinner has not reached such a level, and instead follows his own selfish instincts rather than divine communication.

While in the story where the shaikh is seen drinking wine his doubting disciple only ever tastes honey, even when he is intentionally trying to taste wine on behalf of his shaikh, other teaching stories by Rumi featuring sheikhs and their disciples describe the latter as also contravening the Shariah or Islamic conventions. The most celebrated of these stories is probably the story about Bāyazīd's pilgrimage. In this story, Bāyazīd takes advantage of his journey to Mecca to perform the pilgrimage as an opportunity to discover "his epoch's Khiḍr," or the leading Friend of God of his time. He encounters an old man who tells him to circumambulate him instead of bothering to continue his journey to Mecca, and provides the following justification:

> He judges me much loftier, I swear,
> Than that mere house of His. Let us compare:
> That Kaaba is the home of piety (*birr*),
> But I contain His deepest mystery (*sirr*).
> Inside the Kaaba no one's ever stepped
> And my pure heart none but God will accept.
> When you have seen me, you have seen God too;
> You'll circle then the Kaaba that is true (*kaʿba-yi ṣidq*).
> To serve me is obeying God's decree,
> So don't suppose He's separate from me—
> Open your inner eye, see if you can
> Perceive the light of God inside a man![26]

Bāyazīd is inspired by these words from the old shaikh, which lead him to reach the ultimate end of his Sufi path (*muntahā-yi muntahā*), with the implication that he was well on the way there before this beneficial encounter. A novice disciple whose faith in his master is shaken by seeing him drinking and an advanced seeker who understands that a Friend of God is superior to the Kaaba are naturally very different, and it would appear that Rumi considered their relationship to the Shariah to be one important aspect of the difference. In addition to these stories of *The Masnavi*, Rumi provides one in the

Fīhi mā fīh that conveniently involves disciples with different capacities for appreciating a mysticism that transcends exoteric religious practice. This is the story about the disciples of Rumi's father who decide on different strategies while in his company at the time for prayer:

> The following is a story about the Master Bahā al-Dīn: one day his disciples found him immersed in meditation. When the time for prayer arrived, some of his disciples called out to the master that it was time to pray. The master did not pay attention to their words. They got up and started to pray. Two disciples stayed in conformity with their master and did not rise for prayer.
>
> One of those disciples who were praying, called "Khwājagī," saw manifested to his inner eye (*chishm-i sirr*) that all who were praying alongside him with the prayer-leader actually had their backs to the correct direction of prayer (*qibla*), while those two disciples who had stayed with the master were facing it.
>
> Since the shaikh had passed beyond self-awareness and had become annihilated from self and obliterated in the Light of The Truth (*nūr-i Ḥaqq*) in accordance with the Prophet's saying "Die before you die!," now he had become the Light of The Truth. Whoever turns his back to the Light of The Truth in order to face a wall has certainly turned his back on the correct direction of prayer, for It is the soul of the correct direction of prayer. People face the Kaaba which the Prophet made the direction of prayer for the world. It is more fitting for It (the Light of The Truth) to be the direction of prayer because that Kaaba became the direction of prayer for Its sake.[27]

This teaching story shares with the story about Bāyazīd's pilgrimage the promotion of the Sufi master above the Kaaba, a common trope in Sufi literature. However, in this example, although Rumi's own father is the focus as the Sufi shaikh in question, he does not himself give his disciples instructions or explanations. Instead, the disciples are faced with a decision: whether to follow the guidance of the juristic scholars and pray at the appointed time, or to conform with the actions of their master who had already decided not to stop meditating for the sake of the ritual prayer. One of those who chose the wrong option discovers their error through a mystical vision, and Rumi provides an explanation of why remaining focused on one's meditating shaikh is better than praying toward Mecca. One can regard this as a reiteration of Rumi's teaching that the Sufi's direct engagement with God and spiritual experience is the whole point of formal religion, just as "the Light of the Truth" is "the soul of the direction for prayer." That is to say, the niche facing Mecca, like the legal formulations of religious scholars, has no inherent value that requires it to be followed at all times regardless of whether or not it remains the best direction for proximity to the divine.

Rumi frequently advises the reader to learn from Moses's error in the Qur'anic encounter with Khiḍr, not to question the actions of the Friend of God even if they seem unlawful or wicked, just as he emphasizes the overriding importance of the inner dimension of worship, including notably prayer as well as pilgrimage.[28] His opinion of the correct way to act in this situation should therefore be no surprise. However, the disciples in this teaching story had to make an instant decision without the benefit of an explanation from their master. Their situation may be compared with that of Moses in relation to Khiḍr in the Qur'anic story. It could not have been regarded as easy, seeing as the majority in the story chose the wrong option and only two of those present acted correctly. The view that conventional worship is for the majority, while following one's shaikh in the manner of those two disciples who stayed with Bahā al-Dīn is for the advanced minority, is expressed directly by Rumi in one of his most lengthy homilies on Sufi practice in *The Masnavi*:

> The Prophet told ᶜAlī once: "O ᶜAlī,
> Truth's lion, champion with such bravery,
> Don't count on courage on its own to cope;
> Take refuge too beneath the tree of hope:
> Enter the realm of that pure intellect (*ᶜāqil*)
> Whom no transmitter (*nāqil*) can from truth deflect.
> He shadow is just like Mount Qaf's in size;
> His spirit, like the Simorgh, soars the skies.
> We could continue with this man's applause
> Until the end of time without a pause.
> He is the sun, though human in our sight;
> Please understand that God knows best what's right.
> Of all the good deeds on the path (*ṭāᶜāt-i rāh*), ᶜAlī,
> Choose one of God's elite (*khāṣṣ-i ilāh*) as sanctuary.
> Each man resorts to doing a good deed
> If from his ego he longs to be freed.
> Go to the shade of this wise man, to flee
> The grasp of that rebellious enemy.
> Of all the acts of worship it's the best;
> It makes you far superior to the rest.
> Once he leads you, surrender (*taslīm*) to this guide

As Moses with the master Khiḍr once tried:
Stay calm, don't question what he should commit,
So he won't say, 'Enough! Here's where we split.'[29]
If he destroys their boat, don't you go wild!
Don't tear your hair out if he kills a child!
The Truth has said, 'His hand is as my own,'
And, 'Up above their hands rests God's alone.'[30]
The Truth's hand kills him, makes him live again—
More still, his soul will be eternal then!
Whoever tried this journey on his own
The guides still helped; he didn't walk alone.
The guide's hand is for all across the land;
It has to be then naught but God's own hand.
If absent people can gain gifts galore
Those present with the guide must then get more.
If absent ones receive such gifts for naught
Imagine what his personal guests are brought.
You can't compare his faithful followers
With those who choose to be mere onlookers.
Don't be too squeamish when your guide's around,
As weak as water, crumbly like the ground;
If each blow leaves you bitter don't expect
Without pain like a mirror to reflect."[31]

ᶜAlī is distinguished here from presumably the other followers of the Prophet Muhammad, as someone with the capacity to truly overcome his commanding soul, and the best prescription for this is to follow a master with the kind of complete submission (*taslīm*) Khiḍr had demanded of Moses. It is worth noting that ᶜAlī is warned not to imagine he could cope on his own, and that the master is presented as someone with direct knowledge in contrast with someone who transmits knowledge in the manner of a religious scholar (*ᶜāqil v nāqil*). Moreover, while pious acts of obedience (*ṭāᶜāt*), such as those that may be formulated by those scholars or Sufi theorists, are not dismissed or derided, surrendering completely to a Sufi master (*pīr*) in this manner is considered superior, in agreement with the story about Bahā Walad's disciples at the time for prayer. The underlying point in the above passage is that the challenge for the Sufi is to overcome the commanding soul, and the most effective way of achieving this is through devotion to a Sufi master, not through transmitted scholarship, bold individual striving, or pious devotion to God.

The above examples are representative of Rumi's teaching that the Friend of God is unconstrained by the Shariah or any other code of behavior, because his relationship with God is closer, and therefore at a higher level.[32] Moreover, it is important to note that the disciples of such individuals could also be unconstrained by it when they receive instruction from the Friend of God, which has precedence over any theoretical code of behavior. Behind these examples is the conviction that following obediently one's master is more effective than anything else for completing the Sufi path.[33] Rumi appears to go even further than this by indicating that in addition to giving precedence to the company of their master, those who have the capacity can also follow their own hearts in deciding how to act. He mentions this as part of a follow-up to a dialogue between Jesus and John the Baptist which respectively contrasts their approaches to God as being optimistic of His grace and fearful of His wrath. Rumi adds that one of the Friends of God asked God which is better. God's response takes the form of the hadith in which He expresses preference for the one who thinks better of Him.[34] Following this, Rumi gives advice about preserving one's thoughts for God alone in the eleventh chapter of the *Fīhi mā fīh*:

> Examine yourself to decide which is more beneficial for you out of weeping, laughing, fasting, praying, seclusion, company and other acts. Adopt whichever one is the means by which your states will become more true and your progress will accelerate. "Consult your heart even if the muftis have given you a fatwa!" (*istafti qalbak wa-in aftāk al-muftūn*)[35] means precisely this. You have a spiritual organ within. Let it review the fatwa of the muftis and adopt whatever it agrees with.[36]

The notion that an advanced disciple could find it more beneficial to follow the divine communication received by his own heart than the rulings of a legal expert is a reminder of Rumi's stress on the greater importance of the inner state of an individual over his or her actions. This point is made emphatically in the 34th chapter of the *Fīhi mā fīh*, where Rumi expresses such views in the context of what seems like his lament over a former attendant who was being led astray by means of piety. He refers to that piety as being more harmful than carnal pleasure:

> If the attendant were here, I would go to him, counsel him, and not leave his side until he drives him away and distances himself from [his teacher], because he is corrupting his faith, heart, spirit, and intellect. If only he would lead him towards other corruptions such as drinking

> wine and singing-girls—that could be repaired if the grace of a holy one were to come in contact with him, but instead he has filled his house with prayer-rugs. I wish he were rolled up in them and set on fire, so that the attendant could be free from him and his evil. . . . He has trapped him with rosaries, litanies, and prayer-rugs![37]

Although the above passage refers to a specific situation, Rumi's emphatic protest that pious worship, represented by prayer-rugs, rosaries, and litanies, was doing more harm to the spiritual development of a relative novice than drinking and singing-girls ever could, gives an indication of what might seem like a surprising attitude. However, his writings abound with critiques of false piety, most memorably in the form of humorous tales in *The Masnavi*. For instance, the story about the deaf man who visited his sick neighbor illustrates the emptiness of following a code without completely genuine engagement.[38] The deaf man visits his neighbor because he feels he ought to, and, since he is deaf, prepares what he will say on the basis of guesswork regarding what the sick neighbor might tell him. His visit comically has the opposite effect because all the guesses turn out to be wrong. Rumi concludes that story by condemning the prayers of those who seek rewards from their worship:

> "While being obedient (*ṭāᶜat*) many are astray
> With thoughts of their rewards on Judgment Day;
> It's truly sin (*maᶜṣiyat*), though hidden in this guise
> And all their vileness seems pure to your eyes."[39]

In addition, one can refer to the well-known story of Muᶜāwiya and Satan in the second book of *The Masnavi*, where the latter wakes him up to perform the morning prayer simply so he will miss out on the greater benefit of the inner feeling of anguish after having missed that prayer.[40] Such comments are so frequent that it may sometimes seem that Rumi reserved his criticism for pious acts of worship. This is surely not the case, but can be interpreted instead as symptomatic of the fact that precisely such pious actions are the ones that people around him could be driven to perform for show or out of a sense of obligation in the manner of the deaf neighbor, rather than as a heartfelt expression. Moreover, if it is to be accepted that he inherited students from his father of a very different aptitude, it is understandable that he should have been so concerned about the conditioning of his audience to perform such actions thoughtlessly. Therefore, it may be no coincidence that when Rumi gives a defense of an instance when a shaikh insisted that his disciples perform an outward action, it is actually in relation to actions that do not have religious origins:

> There was a shaikh who made his disciples stay standing up in attendance with hands folded. He was told, "O shaikh, why don't you seat this group, because this is not the manner of dervishes (*rasm-i darwīshān*) but instead the custom of princes and kings!"
>
> He said, "No, be quiet! I want them to have reverence like this, so they will benefit!"
>
> Although reverence is in the heart, still "the outward aspect is the title-page of the inner aspect" (*al-ẓāhir ʿunwān al-bāṭin*). What is the meaning of "title-page"? It means that from the title-page of a book you can tell what sections and chapters it contains. From outward reverence, lowering the head, and standing up, it becomes known what kind of reverence they have within, and how they revere God. If they do not show reverence outwardly, it is then known that they are unconcerned within and do not revere the men of God (*mardān-i ḥaqq*).[41]

Although in this story the shaikh demands his disciples perform an outward act, it is for the sake of an inner quality, namely reverence for him as God's representative. Any Sufi master would necessarily prescribe things for disciples to do as a means to aid them in completing the Sufi path. What is important to note is that the demands of inner development are what determine the action, rather than the constraints of any theoretical system, whether that be the Shariah or indeed Sufism's own past customs. As disciples advance and succeed in the struggle against the self, they would be able to follow the divine communication in their hearts increasingly, at which point they are also unconstrained by any external code. Although a Sufi tradition's own customs may not always be followed rigidly, this is not to imply that Sufis can have a casual attitude toward their actions. In Rumi's view, their actions under guidance must serve the challenge of overcoming the self, a much more demanding task than the Shariah aspires to achieve; in the case of those who have succeeded in this task, their every action becomes compelled by God's direct command.

In previous studies of Rumi's view of the Shariah, the prose introduction of the fifth book of *The Masnavi* has been considered a key passage deserving attention. Having already examined Rumi's many references to the Shariah in his didactic writings, I will now evaluate this passage, given here in its entirety:

> This is the fifth of the books of the poem and spiritual exposition that is *The Masnavi*, clarifying that the *sharīʿat* is like a candle which shows the path; unless you obtain the candle the path cannot be traveled.

Once you have come to the path, your traveling on it is the *ṭarīqat*. When you reach the destination, that is the *ḥaqīqat*. This is why it has been said: *"If the ḥaqīqats were to appear, the sharīᶜats would become void."* This is the same as when copper becomes gold, or was gold originally—it has no need for the theory of alchemy which is the *sharīᶜat* (*ū-rā nahᶜilm-i kīmiyā ḥājat-ast kih ān sharīᶜat-ast*) and neither does it need to rub itself on the philosopher's stone, a process which is the *ṭarīqat*, as it has been said: *"It is despicable to seek a guide after arrival at the goal, and abandoning the guide before arrival at the goal is also blameworthy."*

In summary, the *sharīᶜat* is like learning the theory of alchemy from a teacher or book, while the *ṭarīqat* is applying the chemicals and rubbing the copper on the philosopher's stone, and the *ḥaqīqat* is the transmutation of copper into gold. Those with knowledge of alchemy celebrate their knowledge of it, saying: "We know the theory of this." Those who actually carry out alchemy celebrate applying alchemy, saying: "We are doing such works." Those who attain the truth celebrate the truth, saying: "We have become gold and are free from the theory and application of alchemy. We are God's emancipated ones." *Each group is celebrating what they themselves have* (Qur'an 18/110).

Alternatively, the *sharīᶜat* may be compared with learning the science of medicine, the *ṭarīqat* with restricting one's diet in accordance with the science of medicine or taking remedies, and the *ḥaqīqat* with attaining everlasting good health and being free from the other two. When a man dies to this life, the *sharīᶜat* and the *ṭarīqat* become disconnected from him, and only the *ḥaqīqat* remains. If he possesses the *ḥaqīqat*, he yells: *"Oh, if only my people could know how my Lord has forgiven me!"* (Qur'an 36/26–7). But if he does not possess it, he yells: *"Oh, if only I had not been given my record of deeds and remained unaware of my reckoning! Oh, if only [my death] had been the final decree. My wealth has not availed me; my authority has perished and left me!"* (Qur'an 69/25–9)

The *sharīᶜat* is the theory, the *ṭarīqat* is the action, the *ḥaqīqat* is reaching God: "Let whoever hopes to meet his Lord perform good actions and not associate anything with the worship of his Lord" (Qur'an 18/110).[42]

This passage relates the meanings of three balanced rhyming terms (*sharīᶜat*, *ṭarīqat* and *ḥaqīqat*) to each other sequentially. The *sharīᶜat* (usually translated as "law") shows the way, or provides the theoretical basis, to the *ṭarīqat* (usually translated as "mystical path"), the process of activity that leads one to the *ḥaqīqat* (usually translated as "the Truth"). In addition to providing three different analogies for the relationship between these stages, Rumi stresses repeatedly a specific point he deems so important that it is also the first point he actually articulates, namely that those who have reached the *ḥaqīqat* no longer have any need for the other two. If this point is applied to the Friend of God who has completed the mystical path and reached God, then this prose introduction would be a reaffirmation of Rumi's view that this figure is not constrained by any law or code of behavior.[43] On this basis, the rest of the passage has usually been interpreted as meaning that one must follow the religious law (*sharīᶜat*) in order to be able to undertake the Sufi path (*ṭarīqat*), even if one no longer has any need for either of these once the Truth, or God *(ḥaqīqat)*, has been reached.[44] However, a rush to interpret it in this way risks overlooking the problematic aspects of this passage, which should be taken into consideration.

It is important to appreciate that finding three balanced and rhyming technical terms that can conveniently be used to mean precisely what you need for a given passage is a rare achievement, even for a poet as talented as Rumi. Rumi's usage of the term *sharīᶜat* here is arguably the most forced of the three. This is because *sharīᶜat* usually means the religious law one follows in the Islamic religious system, a factor so distinctive that it has famously led commentators to observe that Islam is more of an "orthopraxy" than an "orthodoxy"; in other words, Islam is more about "doing" than "knowing."[45] The problem with Rumi's use of the term *sharīᶜat* in this passage, though it rhymes excellently with the other two terms, is that it is clearly meant to refer to knowledge rather than action. The only "doing" referred to here is the Sufi path, or *ṭarīqat*. The term *sharīᶜat* is instead used here to represent something closer to "believing," in that it is described as "the theory of alchemy" (rather than its application), or "the candle which shows the path" (as opposed to actually traveling the way). Although, on the basis of these analogies, some have still been tempted to assume that the *ṭarīqat* is simply the application of the formulations of the religious law, the passages presented earlier in this chapter indicate that for Rumi the Sufi path can neither be equated with the religious law nor wholly constrained by it. Moreover, this fifth book of *The Masnavi,* for which the passage above serves as prose introduction, lacks any support that the religious law is meant; rather, according to this book (as well as the rest) of *The Masnavī,* the key to transcending the material world and entering into the mystical path (*ṭarīqat*) is the intervention of the grace of God and His representatives. The answer to what the term *sharīᶜat* means in this passage may therefore lie in its concluding statement, repeated here:

"The *sharīʿat* is the theory (*ʿilm*), the *ṭarīqat* is the action (*ʿamal*), the *ḥaqīqat* is reaching God (*wuṣūl ila Llāh*): *Let whoever hopes to meet his Lord perform good actions and not associate anything with the worship of his Lord*" (Qur'an 18/110).

Both Rumi's statement and the subsequent Qur'anic citation include three elements, which correspond as follows:

Let whoever hopes to meet his Lord = the *ḥaqīqat* is reaching God
perform good actions = the *ṭarīqat* is the action
not associate anything with the worship of his Lord = the *sharīʿat* is the theory

Although the Qur'anic verse is presented at the very end of this passage, the close correspondence demonstrated above may indicate that it was its original inspiration. This would mean that the term *sharīʿat* is not being used to mean "law" here, but rather to mean knowledge of religion in general, or more specifically, the monotheistic view expressed in the above-cited Qur'anic verse.[46] Taking into account the way that Rumi defines these terms in this passage and illustrates them by means of analogies, the above correspondence would be the least problematic, and it is even reiterated in a verse later in this same book of *The Masnavī:*

"Until 'No god but God' you should declare/You will not find the way to the path there." *Tā nakhwānī lā wa illa Llāh-rā/dar nayābī manhaj-i īn rāh-rā.*"[47]

It is worth remembering that, as far as Rumi is concerned, the means of realization of even the Sufi disciple cannot be equated with following the Shariah. Their relationship with a Friend of God, the living bearer of charisma who can offer divinely communicated guidance, is what privileges the followers of the Sufi path (*ṭarīqa*). Similarly, in the example Rumi gives from the time of his own father, at the call to prayer most of his father's disciples turned away from him to pray, but two opted for the more challenging alternative of remaining with their master despite all that they must have been taught in their upbringing about performing daily prayers on time. They were inspired by his example, which was itself understood to be at God's command for a confirmatory vision to be revealed. However, Rumi's views on the Shariah have not usually been interpreted in this way.

William C. Chittick's book *The Sufi Doctrine of Rumi* was republished in 2005, thirty-one years after its first publication, with his explanation that he "agree[s] with practically everything"[48] in the first printing. This work includes a translation of the same prose introduction of the fifth book of *The Masnavi* with the parenthetical comment: "[i.e. unless you follow the Sharīᶜah, you cannot enter the Ṭarīqah]" as his interpretation of what Rumi means when he says, "Unless you gain possession of the candle, there is no wayfaring" (Chittick's translation).[49] At the same time, in his introduction to this passage, he makes the assertion that "once the goal of the Path has been reached, doctrine is 'discarded.'"[50] This leads the reader to presume that his citation of this prose introduction is due appropriately enough to the emphasis in it, above all other points it makes, that those who have reached God have no need for "doctrine." However, by asserting that they must start off by "following the Sharīᶜah" before they can even venture on the Sufi path, or *ṭarīqa,* Chittick seems to be implicitly equating the Shariah with "law" here, even though he mentions that it is "doctrine" that is discarded at the end, but it remains at least ambiguous.

In his 1983 work *The Sufi Path of Love,* Chittick offers an alternative and heavily truncated translation. This excludes the entire section where Rumi underlines his main point in this passage, which had been correctly identified by Chittick himself nine years earlier, about how someone who has reached God no longer needs the path that took him there.[51] Presumably, his selectivity here is due to the use of the passage for a different purpose in this new context. Chittick's 1983 translation also appears to be a completely fresh translation because of his use of a different set of vocabulary. The commentary he provides for his fresh translation suggests that he no longer interprets "the Sharīᶜah" in this passage as "law," whether or not he meant to imply that in his earlier translation. This is because Chittick himself makes the point here that "Sufis understand 'Law' or Sharīᶜah in its widest sense, as embracing 'knowledge' and all the theoretical teachings of Islam."[52] However, he immediately follows this up by asserting ambiguously that "The 'Way' or Ṭarīqah is then the method of putting *the law* into practice."[53] As I have argued above, without any need to refer to anything external to the prose introduction itself, the more obvious reading is that the term *sharīᶜat* here means knowledge of religion in the broadest sense. Chittick most probably perceived this all along, but may have still used inconsistent vocabulary simply due to the weight of interpretation of this term as "law" in Islamic literature. This necessarily affects how *ṭarīqat* is interpreted: if *sharīᶜat* does not mean "law," then one cannot have it both ways by arguing that *ṭarīqat* means "putting the law into practice." In Rumi's view, it is knowledge in a broad sense of Islam's monotheistic message, in accordance with the Qur'anic citation at the conclusion, and not a code of law that determines the actions of the Sufi on the mystical path. If Rumi had wished to equate the Sufi path with the putting into practice of the Shariah, he had plenty of opportunities to do so as unambiguously as he presents his other teachings.

This minor inconsistency in Chittick's translation of the passage discussed above is a trifle when seen in light of the long tradition of interpreting Rumi in contradictory ways in the academy. Annemarie Schimmel attributes to Rumi a "strict adherence to the law,"[54] as well as the opinion that "'Sufism' branches out of the great trunk road *sharīᶜa*."[55] She goes as far as to characterize Rumi as belonging to those Sufis "whose mystical state was deepened by the experience of ritual prayer, not to those whose high spiritual flights were interrupted when turning to the prescribed formulas of the *namāz*."[56] The numerous examples provided in the first section of this chapter show how her influential depictions of Rumi are highly questionable.

The assumptions of Schimmel are often reproduced hand-in-hand with reminders that Rumi was brought up in and taught at a "*madrasa*." Franklin Lewis has thankfully given a useful reminder that *madrasa*s at that time could take many forms, with Rumi's father's certainly not functioning as a place to earn a license to practice as a jurisconsult.[57] In fact, Lewis is putting it mildly when he comes to this conclusion from a passage which reveals that students at other centers actually feared joining Rumi's circle. Their fear is that they would "forget the knowledge they had already acquired and abandon it" (*ᶜilm-rā farāmūsh kunand wa-tārik shawand*), rather than simply that they would not be able to earn a useful qualification.[58] Rumi's acknowledgment of this situation in his *Fīhī mā fīh* indicates that his circle was not simply a less academically intensive version of a seminary, but a place for learning spirituality without privileging the exoteric understanding of Islam. This is also evident from the contents of the *Fīhi mā fīh* itself, not to mention *The Masnavi*, which was after all written for the students there in mind.[59]

Lewis's more recent biographical study also contains some brief summaries of Rumi's teachings. As syntheses of earlier scholarship, they reveal the same tendency to interpret Rumi through preconceptions of a normative Sufism. For instance, Lewis comments under "Outward observances" that "the saints do not fail to pray, to fast, to perform alms, to go on pilgrimage and so forth."[60] While they do not fail to fulfill what God wants them to perform at any given moment, for Rumi this cannot simply be equated with the main rituals as defined by the Islamic religious system. Moreover, his comment at the end of this section that "one observes the outward form with the *qāzi*s and the men of literal legalism," while sounding plausible, is in fact either an unfortunately ambiguous usage of the term "observes" or an unfaithful rendering of the passage in Rumi's *Masnavi* to which he refers (IV, vv. 2175–78): There, Rumi is critiquing legal scholars by way of an analogy (within a typical list of multiple analogies) for making judgments on the basis of appearance without any mention or implication of what one should or should not do while with them, or that anyone but legal scholars should observe the mere outward form.[61] It has almost become common wisdom that Sufism as a whole defers to juristic Islam, and has always done so; the weight of such an assumption can explain why these interpretations of Rumi have been prevalent among academicians. It will therefore be important to consider what the oldest surviving Sufi writings on Friendship with God have to say about this matter.

The Friend of God and the Shariah in Kharrāz's (d. ca. 286/899) al-Kashf wa'l-bayān and Tirmidhī's (d. between 295–300/905–910) Sīrat al-awliyā'

As mentioned in chapter 1, among the very oldest surviving Sufi writings are two treatises that seem to be products of ongoing debates about the Friends of God, namely the *al-Kashf wa'l-bayān* of Abū Sa'īd al-Kharrāz[62] and the *Sīrat al-Awliyā'* of Ḥakīm al-Tirmidhī.[63] They were written in the period when jurisprudence was still beginning to consolidate its authority among the approaches to Islamic sources. Kharrāz, who shows much more concern for theological matters than jurisprudential ones, does not actually make any mention of the Shariah itself in his *al-Kashf wa'l-bayān,* referring instead to God's command (*amr*) and will (*mashī'a*). Kharrāz illustrates this particular point by using an example remarkably similar to Rumi's famous story about the lover who knocked on his beloved's door and said, "It is you" instead of "It is I":[64]

> How can anyone be free to say 'I and you' other than someone veiled from the truth of servanthood (*ḥaqīqat al-'ubūdiyya*). Do you not see that the origin of the claim was with Satan, when he said, "I am better than him: You created me from fire and him from clay" (Qur'an 7/12). If any person says "I," his speech is derived from pride and blindness about servanthood. If the servant says "I," God says, "I, not you." If the servant says, "You," God says, "I and you." The special distinction of the Friends of God then in this case is that not one of them says "I."[65]

The overall point Kharrāz makes about the mystic "servant of God" being subject to God's "command" and "will" can be fruitfully compared with Rumi's notion of the compulsion of the Friend of God to act always at the command of God, who directs him once he no longer has self-consciousness, let alone a will of his own to follow. As Christopher Melchert has importantly pointed out, such a doctrine indicates adherence to a strict degree of servanthood to God rather than an antinomian claim for greater personal freedom.[66]

In her unpublished doctoral dissertation, Nada A. Saab has pointed out that Kharrāz does not consider the Shariah as all-authoritative. In fact, she characterizes him as a Sufi who "endeavored to demonstrate the superiority of ecstatic mysticism over Islamic religious law."[67] This is based on comments such as the following from his *Kitāb al-Ṣafā*:

> Their allotment from God is perfect and all that God had was perfect before and after their existence. . . . Had God created all men deaf, mute and blind, whereby they did not remember Him to the end of time, and as their acts [of worship] were diminished, this would not decrease what they had previously received from Him. If they do acts [of worship] and strive with all their might, this will not add anything.[68]

In Kharrāz's case, the lack of specific reference to the Shariah in his *al-Kashf wa'l-bayān* seems most likely to be a reflection of its relative lack of significance by this date, rather than a strategy of silence on the matter. His more scholastically accomplished contemporary Ḥakīm Tirmidhī considers in some detail the actions of the Friends of God in his *Sīrat al-awliyā'*, even if he too is more concerned with theological aspects of Friendship with God overall. Tirmidhī's Friend of God (*walī Allāh*) and Lesser Friend of God (*walī ḥaqq Allāh*)[69] are distinguished from each other emphatically regarding this issue. The former category are directed by God's command, having lost their self-will and the ability to act of their own accord:

> God nourishes [the Friend of God] with His grace until the will to act does not remain at all in his self, at which point the Most Magnificent Will (*al-mashī'a al-ʿuẓmā*) appears to him from the realm of God's grace. Then the veil is lifted and he is commanded to advance into the state of inability to act by oneself (*ʿajz*).[70]

It is worth noting that Tirmidhī also insists that Friends of God can receive good tidings confirming their security in the afterlife, like the ten companions of the Prophet Muhammad who received such news from him, and were labeled accordingly "*al-ʿashara al-mubashshara*."[71] In his spirited defense of this belief, which is compatible with the above-cited comment by Kharrāz, he responds to the perceived threat that this would allow Friends of God to act as they please, by means of the following reassurance:

> We have learned that good tidings should be forbidden on account of harm they could cause, but [the Friend of God's] heart is in His grasp, he speaks through Him, hears through Him, sees through Him and understands through Him, so how can good tidings cause him harm?[72]

Not only does this underline Tirmidhī's view that the Friend of God ultimately acts under the direct guidance of God's command rather than any particular legal or ethical system, but it also has the effect of asserting that whatever the Friend of God does must be right, because all he does is through the direction of God, whose will is what the juristic scholars attempt to approximate to the best of their abilities in their formulations; therefore, there can be no harm in him receiving foreknowledge of his assured felicity in the afterlife.

According to Tirmidhī, the highest station reached by his Lesser Friend of God (*walī ḥaqq Allāh*) is that of being drawn up by God similarly to his full Friend of God (*walī Allāh*), by virtue of which he too can join the latter category.[73] Before then, however, he must follow some kind of path of struggle. For Tirmidhī, this means primarily the struggle against the self while maintaining sincerity, and not simply the fulfillment of a religious law or formulated code of behavior. It is worth noting that Tirmidhī downplays the significance of the Shariah for this lower category, stressing instead the paramount importance of sincerity (*ṣidq/ikhlāṣ*) in one's actions.[74]

The all-important turning point for Tirmidhī is when God draws up the seeker into Friendship with God and action only under the direction of His command for His purposes. Therefore, the less one is led by his own will and the more he is led by God the better. Ahmet Karamustafa has shown that Tirmidhī's contemporary Abū'l-Qāsim al-Junayd (d. 297/910), who may also have been Kharrāz's student, similarly "seems to close the door to spiritual advancement through personal striving," with comments such as the following: "Know that you are veiled from Him through yourself, and that you do not reach Him through yourself but that you reach Him through Him."[75]

Since acting on one's own initiative is inevitably flawed in Tirmidhī's view, this might explain why, in response to being asked what a lesser Friend of God (*walī ḥaqq Allāh*) should then do, he answers:

> He should carry out what is absolutely compulsory in the law (*farāʾiḍ*)[76] and not transgress the absolute restrictions (*ḥudūd*).[77] There is nothing in this, if he should carry it out, that would make him incapable of the other things (*sāʾir al-ashyāʾ*). What servanthood is more noble than this? Has God compelled His servants to anything besides this?[78]

The two technical terms from jurisprudence he uses here, *farāʾiḍ* and *ḥudūd*, combine to mean the absolute requirements of the law, representing extremities of actions that are compulsory and strictly forbidden, respectively. Furthermore, the above statement appears after two paragraphs where Tirmidhī dismisses the value of actively seeking God through obedience and good deeds, which he views as simply giving pleasure to the carnal soul with the delusion that one can reach God through it.[79] Therefore, his recommendation to Lesser Friends of God here appears to be to follow no more than what is necessary of the law, and to beware of its potential to be counterproductive for the all-important struggle against the self.

The ultimate goal of the mystic contrasts favorably in Tirmidhī's view with the actions of other religious figures who preoccupy themselves with the Shariah. He criticizes the latter for feeding the self through acts permissible according to their own legal formulations, adding that, in place of the forbidden things that initially attract them, they feed the same lusts with something lawful; as a result, they will continue to crave those forbidden things and remain insincere.[80] This highlights the difference between his view of the religious law and the Sufi path, for which the legality of an act is not the criterion, but rather the degree to which it helps subdue the self, at which stage Friends of God will be commanded directly by God Himself and will no longer be able to do anything outside of His command. As Tirmidhī puts it in the forty-third paragraph of the *Sīrat al-awliyāʾ*, the Friend of God is told:

> "We impose on you, along with freedom from bondage to your carnal soul, the condition that you must stand firm here and not go forth to undertake works without permission. If We give you permission, we will send you forth with guardians."[81]

Tirmidhī uses the actual term *sharīʿa* in two contexts in his *Sīrat al-awliyā*, in both cases as something by which the Friend of God is restricted. When this refers to something that the divine communication received by the Friend of God will never contradict, he is evidently using the expression "*sharīʿat al-rasūl*" in the sense of religious knowledge, rather than the formulated law of religious scholars.[82] Tirmidhī also uses the term "*sharīʿa*" while justifying the possibility for Friends of God to receive divine communication that is secure from the intervention of Satan. Here, he depicts messengers (*rasūl*) as bringing a *sharīʿa*, ordinary prophets (*nabī*) as following and propagating it (*wa'l-nabī alladhī lam yursal huwa yatbaʿ sharīʿat dhālika al-rasūl wa-yadʿū al-khalq ilā tilka al-sharīʿa allatī atā bihā al-rasūl*), and Friends of God, who are communicated with by God, as calling people to God through it (*al-muḥaddath yadʿū ilā Allāh ʿalā sabīl tilka al-sharīʿa*).[83] He also adds the reassurance that none of the divine communication received by the Friend of God abrogates the *sharīʿa* or contradicts it. The reference to ordinary prophets "following" it supports the interpretation of the term here as "Holy Law," as Radtke consistently renders it. However, it may be significant that Tirmidhī does not say that the Friend of God himself follows the *sharīʿa*, even though he describes the ordinary prophet as doing so, especially since he is invariably very precise about what he wishes to convey. One should also bear in mind his many references that contradict the notion that the Friend of God should follow legal formulations, and his prescription for the lesser Friend of God of just the bare minimum of the formulations. Significantly, those statements are made while describing the different categories of Friend of God, rather than in a defensive passage where he intends to offer reassurance that Friends of God are subordinate to Prophets and can be trusted with good tidings about their future outcome.

In summary, these two ninth-century Sufi treatises about Friendship with God are more preoccupied with theological aspects of Friendship with God than legal ones. This is representative of the time, as one can also see in Sahl al-Tustarī's (d. 283/896) relative lack of concern for legal issues; he even asserts that Friends of God go directly to paradise without undergoing any judgment process.[84] Both of them also refer to outside criticism, although only Tirmidhī identifies the source with the ambiguous "*ʿulamāʾ al-ẓāhir*" and "*qurrāʾ*."[85] More is perhaps given away by the contexts where he refers to such criticism or implies it, namely with regard to elevating the status of the Friend of God above that of a Prophet. One might add also that he implicitly responds, or at least preempts, a demand from opponents for a greater degree of adherence to the Shariah, such as in the above-quoted passage, where he asks rhetorically in relation to the still aspiring Lesser Friend of God: "Has God compelled His servants to anything besides this?" Tirmidhī also returns criticism of his own by accusing his opponents of transmitting more controversial hadiths than the ones they complain about.[86] Elsewhere, Tirmidhī has identified his opponents as the semirationalist Hanafites, who were a major presence in his region, and he has also indicated his disagreement with their all-encompassing approach to the Shariah by pointing out that the acknowledgment of its limitations by pioneer jurists was being increasingly ignored.[87] Tirmidhī writes as a participant in the discussion about the development of the Shariah and the kind of authority it should have, and this probably best explains why he does not shy away from making direct critiques of its application. Although his criticisms may not have been aimed exclusively at Hanafites, with terms such as "*qurrāʾ*" and references to hadith transmission perhaps indicating more Traditonalist-leaning opponents, when it comes to the Shariah he probably focused on the former group.

Tirmidhī is the only one of this pair who makes a distinction between different levels of Friends of God: for the still aspiring Lesser Friends of God (*walī ḥaqq Allāh*) he recommends the minimum necessary of the Shariah, though they should tread with caution. His treatment of this category is similar to Rumi's treatment of disciples in that their task is the struggle against the control that the self still has over them. Tirmidhī's concern about the psychological aspects of the self is so great that he warns extensively against self-prescribing pious worship, because it could jeopardize one's sincerity and lead to pride and vainglory, not to mention prove counterproductive in the endeavor to be drawn up by God rather than rely on one's own means. There is therefore already an articulated precedent in Tirmidhī's ninth-century work for Rumi's later teaching that the Sufi path that aspirants should follow is designed to defeat the self, and that this cannot be simply equated with the Shariah. Moreover, Tirmidhī already points out the psychological pitfalls in following avidly the formulations of jurists, which Rumi would expand on some four centuries later. It may be no coincidence to find such sentiments dating from a period when juristic scholars were only beginning to consolidate the authority of their knowledge, as well as long after this process had been securely completed, but not during the critical consolidation period.

The main reason why common wisdom has been that Sufism always defers to juristic Islam is the presentation of their relationship in the Sufi manuals of the tenth and eleventh centuries, which became highly influential because of their popularity. In the next two sections of this chapter, I consider their treatments of this topic with close scrutiny, in order to assess them in their historical context and determine whether they may be more nuanced than they are usually assumed to be.

Friendship with God and the Shariah in Sarrāj's (d. 378/988) Kitāb al-Lumaᶜ and Kalābādhī's (d. 380s/990s) Kitāb al-Taᶜarruf

From a cursory glance at the *Kitāb al-Taᶜarruf* of Abū Bakr al-Kalābādhī,[88] the reader immediately notices that, in contrast to the ninth-century mystic authors, this author expresses a greater appreciation of the scholars of jurisprudence. The most conspicuous sign of this is his inclusion of a chapter on "[the Sufis'] opinions on the legal schools (*madhāhib al-sharᶜiya*)."

Here, Kalābādhī asserts that Sufis defer to experts in the law and appreciate their difference of opinion (*ikhtilāf*), even imposing on themselves the most cautious and safest course of action in such situations (*innahum ya'khudhūn li-anfusihim bi-l-aḥwaṭ wa'l-awthaq fī-mā ikhtalafa fīhi al-fuqahā'*).[89] This already reads as a major departure from the "minimum necessary" prescription by Tirmidhī to Lesser Friends of God and the ambiguous "will" and "command" of God referred to by Kharrāz, although that is perhaps not so surprising when one appreciates that Kalābādhī was not primarily a mystic in all likelihood.

Although he does not specify the Friend of God in his chapter devoted to the legal schools, he does so when discussing duties imposed by God on the legally mature (*fī-mā kallafa Allāh al-bālighīn*), and also the station of annihilation in God, which a Friend attains. In the former chapter, Kalābādhī comments:

> [The Sufis] agree unanimously that everything which God has made compulsory for his servants in His book, and the Messenger of God has made obligatory, is indeed compulsory (*farḍ*) and obligatory (*wājib*), and is a mandatory imposition (*ḥatm lāzim*) on mature and rational people; neither abandonment of it nor neglect of it is permissible in any way to any person, including the holy one (*ṣiddīq*), the ordinary Friend of God (*walī*), and the mystic (*ʿārif*).[90]

Although the Shariah itself is not mentioned here, the use of technical legal terms *"farḍ"* and *"wājib,"* as well as the reference to the Qur'an and Prophetic sunnah, indicate what is meant. Moreover, his assertion that even mystics and Friends of God are subject to the law is an indication that he thought this specifically needed to be spelled out. That is to say, he must have thought that some might assume that mystics and Friends of God were excluded otherwise. If any further corroboration were required, he emphasizes his insistence that the Friend of God continue to follow Shariah rules of prayer in his chapter on self-annihilation and subsistence (*fanā' wa-baqā'*).

> The self-annihilated one is preserved (*maḥfūẓ*) with regard to his duties given by God (*waẓā'if al-ḥaqq*), as Junayd has confirmed: he was told, "Abū al-Ḥusayn al-Nūrī has been standing in the al-Shūnīzī mosque for days without eating, drinking or sleeping, and has been repeating 'Allāh, Allāh!' He also does his ritual prayers at their appointed times." Someone present said, "He is sober." Junayd said, "No, rather those who have ecstasies (*aṣḥāb al-mawājīd*) are preserved (*maḥfūẓūn*) before God during their ecstasies."[91]

The obvious reading of this passage is that self-annihilation does not mean transcendence of the Shariah's requirements, such as performance of the ritual prayer at the appointed times calculated by jurists. Its message could not contrast more with Rumi's story about his father remaining immersed in meditation rather than heeding the call to prayer. The meaning of "preserved" here would consequently be that God enables His self-annihilated Friends to continue to fulfill the Shariah, even though their ecstatic state makes it seem unachievable. When one also takes into consideration Kalābādhī's insistence in his chapter on the miracles of the Friends of God, that they continue to be anxious about satisfying God even after being assured about their outcome in the afterlife (an attainment he confirms), then his consistent message appears to be one that insists on the applicability of the Shariah to everyone, regardless of their spiritual development or ecstatic state.[92] The reasoning applied here contrasts strongly with that of Tirmidhī, Kharrāz, and Tustarī from a century earlier. Tirmidhī had argued that there is no objection to the Friend of God feeling secure about the future because his every action is directed by God in any case, and so it is right and good regardless, while Kharrāz and Tustarī had suggested that the Friend of God's actions are irrelevant to his final outcome in the afterlife. In contrast, Kalābādhī's argument is that God intervenes so as to ensure that the Friend of God can fulfill the Shariah despite his ecstasies, and when he is not in ecstasy the Friend of God is self-consciously anxious about pleasing God.

Kalābādhī's contemporary Abū Naṣr al-Sarrāj[93] does not often discuss directly the applicability of the law to the Friend of God, but he does so indirectly in his chapter "Those Who Have Erred Regarding the Essence of Union (*ᶜayn al-jamᶜ*)," which is found in the series of chapters on "erroneous beliefs" among the Sufis. He begins this chapter with the following identification of what he considers an erroneous belief:

> A group have erred concerning the essence of union (*ᶜayn al-jamᶜ*), for they fail to ascribe to creatures what God has ascribed to them, and they do not attribute to themselves action (*ḥaraka*) that they carry out, reckoning that this is as a precaution not to allow anything other than God to exist alongside God. That has led them to leave the religious community (*milla*) and abandon the *ḥudūd* rulings of the Shariah, on the basis of their belief that they are compelled to carry out their actions (*hum mujbirūn ᶜalā ḥarakātihim*), to the extent that they become absolved of blame for transgressing the *ḥudūd* rulings and non-compliance. Among them are some whom this has led to the audacity of licentiousness and idleness, and whose carnal souls have emboldened them to believe that they are excused for doing anything they have been compelled to do.[94]

Sarrāj's assertion seemingly discounts any belief that Friends of God may eventually act on the basis of compulsion to execute God's command without the involvement of their own will. His specific mention of "precaution not to allow anything other than God to exist alongside God" suggests that he is referring here to the sentiment expressed by Kharrāz in the above-quoted illustration about not saying "I." However, he seems to be principally concerned with those of his contemporary Sufis who feel absolved of responsibility for whatever they do, and, on that basis, ignore the absolute *ḥudūd* prohibitions of the Shariah.[95]

The strangest aspect of this chapter is when Sarrāj unnecessarily indicates that his opinion is one that had not been completely shared by earlier Sufis of great renown, by including in this discussion the following saying by Sahl Tustarī:

> He was asked, "What is your opinion of a man who says 'I am like a door: I do not move unless I am caused to move.'" Sahl b. ᶜAbd Allāh said, "Only two kinds of men can say this: a holy man (*rajul ṣiddīq*), or a heretical man (*rajul zindīq*)."[96]

The fact that an author of Tustarī's eminence in Sarrāj's own eyes is quoted here deeming it possible that a holy man (*rajul ṣiddīq*) could legitimately make a statement which seemingly corresponds to the doctrine he wishes to refute, is what makes this problematic. Sarrāj opts to interpret the "holy man" at length in his subsequent commentary as someone who sees God as the supporting basis of all things, making him refer everything back to God, and who "possesses all the necessary theological knowledge, follows commands and prohibitions (*al-amr wa'l-nahy*), carries out good deeds (*ḥusn al-ṭāᶜāt*), maintains good manners (*adab*), and travels the path (*sulūk al-minhaj*) with the utmost steadfastness."[97]

Even with the addition of this commentary, one cannot help wondering why Sarrāj would include such a citation, almost self-defeatingly, in this context. Being attributed to a major early Sufi, this utterance could well have been used previously in support of the actual argument Sarrāj aims to refute, prompting its inclusion and reinterpretation in this polemical chapter. Never one to opt for the easier and more economical route, Sarrāj's relatively lengthy interpretation of Tustarī's "holy man" argues that it could only apply to someone who was already following the commands and prohibitions of God anyway. This is of course an interpretation of Tustarī's "*rajul ṣiddīq*," which is different from what one finds in Tustarī's own writings,[98] but the main significance in this context is that Sarrāj gives mixed signals on whether or not fully fledged Friends of God must endeavor to follow the formulations of juristic scholars.

Sarrāj also gives mixed signals in his chapter "The Group Which Has Erred Regarding Permission (*ibāḥa*) and Prohibition (*ḥaẓr*) and the Refutation of Them," where he identifies the "error" as being based on the belief that everything is permissible in origin, with the prohibitions only necessary to prevent immoderation (*taᶜaddī*).[99] He identifies the causes of this as being an incorrect interpretation of Qur'an 80/27–32 about God's provision of grains, vines, olives, dates, and orchards, as well as the influence of reports about the code of behavior of early Sufis. With regard to the latter, Sarrāj writes:

> They have heard of the noble characteristics and beautiful association and close friendship among a group of the early sheikhs, between whom matters were carried out with the height of decency and consideration towards one another, to the extent that one of them would go to the home of his brother and stretch his hand to eat his brother's food, take what he needed from his brother's earnings, and examine the affairs of his brother as he would his own affairs.
>
> This is like what is related about Fatḥ al-Mawṣilī: he went to the home of one of his Sufi brethren and told the slave-girl, "Bring out here for me the purse of my brother!" She brought it out to him and he took from it what he needed. When his Sufi brother returned home, his slave-girl informed him about what Mawsilī had done while he had been away, and her master told her: "If you are telling the truth, you are free from now on by God's will!"
>
> It is also like what was mentioned about al-Ḥasan al-Baṣrī: he used to eat out of the food-basket of one of his brethren when the latter was absent. On being questioned about that by someone, he said: "Idiot! Were the people before us any different? One of them would go to the house of his brother and partake of his food and money, wishing thereby to bring joy to his brother because he knew that he would like this more than the finest of camels!"[100]

Sarrāj remarkably volunteers, as the proof used by those he identifies as being in error, a nostalgic depiction of the code of behavior believed to have been followed by Sufis living before the establishment of the law schools. The belief in the earlier application of an independent code must therefore have been strong for him to bother citing it as a proof commonly used in support of non-compliance with the formulations of religious scholars. Otherwise, it would have been easier to reconstruct the past by simply claiming that Islamic laws had always applied since the Prophet

Muhammad's time, and that there never was nor ever could be any alternative "beautiful association." Moreover, it is illustrated with anecdotes about two authoritative figures who lived early enough to underline the point about predating the Shariah, namely Fatḥ al-Mawṣilī (d. 220/835) and al-Ḥasan al-Baṣrī (d. 110/728). The fact that such figures have the role of taking someone else's possessions without asking steers the reader to view these actions as acceptable coming from them; at the end of each story the mystery is clarified with the confirmation that being able to provide wealth or provisions to fellow brethren made Sufis happy. The underlying ethical basis of this kind of interaction corresponds with that of chivalry (*futuwwa*), which remained a significant influence in the Sufism of northeastern Persia of Sarrāj's time.[101]

The inclusion of this explanation is significant because it is presented by Sarrāj as the basis of a viewpoint he aims to refute, rather than his own. That is to say, he has no inherent interest in inventing it, and it is not in itself a disparaging depiction, nor dismissed as an inauthentic transmission or reinterpreted drastically as with the Tustarī citation discussed earlier. Rather, his argument is simply that the precedent is abused by those who appeal to it today, because they use it as a pretext "to abandon legal rulings and flout the restriction of commanding right and forbidding wrong, causing them to lose their way out of ignorance and to seek whatever their carnal souls desire with regards to lusts and forbidden things."[102] However, according to the depictions of the anecdotes and Sarrāj's introduction to them, the original "noble characteristics and beautiful association . . . decency and consideration towards one another" were based on the principle of thinking about the needs of one's brethren before oneself; therefore they were not inherently unacceptable. Sarrāj leaves it ambiguous whether or not such an alternative code of behavior remained viable if it were followed properly and not abused. The same impression is gained from reading the works on customs and flaws of the self by the main Sufi author of the next generation, Abū ᶜAbd al-Raḥmān al-Sulamī (d. 412/1021), who gives hardly any emphasis to juristic formulations.[103]

In contrast to Kalābādhī's briefer discussions, Sarrāj's inclusion of this material indicates that his approach was to reason out and qualify his opposition to perceived errors among Sufis, rather than simply declare them invalid without any explanation. His aims are highlighted by the fact that toward the beginning of his *Kitāb al-Lumaᶜ*, he groups Sufis alongside jurists (*fuqahāʾ*) and hadith experts (*aṣḥāb al-ḥadīth*) as followers of three alternative religious disciplines, which were all worthy. Unlike the mystic Tirmidhī's *Sīra* from a century earlier, there is no trace of polemic in his accounts of religious scholars, which are remarkably matter-of-fact, even though he clearly favors the Sufis. Sarrāj finds occasion to flesh out his view of the relationship between Sufis and jurists in the course of the chapter with the lengthy title "What Has Been Related from the Prophet about Concessions and Leniency to the Muslim Community which God has Made Permissible, and How this Relates to the Elite and the Masses when it Comes to Following the Example of the Messenger of God."

The followers of the Messenger of God are divided into three groups:

1. those who are occupied with licentiousness, permissiveness, loose interpretations, and laxity;
2. those who are occupied with the knowledge of compulsory acts, the customary behavior of the Prophet, the *ḥudūd* penalties, and rulings;
3. those who fulfill that (*aḥkama dhālika*) and know enough of the rulings not to be deemed ignorant of them then become occupied with resplendent mystical states, deeds that please God, noble characteristics, lofty matters, the truths behind the laws (*ḥaqāyiq al-ḥuqūq*), realization (*taḥaqquq*), and sincerity (*ṣidq*).[104]

The point Sarrāj makes in this instance is that while Sufis are characterized by their distinctive mystical endeavors, they both possess a basic knowledge of jurisprudence and implement what the experts in that subject have formulated. That is to say, Sufi mysticism has the prerequisite of fulfillment of what is necessary according to the Shariah, and Sufis are to be distinguished from licentious permissivists, who are presumably included in this classification to underline that point. However, the Shariah does not assume a place of special importance to the Sufis. Echoes are therefore still perceptible here of Tirmidhī's earlier reductionist approach to the Shariah for aspiring mystics, even though Sarrāj's contemporary Kalābādhī verges toward the opposite extreme.

Overall, both Kalābādhī and Sarrāj show a greater degree of preoccupation with the issue of the Shariah than the mystics Kharrāz and Tirmidhī from a century earlier. This is probably not simply because of their own differing predilections, but because the jurisprudential issues had displaced theological ones toward the top of the agenda, with the authority of this discipline having become much more established by their time. Neither attempts a critique in the manner of Tirmidhī a century earlier. While Kalābādhī does not indicate any flexibility or ambiguity over this issue, Sarrāj's position is more complicated: he insists on the application of at least the minimum necessary of the Shariah by his contemporary followers of Sufism, but he expresses admiration for different codes of behavior followed by earlier Sufis and also deems it possible for someone very high-ranking to claim "I am like a door: I do not move unless I am caused to move." He seems to consider the application of the Shariah to be at least the safer approach, though not necessarily the only legitimate one: this is not merely apologetics, but, if he is taken at his word, it may offer protection against abuse of the precedent set by the first Sufis to live according to an earlier and more selfless system of ethics: too many of his contemporaries were liable to fall short of the standards of the Shariah if they attempted this, rather than excel them.

The earlier psychological concerns of Tirmidhī with regard to adoption of the Shariah and pious worship are overlooked by Sarrāj in favor of precaution against excessive permissivism, even though he is fully aware of higher codes of chivalrous behavior that predated the Shariah, and has expressed his admiration of them. The openness and flexibility of his discussions of this topic in his highly influential *Lumaᶜ* are likely to have contributed to the preservation of such opinions and attitudes among Sufis, which may have been his intention, since the option of omitting any mention of them in the manner of Kalābādhī would have been much less problematic.

Friendship with God and the Shariah in Qushayrī's (d. 465/1072) Risāla and Hujwīrī's (d. ca. 467/1074) Kashf al-Maḥjūb

If there is one point that Abū al-Qāsim al-Qushayrī[105] communicates immediately to readers of his *Risāla* it is his view that the Shariah is taken seriously by Sufis. In addition to his introductory statement about the very reason why he wrote his *Risāla*, which is discussed in the next section, one can see in the heading of his biographical section just how important the Shariah was for him. It reads: "Section Mentioning the Shaikhs of This Path and Those Aspects of Their Behavior and Sayings Which Show Reverence for the Shariah (*taᶜẓīm al-sharīᶜa*)."[106] Qushayrī would thereby like to assert that Sufi Friends of God from as far back as Ibrāhīm ibn Adham in the second/eighth century all venerated the Shariah. The reader also finds his reiteration of the need for Sufis to follow the Shariah in the appendix of "Advice for Disciples," where the first thing required of a seeker after establishing a connection with God is for him "to study enough about it in order to be able to fulfill it, to consult juristic authorities about what is compulsory, and to adopt the more cautious option when they have differing responsa (*fatāwā*)."[107] Following the Shariah strictly is therefore essential for disciples in his view in order for them to perform what is compulsory as part of their practice. In the same appendix, Qushayrī also describes "maintaining the customs of the Shariah (*ḥifẓ ādāb al-sharīᶜa*)" as the first item in a list representing the very foundation on which Sufism has been built, a far cry from what Tirmidhī had asserted, and even significantly different than Sarrāj's characterizations of Sufism and the role of the Shariah therein.[108] Qushayrī gives prominence to the Shariah also by including a brief entry in his terminology section, entitled "The Shariah and the Truth (*al-sharīᶜa wa'l-ḥaqīqa*)," where he emphasizes the mutual dependence and inseparability of the servant restricting himself to his Lord's laws and witnessing the truth of His Lordship.[109]

The closest Qushayrī comes to discussing the Friend of God's relationship to the Shariah in any detail is in his entry "The Second Separation" after "Union of Union" (*jamᶜ al-jamᶜ*) achieved by the Friend of God. At the end of his entry on the term "Union of Union," he discusses a subsequent experience which he calls "The Second Separation" (*al-farq al-thānī*). While "Union of Union" occurs after one has lost perception of everything but God, due to becoming overwhelmed by Him,[110] the Second Separation is a return to sobriety at specific times, which enables the worshipper to carry out his necessary obligations to God at those appointed times (*wa huwa an yarudd al-ᶜabd ilā al-ṣaḥw ᶜinda awqāt adāʾ al-farāʾiḍ li-yajrī ᶜalayh al-qiyām bi'l-farāʾiḍ fī awqātihā*).[111] This seems to be intended to tackle the difficulty of arguing for the continuation of obligatory duties at all stages of the Sufi Path, by asserting that there is a stage beyond self-annihilation and loss of perception of everything other than God, where the Sufi would be able and compelled to fulfill them. In Qushayrī's "second separation" God enables His Friend to fulfill his obligatory duties (*farāʾiḍ*) to Him in a sober state. He argues that it is different to the experience before union by virtue of the servant being conscious now that his actions are being carried out by God through His will and knowledge; as Qushayrī puts it, it is a return to God through God rather than himself (*fa-yakūn rujūᶜan lillāh billāh lā lil-ᶜabd bi'l-ᶜabd*).[112]

Qushayrī's use of the term "*farāʾiḍ*" creates a certain amount of ambiguity here because it is a technical juristic term for legal obligations. If "*farāʾiḍ*" is interpreted as referring to the obligatory acts as defined by juristic formulations, then Qushayrī would be depicting a situation where God uses His direct control of the Friend of God in order to lead him to fulfill the jurists' theoretical attempts to estimate His will. Although this might sound unrealistic, he seems to stress the same point in his definition of the spiritual moment (*waqt*), commenting that although the Sufi is ruled by his spiritual moment in that he surrenders to whatever comes to him from the unseen without the use of his own will, what God has stipulated as a law (*sharᶜ*) cannot be overridden, neglected, or considered as dependent on fate.[113] While Qushayrī does not make it absolutely clear here whether or not he equates what God has stipulated as a law with the theoretical attempts by juristic scholars at formulating that, his terminology at least opens up the possibility for such an interpretation.

Qushayrī's increased emphasis overall on the Shariah compared with Sarrāj, whose *Lumaᶜ* served as a major source for the *Risāla,* can also be seen in the lower profile he gives to Sufi customs (*ādāb*). He includes only three chapters, on *ādāb* in general, rules during travel, and companionship, respectively. Moreover, they are included among the list of chapters he introduces as dealing with the states and stations of the path, rather than separated into an independent section, as in the *Lumaᶜ*. The effect of this is for Sufi customs to appear more emphatically as supplementary customs to be subsumed by or tagged onto Shariah requirements as defined by jurists, rather than a wide-ranging system in their own right. In spite of this, the material that Qushayrī offers in these three chapters reaffirms the existence of higher ethical ideals among Sufis than the ideals required by the religious law. These transmissions include sayings by Qushayrī's predecessor Sarrāj, such as the following, which implies that he may have held similar views but chose not to give them as much prominence in his work as his predecessor had done.

When it comes to etiquette (*adab*), people can be divided into three categories:

1. the people of the world (*ahl al-dunyā*) . . .
2. the people of religion (*ahl al-dīn*), most of whose etiquette concerns discipline of the carnal soul, restraining their bodily parts, observing God's prohibitions (*ḥudūd*), and abandoning lusts.
3. the elect (*al-khuṣūṣiyya*), most of whose etiquette concerns purification of hearts, contemplating their inner souls, loyalty to pledges, observing requirements of their spiritual moments, paying little attention to idle thoughts, and observing fine etiquette while seeking God and in the moments of presence and stations of proximity to Him.[114]

The definition of "the elect" here identifies them as Sufis on the basis of Qushayrī's usage of this title. Their description also corresponds to Qushayrī's own view on etiquette as it can be interpreted from his *Risāla.* This is because Qushayrī places much stress on the importance of fulfilling the requirements of one's mystical experiences, most notably in his influential definitions of the "spiritual moment" (*waqt*) as mentioned above, and also that of the Sufi station (*maqām*).[115] It should therefore not be overlooked that his chapters on Sufi states and stations, which make up the bulk of the *Risāla*, elaborate on the appropriate attitude and behavior for the Sufi, rather than focusing purely on inward characteristics. Therefore, however indirect such discussions may be, his *Risāla* in its own way contains specifically Sufi ethical guidelines for behavior and interaction.[116]

In his chapter on Friendship with God, Qushayrī offers two meanings for the term "*walī*," distinguished by whether it is taken to be an active or passive participle; the latter reading means that God takes charge of the affairs of the Friend of God perpetually, while in the former the Friend takes charge of them for himself without ever breaking off from acts of obedience to God.[117] This makes it particularly relevant to the question of following religious laws. While Qushayrī insists that both these meanings must be fulfilled at the same time for someone to be truly a Friend of God, the reports he subsequently cites stress the passive meaning, whereby God takes charge of His Friend's affairs for him. Moreover, he also raises in this chapter the question of whether or not a Friend of God can know that he is one and consequently feel secure about his future fate, taking the affirmative view. This leads him to express preference for the view that the Friend of God need not maintain "faithfulness [even] at the very end" (*al-wafā*ᵓ *fī al-ma*ᵓ*āl*), which seems to fit in with his stress on the passive over the active attitude of the Friend of God towards his own affairs.[118] All to say that even Qushayrī, who states so prominently the importance of the Shariah for Friends of God, gives ambiguous teachings about the relevance of juristic formulations for fully fledged Friends of God, with his chapter on Friendship with God implying that following them purposefully may not always be a requirement.

Qushayrī's contemporary in Lahore, ᶜAlī Hujwīrī,[119] shared with him an interest in scholastic Islam (in his case the Hanafite tradition) as well as with Sufism, although he wrote only about the latter subject. This is evident even from the organizational framework of his sole surviving work, the *Kashf al-maḥjūb*: not only does he present the generations of the Prophet's successors according to Sunni Islam as the first Sufis, but he also discusses Islamic rituals ahead of specifically Sufi rituals and customs in the main section of his work. It should be no surprise therefore that Hujwīrī views Sufis and religious scholars as complementary groups both in the service of Islam, which he expresses in the following way:

> [Friends of God] were here before us in previous centuries and they still exist, and will continue to do so until the Day of Resurrection, because God has given this community (*ummat*) pre-eminence over all other

> communities and has guaranteed "I will preserve the religion (*sharīʿat*) of Muhammad." Transmitted and intellectual proofs today exist among the religious scholars (*ʿulamāʾ*), and, similarly, directly experiential evidence (*burhān-i ʿaynī*) exists among the Friends of God and His elite (*awliyāʾ wa-khawāṣṣ-i khudāwand*).[120]

This passage follows a description of the Friends of God that focuses on the miracles God has given them and the degree to which He has purified them from the flaws of human nature. Therefore, it can be assumed that they serve as "evidence" that can be directly experienced, by virtue of being witnesses to God through their behavior and actions. Hujwīrī himself later comments: "God has made the prophetic evidence (*burhān-i nabawī*) persist today, and has made His Friends the means of its manifestation, so that the signs of the Truth (*āyāt-i ḥaqq*) and sincerity (*ṣidq*) are kept continuous."[121] He identifies his opponents as Mu'tazilites and a group of anthropomorphists (*ḥashwiyān*), underlining that he wishes to represent the Sunni tradition and that he refers to the religion brought by Muhammad in general, rather than the law, by his use of "*sharīʿat*" here.

The passage above is representative of Hujwīrī's greater interest in scholastic theology (*kalām*) than jurisprudence (*fiqh*). Nonetheless he includes in the same chapter, among sayings of past Sufis about the Friends of God, two anecdotes which teach that following the customs of the Prophet is a condition of Friendship with God. In the first of these, Abū Yazīd rejects somebody who spits in a mosque, after initially having been keen to meet this man because he had earned a reputation for being a Friend of God. In the second example, Abū Saʿīd b. Abī 'l-Khayr dismisses from a mosque someone who enters it with his left foot first (as opposed to the Prophet's custom of entering with the right foot first). Though the latter would seem an exceedingly minor flaw in comparison, Hujwīrī himself offers the following combined commentary on these two anecdotes:

> A group of heretics have associated themselves with this dangerous path and have opined that service (*khidmat*) is only necessary up until one becomes a Friend of God. When one has become a Friend of God, service is abolished. This is error. There is no station (*maqām*) on the path to the Truth where any pillar (*rukn*) of service is removed.[122]

It is only with a superficial reading that this might be read as an appropriate commentary to the two aforementioned anecdotes, because, on closer inspection, Hujwīrī has changed the terms of the debate. His argument is that the Friend of God always performs service (*khidmat*) to God, an argument that few mystical writers would disagree with. It is after all an inherent quality of a Friend of God to be at God's service, based on the model of Khiḍr. The anecdotes provided by Hujwīrī, however, describe someone who behaves offensively in a mosque and someone who overlooks a detail of the customs of the Prophet in relation to entering a mosque, respectively. This is at the very least a strangely indirect way of describing abandonment of service to God. Khiḍr after all is described in the Qur'anic story as killing a child and destroying property, both seemingly illegal and immoral acts, and yet at the same time this was his way of carrying out service at the command of God.

Hujwīrī may have preferred this way of tackling the difficulty in equating with the Shariah the commands of God that the Friend of God must always follow. While Qushayrī had implied more specifically in his *Risāla* that what God compels His Friend to fulfill are obligations (*farā'iḍ*) at their appointed times, Hujwīrī's contrasting method is to affirm more generally that the Friend of God must always "serve" God, and then to illustrate this notion of service with the following of minutiae of the Shariah. The fact that both of them saw the need to confront this aspect, and resorted to strategies of describing ambiguously the Friend of God's compulsion to act, indicates that it was not something they could simply refute. While Qushayrī's strategy involved implicitly equating God's commands with the fulfillment of the legal formulations of scholars, Hujwīrī imples that following the minutiae of the Shariah is part of one's service to God, though he neither clarifies whether the Friend of God is directed to such actions by God or relies on juristic formulations.

Hujwīrī identifies those who contravene the Shariah as those who believe they have freedom to do as they please, and in this way sidesteps the more challenging issue of the Friend of God's compulsion to fulfill God's command regardless of its compatibility with the theoretical Shariah. However, he does verge on tackling the more challenging issue at one point later in the same chapter, where he asserts that an elite among the Friends of God can know that they are Friends of His by virtue of the miracles He bestows on them and the soundness of their states. In response to the objection that this would cause them to grow conceited, Hujwīrī asserts, with echoes of Tirmidhī's comments from two centuries earlier,[123] that this is impossible because "the condition of Friendship with God is God's preservation (*ḥifẓ*), and he who is preserved from such flaws (*az āfat maḥfūẓ*) cannot succumb to this."[124] This almost circular argument is significant because it implies a broader understanding of "*maḥfūẓ*" than being kept by God vigilantly carrying out one's duties to Him at their appointed times according to the Shariah, which

Kalābādhī had implied a century earlier and Qushayrī had kept alive, albeit ambiguously. After all, there is no law against self-conceit itself.

It should also be noted that although Hujwīrī includes chapters on purification and the main rituals of Islam before chapters on specifically Sufi guidelines for interaction, discourse, and ritual, the latter chapters constitute a much greater amount of material. Moreover, in the introductory section of the *Kashf al-maḥjūb* he includes further relevant material, such as his chapter on patched frocks (*muraqqaʿa*). Therefore in combination, he includes in his *Kashf al-maḥjūb* a more explicitly wide-ranging Sufi code of etiquette than Qushayrī.

In summary, the eleventh-century Sufi scholars Qushayrī and Hujwīrī maintained the emphasis on following the Shariah which their predecessors in the tenth century had first begun to insist upon in earnest. However, in both authors' theoretical works one can find instances of ambiguity and inconsistency, which suggest that their treatment of this topic was to some degree a challenge forced on them by historical circumstances rather than a natural extension of their worldview. While this certainly did not detract from the value of their works for most Sufi readers, since they have gone on to become the most widely read prose books on Sufism ever written in Arabic and Persian, they nonetheless need to be evaluated in their own historical context rather than treated as timeless lenses through which all other expressions of Sufism should be judged.

Conclusions

After expounding Rumi's teachings about the Friend of God and his relationship to the Shariah toward the end of the first section of this chapter, I highlight the fact that academic commentators have opted to interpret them in the least obvious way. The main reason for this has been suggested to be the interpretation of the tenth and eleventh-century manuals of Sufism as normative for the whole tradition. The treatment of this topic in such works, which I have expounded in the preceding section, highlights the contrasts with Rumi's teachings, strengthening the view that they should not be used as the basis for interpreting them in the least obvious of ways. It also underlines the fact that they were themselves elements in a historical process during which religious laws began to assume increasing importance, and should therefore not be treated so readily as normative. This is perhaps best highlighted by examining the introduction of the most influential of all the classical Sufi manuals, Qushayrī's *Risāla,* where he makes the following historically revisionist lament as an explanation of the reason why he wrote the work:

> Know that the majority of the true members of this sect (*ṭāʾifa;* i.e. Sufism) have become extinct, and all that remains in this era of ours from this sect is their trace, as it has been said:
>
> The tents look like their own tribe's tents, however
> Their women aren't the women I remember!
>
> Gone are the shaikhs in whom one could find guidance, and few are the young men (*shabāb*) whose deeds and customs are worth emulating. Piety has disappeared and rolled up its rug; covetousness has gained strength and tightened its grip. Respect for the Shariah has departed from their hearts, for they have considered lack of concern for religion a stronger support, and have rejected the distinction between what is lawful (*ḥalāl*) and what is forbidden (*ḥarām*). They have made abandoning respect and negating shame their religion. They have taken lightly the performance of ritual worship (*ʿibādāt*), have judged trivial the fast and prayer, and have run to the field of negligence, to trust in complying with their lusts and lack of worry about engaging in forbidden things, and utilizing what they have seized from commoners, women, and courtiers.
>
> Furthermore, they have not become content with engaging in such evil actions, but have gone as far as to refer to the highest truths and mystical states: they have claimed that they are liberated from the bondage of slavery and have attained to the truths of union, in that they are now residing with God, and His decrees are fulfilled through them, while they are effaced, such that God cannot censure them for what they do or do not do.[125]

As I have indicated already, the demand for respecting the Shariah is frequently highlighted in Qushayrī's *Risāla,* even if his actual detailed comments appear to be more complicated. The characterization of astray Sufis as holding a casual attitude toward obedience to God in terms of the Shariah presented above can therefore be taken as part of his efforts to highlight this message. While early Sufi authors certainly did not advocate such a casual attitude towards duties to God in general, it is important to point out that they also did not prioritize scrupulousness in following the Shariah let alone equate them with that. Qushayrī's claim that he is proposing a "return to Sufism's authentic roots" should therefore be recognized for what it is, namely a reinvention of the past. For instance, in the ninth century, two hundred years closer to Sufism's roots, mystics stressed the view that the Friend of God acts through the direct command of God, and not simply according to the theoretical formulations of juristic scholars; even Tirmidhī's Lesser or would-be Friend of God follows only what is absolutely required and must guard vigilantly against insincerity in this regard.[126] Moreover, Sarrāj, whose *Lumaᶜ* was the single most influential work for Qushayrī himself, has been shown to refer to a different system of ethics among the earliest Sufis, as well as explaining how "the holy man" can say "I do not move unless I am caused to move," even though he stressed the compatibility of juristic and mystical Islam.

Although the hazardous venture of reconstructing early Sufi history is not the intention of this particular study, it is worth pointing out that the more obvious interpretation of developments in discussions of this issue in early Sufi writings is that they were interrupted by the Shariah's emerging dominance in Islamic society. That is to say, the ninth-century authors showed little concern for apologetics with regard to the Shariah compared with doctrinal theological matters: Kharrāz shows minimal effort in this direction, even though he was concerned about "accusations" against Sufis, while Tirmidhī self-confidently takes a polemical stance against his opponents. The process of irenic harmonization with the theoretical formulations of juristic scholars would appear to have gotten significantly under way only in the tenth century. Throughout this period, alternative viewpoints, including those closer to Tirmidhī's, must have continued to be prevalent for the later authors to continue to argue against them. Nonetheless, Qushayrī would have the reader imagine that the only alternative takes the form of the characterization he presents in the passage cited above from the introduction of his *Risāla* as a lamentable innovation.

What is important to observe in this study, regardless of the exact historical development, is that it is an anachronism to consider juristic formulations as being the original basis for Sufism and the mysticism of this tradition's precursors, as Qushayrī implies. It was preceded by at least one system of ethics comparable with chivalry (*futuwwa*) according to his own influential predecessor in northeastern Persia, Sarrāj, who makes this allusion without any obvious agenda to promote that view of the past. In contrast, belief in the Friend of God's attainment of a proximity to Him, wherein his every action is compelled by God's direct command, clearly predates the interruption of this discourse by the jurists' increasing influence. This latter point is evident not least through the subsequent attempts by Kalābādhī, Qushayrī, and Hujwīrī to transform it into something closer to meaning compulsion specifically to fulfill juristic formulations, and Sarrāj to present adherence to them as a qualification for having the experience of being moved by God "like a door."

Resorting to reinterpretation implies a concession to the impossibility of refuting a belief in compulsion under God's direct control that was too deeply established.

The differences in Rumi's teachings can therefore be best understood as representing not only his use of practical teachings rather than systematic, theoretical ones but also the very different context in which he lived. That is to say, they show that he neither felt obliged to integrate his teachings with those of juristic scholars for irenic reasons nor feared that they might cause difficulties for him and his followers. This change in circumstances can account for his significantly differing teachings about the Shariah from those of Qushayrī, Hujwīrī, Kalābādhī, and even Sarrāj. At the same time, however, the degree of agreement between his teachings and those of Kharrāz and Tirmidhī, with whom he agrees that a strict adherence to the Shariah is neither required of the Friend of God nor a fundamental requirement of the aspirant, demonstrate that he had not simply innovated in this matter. The most likely explanation is that these three lived on either side of a period of interruption between the tenth and eleventh centuries when the Shariah's all-authoritative and all-encompassing position was being consolidated in Islamic society. They therefore were spared the kind of pressure the Sufi theorists living during that period were under to respond to those developments in the religion. However, in Rumi's time, after the secure consolidation of the jurists' position, and the success of these earlier irenic scholars at harmonizing, there was a greater degree of accommodation of allowances and concessions to mystics than there could have been when juristic Islam's supremacy had not yet been safely secured beyond any challenge. In any case, Rumi was not advocating an abolishment of any notion of the Shariah, but rather he wished to remove the hindrance that would be caused by prioritizing juristic formulations over a direct experience of God, which he considered the whole point of the mystic endeavor. Rumi provides a memorable example in the following story from the fourth chapter of the *Fīhi mā fīh* of how the juristic approach to religion may stifle the progress of aspiring mystics, even if they were at a relatively early stage.

> This is like the story they tell about a king putting his son in the care of a group of scholars, so that he would be taught astrology, geomancy, and other sciences to become a complete master of them, despite the fact that he was dim-witted and stupid. The king one day hid a ring in his fist, and tested his son by saying, "Come and tell me what I am holding!" He said, "You're holding something round, golden in color, and with a hole in the middle." His father said, "Since you have described it accurately, confirm then what that thing is!" The son

answered, "It must be a colander!" The father exclaimed, "You have given several accurate descriptions, which boggle the mind. With such a level of education and knowledge, how did you manage to overlook the fact that a colander cannot be hidden in a fist!"

It is like that now with the ulama of our time. They split hairs in their sciences, and know so much about other irrelevant matters, having acquired a complete mastery of them. However, the most important and relevant thing is one's self, and they do not know their own selves. They are busy declaring everything either halal or haram, saying "This is allowed" or "That is forbidden" or "This is halal" and "That is haram," but they do not know whether their own selves are halal or haram, permissible or not, clean or unclean.[127]

This anecdote is consistent with Rumi's critiques of religious scholars in the *Fīhi mā fīh* as well as his other works, including the examples cited earlier in this chapter, and conveniently serves to shed light on why he considered their approach to religion inadequate. It is worth contrasting these frequent critiques by Rumi with the relative dearth of such critiques among the Sufi theoreticians of the tenth and eleventh centuries; their concern was to reassure religious scholars. The fact that Tirmidhī was virtually ignored for a couple of centuries arguably further corroborates this point. He is likely to have been singled out among the early mystics as the target for so many accusations because of his articulation of specific criticisms of contemporary jurists and their understanding of the Shariah.

Finally, it is worth noting that Sarrāj's description of an obsolete chivalrous code of behavior of Sufis in the eighth century actually corresponds remarkably to the codes of behavior later instituted by many Sufi orders and maintained until the present day, including Rumi's own followers in the Mawlawiyya tradition. The same can be said for beliefs about the Friend of God's receipt of direct commands from God in preference to the less specific (or demanding) approach of fulfilling the formulations of religious scholars. Sufis are one of the communities of Muslims that has always included among its number many who do not consider jurisprudence to possess ultimate authority. Of course, their articulation of this has depended on the circumstances, as has their practice, with most institutionalized Sufi orders in the pre-modern period having developed close relations with jurists and also having integrated the Shariah into their order's code of behavior and etiquette to some degree.

5

The Friend of God and Miracles

In those days there was a big debate between the physicians and the religious scholars (*ʿulamāʾ*) about whether the human soul is kept alive by blood or by means of something else. The physicians all argued in unison: "Of course, it is kept alive by blood, because if all of someone's blood comes out then he will die immediately!" They thereby made a more compelling argument than the jurists (*fuqahāʾ*).

The religious scholars came altogether to Rumi and presented this question to him. He said, "Of course it has been affirmed that humans are kept alive by blood." All of them then said, "According to the school of thought of the physicians, it is like this, and they also articulate rational and philosophical proofs." Rumi then said, "The school of thought of the physicians is not so great, and, in fact, a human is kept alive by God, not blood." No one had the chance to say, "How?" and "We do not agree!"

Philosophers don't dare to say a word,
For God would pull apart that as absurd.

Then Rumi asked them to bring someone to bleed him. Having allowed himself to be bled from his two blessed arms, he let it continue to such an extent that all the blood came out of his veins and only the pale serum remained at the incisions. Then, he looked at the physicians and said, "What about this then? Are they kept alive by blood or by God?" Everyone lowered their heads and expressed belief in the power of the men of God. Then, Rumi got up straight away and went to the bathhouse. Once he had come out of there, he started a musical session.[1]

This example of a miracle-story is one of the most extraordinary of those recounted in Aflākī's *Manāqib al-ʿĀrifīn*, because it depicts him as staying alive in physically impossible circumstances; it is a case of cheating certain death, thereby coming close to the miracle of restoring life.

This miracle-story is also significant because of the characters who are mentioned, or rather categories of people, and the alliance depicted. Rumi by means of this miracle comes to the rescue of religious scholars, who have found themselves helpless in the face of the argument of physicians that blood keeps humans alive, since without it one would die. Nonetheless, Rumi is portrayed as an outsider to the religious scholars as well as the rationalist physicians. In fact, he asserts at the beginning that the argument of the physicians has "of course been affirmed" (*albatta muḥaqqaq shuda*), even though he decides to prove them wrong on epistemological grounds. It is as if he agrees with the latter's understanding of physical nature, but differs with them when it comes to the belief in a higher dimension beyond their rationalist epistemology. The knowledge of the religious scholars is something he considers even more inadequate, and he shares with that category only the belief in something higher than the physical dimension. Rumi then uses his ability to demonstrate the reality of what he believes, for everyone to witness directly. This proves the rationalists wrong and at the same time astonishes the religious scholars, who previously possessed only blind faith in the matter rather than certain knowledge, having succumbed to misgivings in the face of the physicians' arguments. In fact, the story concludes with all present, both religious scholars and physicians, "expressing belief in the power of the men of God" (*bi-qudrat-i mardān-i khudā īmān āwurdand*)–men like Rumi, Friends of God.

This miracle-story evokes the way that mysticism came to play a key role for the religious scholar Abū Ḥāmid al-Ghazālī (d. 505/1111), to restore his faith in the reality of Prophethood after a personal crisis in the face of formidable rationalist arguments; religious scholarship was impotent in the face of such a challenge, as Ghazālī explains in his *al-Munqidh min al-ḍalāl*, but Sufi mysticism provided him with an answer through direct experience, or "tasting" (*dhawq*).[2] It is therefore not difficult to see why a miracle by a Sufi should be presented in this way at the time of the composition of Rumi's biography, as a means to manifest direct, experiential evidence that can refute the rationalist theory of physicians. Miracles, however, had been discussed in Sufi writings since the very first treatises on the Friends of God, long before Ghazālī and such an alliance between religious scholarship and mysticism. Therefore, after presenting Rumi's own writings about miracles and his illustrations of them through miracle-stories about Sufi predecessors, I will consider the earliest discussions of the miracles of the Friends of God in their historical context, in order to situate Rumi's own teachings more accurately.

Rumi's Teachings about the Miracles of the Friends of God

As well as later featuring in numerous miracle-stories himself, such as the example presented above, Rumi includes many of them about other individuals in his own didactic writings. He also discusses his opinion on miracles in both *The Masnavi* and the *Fīhi mā fīh*. One thing that he does not bother with is making any theoretical distinction between the miracles of the Friends of God and those of the Prophets. He does not even refer to such distinctions for the purpose of dismissing them as being purely for the benefit of the masses, as he does with divine communication.[3] By contrast, Rumi uses interchangeably the different terms for miracle, which most Sufi theorists before him had applied either to Friends of God or to Prophets exclusively, namely "*karāma*" and "*muʿjiza.*" A specific story stands out in this regard because it compares the miracle of a Friend of God directly with that of the Prophet Muhammad. In this story, which is found in the fourth book of *The Masnavi* and has been discussed already in relation to Rumi's dismissal of distinctions between different kinds of divine communication, Bāyazīd Basṭāmī receives news miraculously, through a scent in the breeze, that after his own death a Sufi called Abu 'l-Ḥasan Kharaqānī will be born at its specific location. Rumi compares this miracle with that reported in the famous miracle-story about the Prophet Muhammad and Uways al-Qaranī in Yemen, who becomes his devoted follower without ever meeting him.[4] In the course of Rumi's story, Bāyazīd replies to questions from disciples about the reason for his dramatic change of state by referring to the experience of the Prophet Muhammad: "A marvelous scent reached me all of a sudden / Like that which reached the Prophet once from Yemen."[5]

This miracle-story is worth considering further in order to gain insight into Rumi's teachings about the miracles of Friends of God and Prophets. The nature of the miracle in these stories is communication from God through a scent. In the famous story about Muhammad it is clearly a miraculous communication because Uways is in remote Yemen and has never met the Prophet. In Rumi's story about Bāyazīd, the miracle seems greater if anything. This is because Kharaqānī is not simply in a remote location, but he has not even been born yet. However, this distinction is arguably negligible from Rumi's wider perspective, and when one appreciates that the stories surrounding the Prophet Muhammad's relationship with Uways, which would have been familiar to him, also include predictions about his future greatness. Rumi simply wishes to make the point that this miracle of Bāyazīd is not in any way less than that of the Prophet Muhammad.[6]

Like his biographies, Rumi's own writings take for granted the ability of Friends of God to perform miracles of the most extraordinary kind. In his teaching stories, the Friends of God can change the course of fate and revive the dead, among other types of miracles, as much as Prophets can. And yet rather than simply celebrating the miraculous powers attributed to Friends of God, the miracles in his stories invariably function to express teachings that would be valuable for the mystic aspirant to learn. Rumi is perhaps nowhere more blasé about the actual miracles themselves than in the following passage from the twenty-sixth chapter in the *Fīhi mā fīh*:

> Speaking about miracles, Rumi said, "Someone can go from here to the Kaaba in one day, or even in an instant—that is no marvel or miracle. The desert wind that we call 'Simūm' can also perform this 'miracle' (*karāmat*), going in one day, or in just one instant, however far it wants to. The real miracle is that which takes you from a low condition to a sublime one, so that from there you travel to here, from ignorance to intelligence, from inanimateness to life."[7]

The reason Rumi gives for his nonchalance toward spectacular miracles is to highlight the magnificence of becoming transformed as a human being from "a low condition to a sublime one" (*az ḥāl-i dūn bi-ḥāl-i ᶜālī*), which involves acquiring knowledge. By pointing out here the relatively low importance of miracles in themselves, Rumi may give the impression that he does not consider the miraculous to have a significant role in Sufism. However, in the following passage from the sixth book of *The Masnavi*, he clarifies his viewpoint by asserting that the real point of the miracle is its transformative effect on a human's inner being. That is to say, the significance of the outward wonder in itself may be relatively low, but that is not the main purpose:

> *Muᶜjizāt* and *karāmāt* take effect
> On hearts, when they're by *pīrs* of the elect,
> Inside whom are a hundred resurrections,
> Least of which is to give intoxication:
> Becoming close to men who have this fortune
> Will make a lucky man thus God's companion.
> The *muᶜjiza* through what's inanimate,
> A rod, the waves, or that moon which was split—
> Once it moves you without such mediation,
> Then it's joined you through a concealed connection.
> Effects on such things are just secondary;
> The hidden spirit is what's primary.[8]

In *All the King's Falcons*, John Renard has identified this passage as Rumi's "most complete single statement" about the miracles of the Prophets.[9] However, the most interesting thing to note about this passage is that Rumi is actually referring here to the miracles (*muʿjizāt*) of the elect Sufi master (*pīr-i ṣafī*), or Friend of God, and not a Prophet. He does so without making any distinction between this figure and the Prophet Muhammad, the mention of whose miracles immediately before this passage is what seems to have generated it in the first place. Rumi's main teaching here, however, is that by becoming a devoted disciple of a Friend of God, one can come to experience such miraculous inner effects, including intoxication as its most modest example. Moreover, this can eventually be experienced directly without the need for him even to perform a miracle to serve as the outward intermediary to one's inner transformation. This is all made possible by God's Power, and so moving close to a Friend of God makes one become effectively a companion of His, or someone who sits close to God (*jalīs Allāh*). For Rumi, herein lies the value of miracles.

The notion that sitting with Sufis is the same as sitting with God is one that Rumi frequently refers to.[10] One of the most memorable instance is the following anecdote from the second book of *The Masnavi* about Moses, which serves at the same time to underline the fact that, in Rumi's portrayal of the spiritual elite, Prophets are not necessarily at a higher level than Friends of God.

God once told Moses off, "You who've been blest,
And even seen the moon rise from your breast,
With My own Holy Light I made you thrive—
When I was ill why didn't you arrive?"
Moses said, "God, who's free from any flaws,
What riddle is this? Please explain the cause!"
God asked him next, "Why didn't you enquire
About me then, as friendship would require?"
Moses said, "Lord, You've no deficiency;
My mind's confused—explain this please to me!"
"A special slave of mine fell ill" God said,
"He is I: understand this with your head!
His weakness is as if it were my own,
His sickness too; I don't leave him alone."
Whoever wants to be near God must sit
With God's Friends—this has the same benefit.
If you're cut off from them, then your starved soul

Will seem a part kept separate from the whole,
For if the devil keeps you separated
From such great people, you'll feel alienated.
If you should stay apart a little while,
I warn you—it's due to the devil's guile![11]

The point of this passage is to emphasize the close identification of the Friend of God with God, rather than to make any categorical assertions about the relationship between Moses and the Friend of God, though it may be more than a coincidence for the former to have been chosen in view of the Qur'anic story about his encounter with Khiḍr. Such a close identification is frequently alluded to by Rumi in all of his writings. Well-known instances include his defense of al-Ḥusayn ibn Manṣūr al-Ḥallāj's statement "I am God (*anā'l-Ḥaqq*)" and the story about the painting competition between the Greek and Chinese artists.[12] This is what enables dramatic transformations in the inner being of the Friend of God's companions, or even potentially those with the briefest exposure to them, as the following anecdote from the tenth chapter of Rumi's *Fīhi mā fīh* illustrates:

A dear friend made a forty-day retreat (*chilla*) in search of a spiritual goal. Someone called out to him: "Such a lofty goal cannot be achieved by means of a forty-day retreat! Come out of the retreat so that the gaze of a spiritual adept might fall on you—your goal can be achieved by that."

He replied: "Where can I find that adept?"

The other person answered: "In the congregational mosque."

He asked, " Among such a lot of people how will I be able to tell which one he is?"

He was told, " Just go, and he will recognize you and look at you. The sign that he has looked at you will be that the ewer will fall out of your hand and you will faint. You will then know that he has looked at you."

He followed the instructions, taking an ewer full of water with him, and serving water to the congregation as he walked across all the rows of worshippers, until suddenly an inner state emerged in him, he screamed and the ewer fell from his hand. He then was left behind, lying unconscious in one corner, when all the people left. Once he regained consciousness, he found himself alone and could not see that spiritual king who had cast a glance on him, but he had reached his goal nonetheless.[13]

In the process of making the general point that receiving such a glance is a much more powerful way to develop spiritually than to go on an arduous retreat, this story memorably underlines that the aspirant's role can involve little more than being receptive. Rumi frequently refers to this miraculous power that Friends of God have over aspirants, such as in the story about the Byzantine emissary's very first encounter with the caliph Umar, which makes him lose control and feel awe even though the caliph is asleep.[14] Occasionally, Rumi describes more specifically the nature this process of spiritual attention can take between a Friend of God and his disciple. For instance, the following anecdote about a "Shaikh Sarrazī" and his clairvoyance is found immediately before the passage quoted above in the tenth chapter of the *Fīhi mā fīh*:

> Shaikh Sarrazī was sitting among his disciples when one of the disciples was craving a roasted lamb's head. The shaikh indicated that a roasted lamb's head should be brought to him. The disciples asked, "How did you know that he couldn't do without a roasted lamb's head?"
>
> He replied, "Because it has been thirty years since I felt I had to have something, having purified myself and transcended all such cravings. I have become like a clear mirror with no image in it. When the thought of a roasted lamb's head came to me and I craved it and felt compelled to have it, I knew that this was someone else's craving—when the mirror has no image of its own, any image which appears in it must be something else's reflected there."[15]

The explanation Shaikh Sarrazī gives in this anecdote not only offers an insight into one way in which miraculous clairvoyance might be processed but also highlights the extent of the knowledge and influence of a Sufi master over his disciples who aspire to reach his level one day. The miraculous power such fully-fledged Friends of God possess is attributed to their spiritual elevation as a result of completing the mystical path and subsisting in God, like a clear mirror with no image of its own. Rumi comments on the effect that companionship with them can have and what it says about the rank of the Friends of God in the following verses in the first book of *The Masnavi:*

> Even if you should shun God's bondsmen, they
> Are sick of your existence anyway.
> They've amber which affects you just like straw,
> Inducing frenzy in your being, and awe,
> But when they hide their amber, your submission
> You quickly turn again to fierce sedition:

Your rank becomes mere animality;
This is bound by and needs humanity,
While that humanity God's Friends control.
Like animals we need them in this role.[16]

Rumi compares here the effect of the attention or close presence of a Friend of God to a disciple's being with that of amber on straw; when no longer in that presence, the disciple no longer feels the effect as strongly and may rebel. It is therefore characterized as a relationship that is affected by physical presence to some degree, which corresponds aptly with the notion that Friends of God represent the means by which God executes His wishes in the world. It is through God's power, Rumi explains, that the calling of God's Friends can raise the dead.[17] Moreover, not only are God's Friends beyond the jurisdiction of cause and effect, but through God's power they can change the course of fate, as Rumi asserts in the following passage from the first book of *The Masnavi*:

God's Friends possess from God such awesome might
That they can pull back arrows in mid-flight:
Effects which stem from the original cause,
When God's Friend prays, God's power compels to pause:
By grace he makes unsaid what has been said
So no harm comes to anybody's head:
From all the hearts which heard that harmful word
He wipes it out, unseen now and unheard!
Dear gentlemen, if you need proof it's true
"A verse we cause you to forget" should do.[18]

In addition to possessing the miraculous ability to break the sequence of cause and effect and bring about its reversal through the help of God's power (*qudrat az ilāh, z'ān dast-i rabb*), Rumi teaches that the Friends of God enjoy an elevated spiritual status whereby the material realm fulfills their every need at their convenience. This is depicted most memorably in the story about Aḥmad b. Khiḍrūya (d. 240/854) on his deathbed, which is found in the second book of *The Masnavi*.[19] He is surrounded by his creditors, who demand that he pay his debts, and are left frustrated at his lack of concern as well as his seemingly mean-spirited exploitation of a boy selling halva (by not paying after eating a trayful). When it looks like he will pass away leaving debts, for which he shows no remorse, a gift suddenly arrives that includes the exact sum of his debts and the price of the tray of halva. Although the ending of the story involves an astonishing miracle, the reader is alerted at the beginning to the shaikh's lifelong habit of taking on loans which God would pay off for him miraculously: "God paid his debts for him across the land / As he made flour for Abraham from sand."[20]

The story about Ibrāhīm ibn Adham's (d. 160/777) miracles by the shore bears a similarity in that just as Aḥmad b. Khiḍrūya reacted to the bitterness of his creditors by asking God to pay them off, it is in response to the thoughts he reads in the mind of an onlooker that Ibrāhīm reveals his miraculous power:

About Ibrāhīm-i Adham they say
That he stopped on the ocean's shore one day,
And sewed his cloak while resting briefly there.
A prince arrived and soon began to stare;
As a disciple of this shaikh, he knew
Just who he was, and bowed as he should do.
He was astonished at the garb he wore,
For he'd transformed from what he was before:
A life of comfort and prosperity
He'd given up to live in poverty.
He thought, "He has renounced enormous riches.
Now, like a beggar, woolen cloaks he stitches!"
The shaikh could read this person's thoughts with ease—
Hearts are the jungles which this lion sees:
He enters in their hearts like hope and fear.
The secrets of the world to him are clear,
So guard your hearts, you useless slaves of greed,
When near the masters of your hearts—take heed!
The shaikh then tossed a needle in the sea
And called for its return immediately.
Myriads of divine fish came to sight,
Gold needles in their lips, which were pressed tight—
They raised their heads thus from God's ocean and
Said, "Take God's needles, shaikh, with your pure hand!"
He turned his face toward the prince and said,
"The heart's wealth or the wretched kind instead?"
This is the outer sign, and nothing more—
Wait till you see within what lies in store!
Just one branch from the garden men bring down—
They can't bring the whole garden to your town;
When heaven's just one leaf of it—heed well
That it's the kernel while this is the shell.[21]

This story serves as an appropriate illustration of Rumi's teaching of the dominance of the spiritual realm over the material, because Ibrāhīm ibn Adham is famous for the portrayals of his renunciation of princely riches for a life of poverty and spiritual devotion. In this particular story, Ibrāhīm detects a disciple wondering at his outward transformation, and responds by displaying his spiritual gifts, or "wealth of the heart" (*mulk-i dil*), which is manifested as the miracle of commanding fish to retrieve his needle and receiving thousands of gold needles from them. This miracle serves to teach the onlooking disciple that Ibrāhīm gained so much more than he had renounced, despite first appearances, and it achieves this by demonstrating that the material realm is at the command of the spiritual realm he now inhabits.

The miracles Rumi attributes to Friends of God in his didactic writings place them in their mediatory role between God and humanity, between the divine and material realms. They serve as a means by which God executes His commands in the world, and at the same time that material realm serves their needs. This situation of fulfilling God's will without thought of themselves, and having their own wishes fulfilled for them, portrays a state of harmony with the destiny of creation. What is perhaps most interesting of all about this worldview is that, while for Rumi the Friend of God represents the ultimate degree of harmony and integration with the flow of destiny, others are able to partake of it in varying degrees. He expresses this teaching in the forty-ninth chapter of the *Fīhi mā fīh*, where he comments:

> I know truly the basis for God's provision of daily bread, and it is not in my nature to run around in vain or to suffer needlessly. Truly, whatever my daily portion is of wealth, food, clothing, or the fire of lust, if I sit there it comes to me. But if I run around after my daily bread, it makes me tired, weary and debased. If instead I am patient and stay in my place, it comes to me without toil or debasement, because that daily bread is also seeking me and drawing me to itself. When it cannot draw me to itself, it comes, just as when I cannot draw it to myself, I go to it.
>
> The teaching from this is that you should be engaged in matters of faith, so that the material world chases after you. . . . The Prophet said, *"If someone makes all his concerns just one concern, God will free him from his other concerns."* Let whoever has ten cares focus on the one about faith, and God will sort out the others for him without him having to try to do that for himself. The Prophets were not attached to fame or provisions. They were only attached to seeking God's satisfaction, and yet they also gained fame and provisions. Whoever seeks God's satisfaction will be with the Prophets in this world and the next, and a

bedfellow to *"Those with the prophets, the holy ones (ṣiddīqūn), and the martyrs"* (Qur'an 4/69).[22]

What distinguishes this passage from the others about the provision of material needs as part of the flow of divine ordainment is that, after speaking about his own experience, Rumi urges his audience to strive to follow him in the same direction. He thereby extends the principle exemplified by his stories about how Friends of God are miraculously aided and supported as a privilege of their spiritual purity and their role as God's representatives in the world, to accommodate aspirants as well. The message he gives is that the more you prioritize striving for God's, or your faith's (*dīn*) sake, the more He will free you from worldly (*dunyā*) concerns. In this way, just as with divine communication, Rumi teaches that aspirants to Friendship with God may begin to partake in their experiences at the start of a process of self-transformation, and acquire tastes of the completed vision of reality possessed by God's Friends. When mystic aspirants report that, while they are in the presence of a Friend of God or engaged in the remembrance of God otherwise, they experience a special harmony with the flow of events, which incredibly meets their needs and those of others even though it would have been impossible to predict or arrange, in Rumi's teachings this could be interpreted as falling into the category of such miracles.

The Friend of God and Miracles in Kharrāz's (d. ca. 286/899) al-Kashf wa'l-bayān and Tirmidhī's (d. between 295–300/905–910) Sīrat al-awliyā᾽

While Rumi makes no distinction between the miracles of the Friends of God and those of the Prophets, the first thing one discovers from the earliest theoretical writings about the Friends of God is that such distinctions were considered significant enough to debate. In his *al-Kashf wa'l-bayān*, Abū Saᶜīd al-Kharrāz reveals the existence already of debate over the exact types of miracles Friends of God can have, with some types being considered as the exclusive preserve of the Prophets.[23] In the following rendering of the relevant paragraphs of Kharrāz's treatise, the terms for different types of miracles are given in transliteration, rather than attempting to create new words for miracles in English, and thereby obscuring the main issue at stake:

> Some of them said: God made *ᶜalāmāt* and *āyāt* miracles for Prophets, exclusively for them and not anyone else. No one is to claim them, and

they are not given to anyone other than the Apostles, who have *karāmāt* as well as *āyāt*.

As for *āyāt*, no one is given them other than Apostles, while the *karāmāt* are a mercy (*raḥma*) with which God honours whom He wills from among His servants, and they are knowledge, wisdom, and favours.

As for *āyāt*, they are only for Prophets and it is not possible for anyone else to claim them. Do you not see the story of Abraham, when He said to the fire: "Be cool and safe for Abraham" (Qur'an 21/69). Among the *karāmāt* are when He revived the birds when Abraham asked his Lord for that (Qur'an 2/260). Similarly among the *karāmāt* is his raising of [Muhammad] to the angelic realm, where he was shown what he was shown of His Might and Glory. Among the *karāmāt* which are for the Prophets some are also given to God's Friends. However the *āyāt* are only for Prophets. There are also among the *karāmāt* those which are exclusively for Prophets, and those which are for the holiest Friends of God (*ṣiddīqūn*) exclusively and not the rest of the believers, when His mercy is given to them at a time of necessity. Look at the effect of God's mercy and His kindnesses to His creation. It is not excessive for His generosity and magnanimity, and He does as He wishes.[24]

To begin with, Kharrāz's teachings contrast with those of Rumi by his repeated and uncompromising assertion that a certain category of miracles, called "*āyāt*" (lit. signs),[25] are the exclusive privilege of Prophets. In fact, he says this four times above, such an excessive amount that it suggests, along with the redundant mention of "*ᶜalāmāt*" in the opening sentence and the interchangeable use of Prophets (*anbiyāʾ*) and Apostles (*rusul*), that this passage of the original text was considered so important that it may have even been tampered with. According to Kharrāz, Friends of God share only the *karāmāt* type of miracles received by Prophets, and among these are some which are exclusively for Prophets. The implication is that *āyāt* are superior to *karāmāt*, although the example of the former he refers to is Abraham's ability to feel the fire as cool, while examples of the latter are the revival of sacrificed birds and Muhammad's ascension. Therefore, the text suggests Kharrāz felt a need to distinguish Prophets as superior to Friends of God in this regard, but this did not mean that the latter were denied very lofty miracles.

In his *Sīrat al-awliyāʾ*, Ḥakīm Tirmidhī mentions miracles only very briefly.[26] It is in fact presented simply as one of the signs of the ignorance of the "exoteric scholars" (*ᶜulamāʾ al-ẓāhir*) that they deny the reports of the miracles of the Friends of God, such as walking on water and traveling across large distances in inexplicably short time (*ṭayy al-arḍ*). Tirmidhī explains that their motive is to preserve the distinction of Prophets, which would make Mu'tazilites likely candidates for those whom he calls "exoteric scholars" in this instance.[27] Tirmidhī dismisses this restrictive attitude as a folly resulting from the exoteric scholars' failure to distinguish between different types of miracles, between "*āyāt*" from God's power (*qudra*) and "*karāmāt*" from God's generosity (*karam*). This typological distinction could arguably be what his contemporary Kharrāz also had in mind, since God's power could have changed the nature of fire for Abraham's sake, while it could have been His generosity that allowed the Prophet Muhammad to ascend to Him. Tirmidhī specifies that what the Friends of God receive are the latter type of miracle by means of the following put-down of exoteric scholars, with which he closes his brief discussion:

> [The exoteric scholars] refuse to acknowledge the *karāmāt* because they have lost hope in ever receiving these *karāmāt* themselves on account of their own corruption and impurity.[28]

These ninth-century treatises indicate that the denials of the miracles of the Friends of God were motivated by a concern to preserve the distinction of Prophets from other human beings through their ability to perform miracles, whether on account of rationalist theories or religious rivalry. While Tirmidhī refers to this motivation in explicit terms, Kharrāz alludes to it indirectly through his unnecessarily repetitive assertion that some miracles belong exclusively to Prophets. It is also worth noting that at this early stage both of them use the term "*āyāt*" for the miracles of the Prophet, and not "*muʿjizāt*," which would become the standard term in the manuals written a century later. Their greater concern to place the miracles of the Friends of God below that of the Prophets than their successors in later generations may be taken as a sign of their greater preoccupation in the ninth century with theological issues than legal ones.[29]

Friendship with God and Miracles in Sarrāj's (d. 378/988) Kitāb al-Lumaʿ and Kalābādhī's (d. 380s/990s) Kitāb al-Taʿarruf

In contrast to the distinctions made by his predecessors in the ninth century CE, Abū Naṣr al-Sarrāj asserts that the miracles of followers of Muhammad are counted as further "honors" (*ikrāman*) for him, thereby linking together the miracles of Friends of God with the Prophets'.[30] Sarrāj argues that the miracles performed among ancient communities counted as honors for the

Prophets of their time, so those performed by followers of Muhammad until the end of time will all honor him; these miracles will ensure that he, as the greatest Prophet, and his community, as the best of communities (*khayr al-umum*), surpass all who came before them.[31]

Unsurprisingly then, in the section of his *Kitāb al-Lumaᶜ* on "the affirmation of miracles for both Prophets and Friends of God," Sarrāj critiques denial of the miracles of the Friends of God. In the course of this, he chooses to adopt Tirmidhī's identification of the reason for their denial, by asserting in very similar terms:

> The exoteric people (*ahl al-ẓāhir*) do not accept that anyone other than the Prophets can have these miracles (*karāmāt*) because they consider the Prophets to be special only because of them, and consider *āyāt, muᶜjizāt* and *karāmāt* to be one and same. They also reckon that *muᶜjizāt* were named thus only because of the inability (*iᶜjāz*) of other people to perform anything comparable, meaning that whoever attributes any of that to those other than the Prophets has considered them to be of equal status, and has failed to distinguish between them and the Prophets. [32]

In addition to the identification of "exoteric people," presumably here referring to Mu'tazilites, as the opponents who deny that miracles are possible for anyone other than a Prophet, Sarrāj's use of *"āyāt"* may also be a sign of the direct influence of Tirmidhī's treatise, since he does not use the term elsewhere apart from when citing earlier Sufis. If he had indeed used this predecessor's work here, it makes it all the more interesting that he does not acknowledge this in his *Lumaᶜ*. Sarrāj's method of arguing for the positive embrace of *karāma* miracles in his subsequent discussion is to argue that one would be disbelieving in God's omnipotence (*qudra*) otherwise, because he attributes every kind of miracle to God.[33] His perspective therefore is that anything is possible for God: He can bestow what He wants to whom He pleases. The distinction between the miracles of the Prophets and those of the Friends of God that the exoteric people overlook must therefore lie in the way the miracles are used by each category of devotee and the different effects that they have on them. In this regard, Sarrāj specifies the following three distinctions:

1. The Prophets, out of obedience to God, display their miracles to the people to whom they have been sent on a mission.The Friends of God, out of obedience to God, hide their miracles from people, and do not display them for the purpose of improving their standing among them.

2. The Prophets use miracles as evidence against polytheists, whose hearts are hardened against believing in the One God.The Friends of God use miracles as evidence against their own souls which command to evil (*al-ammāra bi'l-su'*) and cause doubt and uncertainty, until they have transformed by becoming pacified (*taṭma'inn*) and reassured with certainty about God's future provision of means and sustenance.
3. The more miracles the Prophets receive from God, the more steadfast and perfected they become, with Muhammad receiving the most and becoming the most steadfast and perfect of them all.The more miracles the Friends of God receive the more worried they become that it might be their portion from God to be deceived, and that they might fall from their station.[34]

Sarrāj's list highlights that his aim in devoting a section of his *Kitāb al-Luma'* to miracles was both to affirm that Friends of God can also have them and to argue that their miracles are not necessarily any less powerful than those of the Prophets: They are all brought about by God's omnipotence and not His individual Friend's or Prophet's power, and to make such a distinction would actually encroach on God's omnipotence. Moreover, consistent with his maintenance of a distinction between Prophets and Friends of God, Sarrāj points to the rank of the individual as the marker of distinction. It is not much of an exaggeration to argue that he is saying that the miracle of the Friend of God is different from that of the Prophet only because he is a Friend of God, and will therefore utilize or react to the miracle in a contrasting way. The inconsistency between the descriptions of the Friends of God's doubts in the second and third points listed above suggest that Sarrāj's aim was simply to differentiate between the Prophets and them in some fashion without limiting the scope of the Friends' actual miracles.

Of the three differences which Sarrāj lists here, the second one focuses on the effect that experiencing miracles may have on the aspirant. It is worth noting that Sarrāj discusses the aspirant's experience of miracles at such length, clarifying emphatically that miracles are far from being restricted to the highest-ranking Friends of God.Those Sufis still struggling to complete the path must be the ones referred to by Sarrāj when he discusses souls at the stage of "commanding to evil" (*al-ammāra bi'l-su'*) and not yet "pacified" (*muṭma'inna*). In fact, toward the beginning of this section on miracles,he presents a saying of Sahl al-Tustarī which makes the matter-of-fact assertion that miracles will appear for anyone who completes forty days of renunciation with sincerity; if they do not come, Tustarī explains that this must be because the renunciation lacked sincerity (and not because of their status or rank).[35]

Sarrāj's list of differences is also in harmony with the rest of his section devoted to miracles, because the additional discussions included there, aside from the proofs for miracles from Islamic sacred history, focus on the following points: the importance of avoiding becoming dazzled and distracted by miracles from one's focus on God, the greater achievements (mostly self-mortifications) of the Friends of God, and the situations when Friends of God showed their miracles to companions (in order to teach a higher point).[36]

As already mentioned earlier, Abū Bakr al-Kalābādhī includes a chapter entitled "Their Doctrine Concerning the Miracles of the Friends of God" in his *Kitāb al-Taʿarruf li-madhhab al-taṣawwuf*.[37] This chapter was mentioned previously because, while it begins with a discussion of the miracles, it proceeds to discuss more general issues about Friendship with God that have been found to be relevant for earlier parts of this study. The actual discussion of miracles is deceptively short, less than half of the chapter ostensibly devoted to this topic.

Kalābādhī's treatment of this subject at first appears similar to that of Tirmidhī in that he affirms the existence of miracles (*karāmāt*) of the Friends of God in the face of denials. However, al-Kalābādhī does not uphold the distinctions between their miracles and the miracles of the Prophets so strictly, as is evident from the first sentence of the chapter:

> "They unanimously affirm the *karāmāt* of the Friends of God, even though they may enter the category of the *muʿjizāt* (*wa-in kānat tadkhul fī bāb al-muʿjizāt*), such as walking on water, speaking with animals, traveling across large distances in inexplicably short time, or making something appear in another place or time."[38]

Kalābādhī continues by presenting reports and arguments in support of the Sufis' unanimous affirmation of the miracles of the Friends of God, in the course of which it becomes clear that by "*muʿjizāt*" in the previous passage, he means the miracles normally attributed to Prophets exclusively. This term appears to have replaced "*āyāt*" by his time as the preferred term for the miracles of Prophets, and this is attributable to the development of the theory of the inimitability (*iʿjāz*) of the verses (*āyāt*) of the Qur'an in the third/tenth century.[39] What is important to note here, regardless of his differing classification to that of Kharrāz and Tirmidhī before him, is that the usually more conservative traditionist Kalābādhī does not appear unduly concerned at the possibility that Friends of God might be able to perform the same kinds of miracles as Prophets.

The first proofs for miracles Kalābādhī cites include Qur'anic stories, namely the miracle of Āṣaf b. Barkhiya, the member of Solomon's entourage who transfers the Queen of Sheba's throne to his palace in the blink of an eye

(Qur'an 27/40), and the provision of fruit to Mary while alone and pregnant (Qur'an 19/25). Kalābādhī considers neither of this pair to have been Prophets.[40] He also mentions a miracle of ᶜUmar, the Prophet Muhammad's companion, after his passing, in order to clarify that miracles are still possible without a living Prophet.[41]

While Kalābādhī attributes the denial of the miracles of the Friends of God to the same concern Tirmidhī identifies, namely that this could remove the evidence of Prophets and their distinction from other people, he does not blame this on a failure to distinguish between different kinds of miracles. Instead he argues that the miracles are not what make a man a Prophet, but rather his mission's teachings.[42] Since for Kalābādhī the miracles in themselves are not the means by which Prophets are distinguished by God from others, he presents reports from Sufis about alternative criteria based on how each respective category actually experiences the miracle. For instance, Prophets are said to be aware of the origin of the miracles, while Friends of God are not. After all of these reports, he cites one that does distinguish the miracles themselves, arguing that those of the Friends of God are restricted to answers to prayers, the completion of a spiritual state, the power to perform an action, or the provision of sustenance in an extraordinary fashion, while those of the Prophets are to produce something out of nothing, or to change the essential nature of things (*taqlīb al-aᶜyān*).[43] However, Kalābādhī does not appear to favor this proposed distinction, which he reports last of all, because he begins this whole chapter by volunteering that the miracles of the Friends of God may enter the category of those of the Prophets.

Overall, Kalābādhī's discussion steers away from distinguishing between the miracles of the Friends of God and those of the Prophets on the basis of the nature of the miraculous occurrence itself. He indicates that such a distinction had been used as the basis of a classification through reports and also indirectly by asserting that the ones of the Friends of God may even "enter the category of *muᶜjizāt*." However, the distinctions he prioritizes are those concerning the knowledge of the recipients about the miracle, and the effects it has on them. The extent to which Kalābādhī is unworried about the possibility that Friends of God can share this privilege with the Prophets is emphasized by the following positive interpretation he offers:

> If a Friend of God is sincere and not a Prophet, then he will not claim Prophethood, nor anything false or futile, but rather he will only invite men to what is true and honest. If God makes a miracle appear in [the Friend of God], this does not infringe on the Prophethood of a Prophet, nor necessarily cause doubt about it, because the sincere Friend of God

> says the same things as the Prophet and invites others to what he had invited them, so the appearance of the miracle in him is really corroboration of the Prophet, a further manifestation of his mission, a confirmation of his proof, and an affirmation of what he had been claiming regarding Prophethood as well as the Unity of God.[44]

With this passage, Kalābādhī argues that there is no reason to worry that sincere Friends of God might receive the same miracles as Prophets, because they would never claim to be Prophets themselves. He is effectively saying that the only difference between their miracles is that one is a Prophet, while the other is a Friend of God who would never claim to be a Prophet because a prerequisite of his own status is sincerity.

While this position that he takes may not seem so surprising for Sarrāj, the fact that Kalābādhī also accepts that the miracles of the Friends of God may overlap with those of the Prophets stands out as being somewhat out of character. It is therefore worth noting that these authors did not feel as much need to affirm the superiority of the miracles of the Prophets over those of the Friends of God as they evidently did with regard to divine communication. One might be tempted to accept at face-value that this is due to the theological dogma of God's omnipotence, which may be compromised by distinctions between miracles by different kinds of devotees when they are all dependent on His power, as argued by Sarrāj. However, it is not difficult to see how God's omnipotence or omniscience could have been brought in to assert a similar equivalence for divine communication, a strategy Rumi himself uses by arguing that the Light of God can never be restricted.[45]

Friendship with God and Miracles in Qushayrī's (d. 465/1072) Risāla and Hujwīrī's (d. ca. 467/1074) Kashf al-Maḥjūb

Abū'l-Qāsim al-Qushayrī[46] begins his chapter entitled "The Miracles of the Friends of God" (*Bāb karāmāt al-awliyā*ʾ)with the assertion that "the appearance of miracles in the Friends of God is possible."[47] One may therefore be tempted to assume that his aims in this chapter would be restricted to supporting this modest statement, especially in view of his tendency toward cautiousness. It is therefore remarkable that one finds significantly more among his teachings, ranging from an acknowledgment of the Friend of God's ability to display his miracles, to support for additional claims that they are able to perform miracles which even surpass those of the Prophets.

Qushayrī begins this chapter, the longest chapter in his whole *Risāla*, with the more conventional arguments his predecessors among Sufi authors and Ash'arite theologians had used already, linking acceptance of miracles to belief in God's omnipotence (*qudra*), for instance. He cites the Ash'arite theologians seemingly just to add more weight to the aim of increasing acceptance of the miracles of the Friends of God, because each of the theologians is quoted distinguishing between the miracles of the Prophets (*muʿjizāt*) and the miracles of the Friends of God (*karāmāt*), such as by asserting that the latter are limited to answers to prayers, or that they are to be kept hidden. Yet Qushayrī volunteers that he himself follows the view of the theologian Abū Bakr al-Ashʿarī al-Bāqillānī (d. 403/1013), which he presents in the following way:

> The peerless one in his science during his era, Judge Abu Bakr al-Ashʿarī said, "*Muʿjizāt* are exclusively for the Prophets while *karāmāt* are for the Friends of God as well as for the Prophets. However, Friends of God cannot have a *muʿjiza*, because it is the condition of the *muʿjiza* to be accompanied by a claim of Prophethood (*nubuwwa*). The *muʿjiza* is not a *muʿjiza* in and of itself, but rather it becomes one by fulfilling many conditions. When a single one of these conditions is missing, then it is not a *muʿjiza*. One of these conditions happens to be the claim to Prophethood. The Friend of God does not claim to be a Prophet, so what appears in him cannot be a *muʿjiza*."
>
> This is the opinion that we base ours on, profess, and believe in. All, or almost all, of the conditions exist in the *karāma*, this one condition being missing.[48]

Qushayrī in this way surpasses all his predecessors among the Sufi authors discussed in this chapter with his liberal assertion of a virtual equivalence between the miracle of the Friend of God and that of the Prophet. Since according to the final comment above, the only difference is the lack of a claim to Prophethood, it would be no exaggeration to say this means that the Friend of God's miracle can be exactly the same as the Prophet's except that it is manifested in a Friend of God instead.[49] Qushayrī follows this volunteering of his own conviction with further accommodating assertions about the miracles of the Friend of God, which include his view that it need not necessarily be an answer to a prayer (and could even occur involuntarily), and that the Friend of God may be seen performing miracles though he would not be deliberately displaying them as part of a mission like a Prophet.[50] In other words, he does not follow the view of the authoritative theologians whose opinions he had initially cited; that was evidently in order to give weight to the acceptance of miracles by the Friends of God.

There is a further significant way in which Qushayrī increases the potential of the miracles of the Friends of God. This is found in his justification of the view that the miracles of the Friends of God can surpass those of the Prophets:

> Someone asked, "How is it possible for these miracles (*karāmāt*) to be greater than the miracles of the Apostles of God (*muʿjizāt al-rusul*)? Is it possible for Friends of God to be superior to Prophets?"
>
> He was told, "Such *karāmāt* are an adjunct to the *muʿjizāt* of our Prophet, because whoever is not truthful in Islam cannot have a *karāma* manifested in him. Moreover, whenever a *karāma* is manifested in a follower of a Prophet, it becomes counted as one of his own *muʿjizāt*. If that Apostle of God had not been truthful, then no *karāma* would have been manifested in one of his followers. The rank (*rutba*) of the Friends of God does not reach that of the Prophets, according to unanimous agreement on that."[51]

While Qushayrī's predecessors from the tenth century, Kalābādhī and Sarrāj, held the view that the miracles of the Friends of God are positive confirmations of the missions of their Prophets or add extra honors to the latter, respectively, they had not gone as far as to suggest that those miracles could actually surpass those of the Prophets themselves. Qushayrī uses a similar argument to theirs by implying that Friends of God can have greater miracles than Prophets because of the fact that their miracles would become counted as one of their own particular Prophet's miracles, since his Prophethood is what has enabled them. The possibilities for the miracles of the Friends of God therefore become virtually limitless, but without any danger that they could be considered superior to Prophets, or at least their own Prophet.

The miracle-stories that make up the bulk of Qushayrī's chapter "The Miracles of the Friends of God" begin with those taken from Sarrāj's *Lumaʿ*, reminding readers of the latter's emphasis on miracles being secondary to the devotee's relationship with God and the need for discretion. However, although the additional stories Qushayrī presents mainly depict how God provides for the needs of His Friends, coming to their rescue through miracles, as well as enabling them to fulfill what He has ordained for them in their capacity as His representatives, a few also depict Sufis as displaying outwardly the power of their miracles.[52] The overall impression this gives is a reinforcement of the perception that Qushayrī wrote more openly and liberally about this topic than his main predecessors among the authors of Sufi manuals.

This stands out in contrast to his more circumspect teachings about the shariah, as has been discussed earlier.

Qushayrī's contemporary in Lahore, ᶜAlī Hujwīrī,[53] is even more emphatic about the similarity between the miracles performed by the Friends of God and those performed by the Prophets. In a section of his chapter on the relationship of Friendship with God with Prophethood entitled "Discourse in Confirmation of the *Karāmāt*," he goes as far as to assert that "the miracle of the Friend of God is exactly the same as the miracle of the Prophet" (*karāmat-i walī ᶜayn-i muᶜjiz-i nabī buwad*).[54] In his idiosyncratically dialectal style, Hujwīrī brings up the view of some of the Traditionalists that Friends of God can only have *karāmāt* and not any *muᶜjizāt*, but he does so only in order to refute it.[55] He uses Qushayrī's argument that the latter type requires the recipient to be a Prophet, otherwise they are the same, which implies that the Traditionalists opinion had assumed a bigger difference.

Hujwīrī does discuss differences between the two types of miracles in the next section of the same chapter, which is devoted to this purpose according to its heading, but this largely consists of citing others' opinions without necessarily agreeing with them or bothering to refute them. The main point he asserts is that the miracles of the Prophets aim to have an effect on others, while those of the Friends of God are designed to have an effect on themselves, thereby echoing Sarrāj's second distinction in his *Lumaᶜ*, which was a major influence on his own work. Although this would imply that the latter should not display their miracles, Hujwīrī later cites the opinion of his own teacher allowing them to.[56]

Later in this chapter a debate is mentioned over whether the Friends of God perform miracles while in a state of drunkenness (*sukr*) or sobriety (*ṣaḥw*). The view that it is in a state of drunkenness would lend itself best to viewing Prophets as superior, because in that theory Prophets are continually able to perform miracles and Friends of God only temporarily, or as Hujwīrī puts it: "The sobriety of the Friends of God is the level of ordinary people, while their drunkenness is the level of the Prophets" (*maqām-i ṣaḥw-i awliyāʾ daraja-yi ᶜawwām buwad wa-maqām-i sukrishān daraja-yi anbiyā'*).[57] However, Hujwīri attributes the counterargument to Junayd, whose opinion he invariably follows, and that would imply that Friends of God are as often in the right (sober) state to perform miracles, as Prophets are.[58]

Conclusions

It is apparent that by the late eleventh century distinctions between the miracles of Prophets and those of Friends of God had become virtually nonexistent, to the extent that justification was found for the latter to have even greater miracles. Rumi's teachings about the miracles of the Friends of God therefore appear in harmony with those of Qushayrī and Hujwīrī in the eleventh century. However, he makes no attempt to offer justifications based on the accrual of honors to Prophets, or to distinguish those of the Friend of God by their dependency on spiritual states. This all stands in stark contrast to the treatises of the ninth century, which reveal a theological concern to preserve the distinction of Prophetic miracles while arguing for the possibility that Friends of God can have a lesser variety of miracles.

The pattern of development seen in discussions of the Shariah and divine communication, which revealed increasing concerns to restrict the possibilities of Friends of God through to the eleventh century, are almost reversed when it comes to miracles: initial circumspection is followed by increasingly indulgent approaches through the next two centuries. The most conspicuous signs of this contrasting pattern of development can be found in the treatments by Kalābādhī and Qushayrī; while these authors were the most conservative in discussing the Shariah and divine communication, they appear to hold a laissez-faire attitude when it comes to miracles. Kalābādhī even implies that miracles are possible for aspiring Friends of God who are not yet perfected mystics, in agreement with his contemporary Sarrāj, nearly three centuries before Rumi.

The most likely explanation for this stark contrast is the fact that the appearance of miracles posed little or no threat to the institutionalization process of Islam under way at the time, unlike the belief in continued divine communication of the highest kind or transcending the Shariah. Establishing that the miracles of the Friends of God differ from those of Prophets only by virtue of the fact that they are not Prophets would also allow a huge accrual of the loftiest miracles among the followers of Muhammad in later generations, thereby taking his honors beyond all other Prophets'. The ambivalence among early Muslims to attributing extraordinary miracles to Muhammad could now be compensated for in abundance, in the process of establishing Muhammad as both the last and the greatest of the Prophets.

Acceptance of the Friends of God's miracles is also likely to have been favored for polemical reasons due to the fact that the Mu'tazilites denied their possibility for anyone but Prophets. A similar approach toward divine communication was not adopted by the Sufi systematizers of the tenth and eleventh centuries, because though this may have achieved a similar goal, it would at the same time have meant dangerously rivaling the supreme authority of the formulations of religious scholars, which depended on Muhammad's divine communication being considered final and unrivaled. As a result of these circumstances and determinants, Friends of God become attributed regularly with limitless miracles, yet at the same time they are portrayed by Sufis more circumspect than Rumi as being dependent on the legal formulations of religious scholars who lacked such divine graces; their influence is seen as being capable of powerfully transformative effects on aspirants to Friendship with God, and yet they are said to prescribe practices strictly within the framework of the religious system constructed by textual scholars.

Rumi's contemporary in Anatolia Najm al-Dīn Rāzī (d. 654/1256) shares with him the view that miracles need not be divided into those of Prophets and those of Friends of God. Once the latter had become presented as an accumulation of Muhammad's honors in any case, this was hardly a surprising development. To be precise, in his *Mirṣād al-ʿIbād* Rāzī uses the term "*karāmāt*" for every kind of miracle and distinguishes only between those that are truly miracles (*bi-ḥaqīqat karāmāt*) and those that can be performed by evil as well as good people.[59] Most significantly for this discussion, those that are truly miracles are said to be exclusively for "the elite" (*khāṣṣ*), who include both Prophets and Friends of God, since Muhammad is among their number as are other members of the "servants of God" (*bandagān*) and "religious folk" (*ahl-i dīn*).[60] Rāzī belittles miracles also like Rumi, seeing them from his perspective as a potential trap that can allure the wayfarer away from the path toward the presence of God.[61] Rumi stands out, however, for his assertion that the greatest miracle is the effect that a Friend of God can have on another person's inner being, which fits well with practical instruction. Although this quality of the Friend of God is discussed by other authors, he raises it specifically in relation to miracles, making it seem all the more appropriate that miracle-stories should be predominant among the variant reports of his much celebrated encounter with Shams-i Tabrīzī.[62]

Conclusion

THE MOST POPULAR teaching-story that illustrates Rumi's prioritization of experiencing closeness to God over following religious dogma is undoubtedly the story about Moses and the shepherd in the second book of *The Masnavi*. This story describes how Moses rebukes a shepherd for expressing his devotion to God in a simplistic anthropomorphic way (e.g., "Where do You live that I might serve You there? / I'd mend Your battered shoes and comb Your hair").[1] The twist in this story's plot comes when God sends divine communication (*waḥy*) to Moses, telling him off for driving this simple devotee away from worship by means of his interference, and clarifying that the inner spiritual state is what counts rather than the outward expression:

> I don't look at what men articulate,
> But at their spirit and their inner state;
> I check that men's hearts have humility,
> Even if they should speak too haughtily.[2]

It should not be difficult to see why this story with its message of tolerance and critique of judgmental attitudes should have proven to be so popular. What is often overlooked, however, is that the shepherd in the story transforms from a simpleton to a Friend of God, who tells the subsequently remorseful Moses that their past negative encounter no longer bothers him, because he has now ascended to the loftiest levels of heaven. Rumi transforms this character by proceeding in his commentary from a message of tolerance to an affirmation of the position of those close to God, beyond all dogma and laws. Although Rumi refers to them here simply as "lovers," when interpreted in the context of his teachings elsewhere, he is clearly referring to Friends of God in commenting:

Beyond all the religions stands love's nation;
God's their sole dogma and denomination.
(millat-i ʿishq az hama dīnhā judā-st
ʿāshiqān-rā madhhab-u millat khudā-st).[3]

Having explored Rumi's ubiquitous teachings about Friends of God in this study, we should not be surprised that he makes this transformation of the shepherd in the context of prioritizing inner experience over outward appearance, and as part of a story that involves confounding the Prophet Moses. This story arguably highlights what is most distinctive about Rumi's teachings on Friendship with God, namely his emphasis on its accessibility. He repeatedly exhorts his audience to strive to reach the same goal as past luminaries with realistic hope of success; the distance between the simpleton shepherd and the Friend of God is not so unbridgeable in his view that he should have hesitated to transform this character in the story almost seamlessly.

As the hugely popular Moses and the shepherd story illustrates, in teaching about Friendship with God Rumi's focus is on a universal and immediate experience of the Divine. He regards it as the actual motivation for any urge to worship God, even if it is not understood in such terms by the majority of people. From this perspective, there is little point in distinguishing between the categories of Friend of God and Prophet. For Rumi, the Prophet Muhammad's distinction is that he was the first to travel the path that all subsequent Friends of God follow similarly to its completion; they do so thanks to his pioneering efforts, whether they acknowledge his role in this or not. Indeed, in Rumi's view, the Prophet Muhammad "set up signposts" precisely to enable subsequent mystic wayfarers to reach the same destination, rather than do anything to prevent such an endeavor or block later opportunities. He thus serves as their own apotheosis. Moreover, beyond personalities who can be compared with each other and ranked, Rumi describes the reality of Prophets as being a special "love and affection" inside the souls of all people inclined toward the mystical path, regardless even of their religion. This can help explain why, in his scandalous-sounding story about the claimant to Prophethood, Rumi takes a more critical stance against the denial of the claim than the actual claim itself.[4]

The key virtue of Prophethood cited by the claimant in the claimant to Prophethood story is divine communication (*waḥy*). This appears to be representative of Rumi's own opinion from the evidence of his various writings on this topic. Having the opportunity to become close to God, mystics who are not classified as Prophets nonetheless also receive direct communication from Him. For fully fledged Friends of God, including himself of course,

Rumi considers this to be the very same kind of divine communication that Prophets receive, no less than God's speech (*kalām Allāh*). One important consequence of this is that the routinized charisma of the Prophet Muhammad, as expressed in the material originally compiled about him by religious scholars, becomes of secondary importance to Friends of God and their followers. While this is not a new approach, Rumi boldly highlights that it applies not only to fully fledged Friends of God, but also to aspirants aiming to reach that status eventually: in his view, they too can receive divine communication with increasing permanence as they progress with their endeavor, and they should keep striving for more.

Disciples of the Friends of God must also appreciate that the teachings they receive from them have originated from divine communication, and are therefore of more direct consequence than the textually routinized Prophetic heritage transmitted by religious scholars. It is perhaps largely on account of the master-disciple relationship, the importance of which Rumi stresses so emphatically in his writings, that he presents in this way the rationale for following contemporary Friends of God unconditionally, just as Khiḍr had demanded of Moses, without deferral even to the laws of a religious system. The aim of this training is for the disciple to overcome the self and increasingly act at the direct command of God like Khiḍr until one is unable even to consider acting otherwise.

Rumi's particular approach to miracles supports further the view that he prioritized the master-disciple relationship above everything else, seeing as their role in intensifying this bond represents what is most important about them. The whole purpose of miracles for him is to inspire others in the most worthy miracle of all, namely inner transformation through the attainment of Friendship with God to one's own capacity. For Rumi the closeness to God that His Friends achieve is dynamic and interactive, in that their devotees also partake of it to some degree through such miracles. One does not have to look too far among his own references to Shams-i Tabrīzī, not to mention the biographical stories about their relationship, to find an inspiration for this perspective in his own experience on the path.

Rumi's teachings about Friends of God, their relationship with Prophets, their divine communication, their miracles, and their relationship with the Shariah are remarkably consistent. Not only is this evident throughout his six-volume *Masnavi,* it is also evident in his teachings recorded within the *Fīhi mā fīh,* in spite of the fact that these two works probably represent two different periods in the last two decades of his life. These practical teachings clash clearly with the most influential theoretical writings of Sufis. The outcome of relying on those manuals of the tenth and eleventh centuries C.E. for the interpretation of his mysticism, rather than as a source for understanding irenic harmonization efforts by Sufis interested in religious scholarship, is to obscure fundamental elements of Rumi's teachings. In the specific case of Friendship with God, some have suggested that strict adherence to the Shariah must be a prerequisite and that Friends of God are always clearly subordinate to Prophets, despite Rumi's repeated teachings about the immediacy and universal accessibility of this experience. It should be noted that Rumi encourages even his own disciples to rely as soon as possible on divine communication they themselves receive ahead of both theory and imitative practice, in order for the following to become applicable to them as soon as possible: "Without hadiths and their transmitters too / Water of Life they drink to know what's true."[5]

If one were to take the theoretical manuals of the tenth and eleventh centuries at face value, one could be forgiven for imagining that Sufis always accepted that Friendship with God was inferior to Prophethood, and that any contrary position expressed by Rumi and other Sufis can represent no more than a marginal later deviation. This is why it is valuable to examine closely the discussions in these manuals, especially in light of the oldest surviving texts about this issue. The latter indicate that the opposite position, namely that Friends of God are superior, was as old as one can possibly verify, since they were either written to refute it or repeatedly offer reassurance that it is not the position being advocated. Moreover, that position, which may seem scandalous from the perspective of the later manuals, actually proved remarkably formidable to argue against, even though developments then in scholastic theology surrounding the understanding of Muhammad's status as "Seal of the Prophets" compelled authors to try. This is evident in the use of last-resort arguments, such as the earliest version of the claim that Prophets are at the same time Friends of God, and that they receive the same divine communication as them in addition to their Prophetic kind, instead of making a convincing argument in favor of Prophethood on its own merit. When one remembers that the Qur'an includes the story of Moses failing to follow Khiḍr satisfactorily and early exegetes insisted that Prophetic divine communication is mediated by an angel, leaving other forms potentially more explicit, one can better appreciate why the argument proved so challenging. Moreover, its resilience is testified to by the fact that the notion of Friendship with God being superior to Prophethood has survived in one guise or another (most famously through Ibn ʿArabī's theory of Friendship with God) far beyond the time of the irenic attempts of the manuals to refute or downplay it.

In much of the secondary literature, the legal system constructed by religious scholars has been commonly assumed to represent the foundation of

Sufism, both for an individual's mystical itinerary, and even historically for the emergence of Sufism. It makes it all the more interesting then to witness that the oldest surviving mystical texts present a contrasting situation, expressing little if any encouragement to follow juristic formulations. Rumi's emphasis to aspirants on the priority of overcoming the self above all else and his belief in the superiority of acting on the basis of direct divine communication rather than through theoretical formulations are therefore hardly innovative. There is arguably some justification for assumptions that Rumi's teachings insisted on deferral to religious laws and dogmas, since it is rare to encounter the open expression of the opposite view among high-profile Sufi authors living after the eleventh-century consolidation of juridico-theological Islam's authority. However, it is worth remembering that the first expressions of deference to scholastic Islam, in the Sufi manuals, represent a sudden change in approach from that of the oldest mystical writings, and that even works of this irenic genre only came to defer to juristic formulations through a gradual process: it ranged from an insistence on the minimal amount of compliance necessary to the adoption of the most conservative approach in any areas of ambiguity. The background of the author was a major factor, with Kalābādhī, who had the least Sufi credentials, being the most conservative. Although the manuals of Qushayrī and Hujwīrī may appear at first, through their stated aims, to be similarly conservative, in contrast they include enough ambiguity to facilitate the preservation of divergent viewpoints, especially with regard to fully fledged Friends of God.

The contrasting ways in which Sufi discourse on divine communication and miracles have developed is also worth considering further. For Rumi, the former takes on much greater importance. However, while the oldest mystical treatises imply that divine communication of the Friends of God had been considered superior in certain ways to that of the Prophets, by the time of the eleventh-century manuals of Qushayrī and Hujwīrī one encounters only silence about this issue. In contrast, while the oldest mystical treatises distinguished the miracles of the Friends of God as inferior to those of the Prophets, the more scholastically-minded Kalābādhī accepted that there could be an overlap, while Qushayrī provided the rationale for accepting miracles of the Friends of God to be superior even to those of Prophets. In the search for a reason why miracles should have been set apart in this way, one likely explanation is that, unlike continual divine communication, they posed no substantial threat to the authority of juristic scholars, which became increasingly important during these centuries. By contrast, there is a strong emphasis on the distinction of the miracles of Prophets in the mystical treatises of the ninth century, when theological matters were much more a priority than juristic ones.

The contrasting silence of Qushayrī and Hujwīrī concerning divine communication may at first seem more difficult to interpret. However, once it is remembered that their predecessors struggled with this particular quality of the Friends of God more than any other during attempts to argue for the superiority of Prophets, their silence can be interpreted as simply a way of avoiding comment. When they faced the challenge to affirm their direct divine communication at the same time as expressing deference to the textually-based religious system of juridico-theological scholars, this might have then been the best option. The fact that Qushayrī is the most liberal in accepting miracles of the Friends of God superior even to Prophets' but at the same time remains silent about their divine communication highlights how miracles represent here the exception that proves the rule. It furthermore suggests that the juridico-theological scholars' concerns about divine communication and abiding by the Shariah were more about their own authority as interpreters of the religion than the status of Prophets, whose cycle they had effectively sealed. They did not see miracles as posing any such threat.

The analysis here of the treatment of Friendship with God in the theoretical manuals corroborates and develops Ahmet Karamustafa's recent assertion that they are more complex than apologetic writings.[6] Even if out of necessity, their use of ambiguity, silence, or categorical statements followed by qualifying elaborations all show their commitment to the fundamental importance of Friendship with God to Sufism; if they had been prepared to write whatever would reassure the critics of Sufism the most, their works would not display these characteristics, which are the consequence of balancing an unwillingness to compromise the basis of the mystical endeavor out of desire for integration with the dominant religious discourse.[7] One way of appreciating their use of such strategies is to consider how they facilitated the endurance of opinions such as those expressed by Rumi so explicitly two centuries later in his practical teachings about Friendship with God, something which would have been more difficult to imagine if they had instead been categorical and unambiguous in their deference. To bring this into perspective, it may be worthwhile to consider how tendencies prevalent in early Shi'ism became marginalized as a result of their renunciation by leaders of the later Imami Shi'i community's scholarly hierarchy; if the authors of the Sufi manuals had similarly renounced the controversial teachings of the early mystic leaders, rather than deal with them using their preferred strategies, then it is likely that such teachings would have similarly survived only on the fringes of the Sufi tradition rather than being propagated so explicitly by leading spokesmen of later centuries. The approach of the manual authors had the virtue of leaving open for Rumi and other prominent Sufis in differing later circumstances some flexibility in redrawing the boundaries of Friendship with God.

If Rumi's teachings about Friendship with God often appear closer to the theories in the oldest surviving mystical treatises than the irenic manuals, this is because, in common with their ninth-century authors, he was not under the same pressure as the Sufi theoreticians of the tenth and eleventh centuries, when juridico-theological scholars were still consolidating their supremacy. Rumi's own teachings are not simply the same as those of the earliest mystics, since he teaches that no substantial distinction exists between Prophets and Friends of God, rather than that one category is superior to the other. However, the similarities with the oldest writings highlight the extent to which the theories articulated in the Sufi manuals of intervening centuries were responding to external developments among juridico-theological religious scholars that constituted an interruption rather than continuity.

Far from being an isolated case, the greater similarity between Rumi's teachings on Friendship with God and that of the earliest mystics is arguably an example of a wider phenomenon. For instance, the theories of Ḥakīm Tirmidhī, the most prolific mystic author of his generation, are ignored, marginalized, or drawn upon only selectively during the tenth and eleventh centuries, when irenic efforts at legitimizing the Sufi tradition were top priority. However, after this period he becomes the subject of a revival of interest, most famously in the writings of Ibn ᶜArabī.[8] Tirmidhī had dared to critique the juridico-theological scholars' own understanding of the Shariah and was accused of claiming to be a Prophet, which seems to have been considered serious enough to make recourse to his idiosyncratic efforts at actually expressing deference to Prophets no longer an option for his immediate successors. This was in spite of the fact that the next generation of Sufi theoreticians could have avoided many of their own struggles with the help of those efforts. Joseph Lumbard has recently shown that the understanding of love as an essential attribute of God, initially expressed by Tirmidhī's contemporary Ḥallāj, was similarly overlooked, only to be revived emphatically in the twelfth century and developed further by Aḥmad Ghazālī (d. 520/1126).[9] He has even traced an instance where Hujwīrī asserts that Sufis prefer that their actual doctrine of divine love remain hidden, which is comparable with Rumi's volunteering that the Sufis' tendency to distinguish between the divine communication of Prophets and that of Friends of God is only on account of the general public's limited capacity for understanding. Lumbard interprets this as an allusion to "an oral tradition that has not been preserved."[10] However, it may be more accurate to point out that they were preserved both orally and to a restricted degree in writing, such as the case of Ḥallāj's own writings.[11] In this regard, it is important to remember that one can find alternative views about Friendship with God in the writings of the leading Sufis living when the theoretical manuals were composed. Though these individuals did not themselves write extended theoretical discussions on this issue, let alone rival manuals, it is likely that their practical teachings continued to be transmitted by their disciples during this period nonetheless. The fact that the manual authors repeatedly return to the topic is also in itself an indication that it was still being contested.

In recent decades Rumi has been at the center of a tug-of-war between those who would dissociate him from Islam and those who respond to this by stressing his proficiency in the Islamic religious sciences. The latter reaction, which is common among academicians, is understandable when one bears in mind early Orientalist assumptions that Rumi, and Sufis in general, were foreign to Islam, because they regarded the religion as a spiritually deficient Semitic legalism.[12] However, a close reading of Rumi's writings is unlikely to find that response any more convincing, which can explain why opinions have remained so polarized. It also highlights what is most problematic about such arguments, on either side of the debate, namely their common assumption that deference to the religious system of Muslim juridico-theological scholars should be the criterion for determining what is Islamic. While this is not an unreasonable position to take, since this is what is usually meant when referring to "Islam," it needs to be acknowledged that the religious system of Islam was consolidated over centuries and with substantial debate and disagreement. That is to say, there have been Muslim communities from before those centuries who have not regarded the systematized religion to be the supremely authoritative representation of their faith.[13] The mystical writings on Friendship with God examined here show that the rising influence of scholastic Islam in fact constituted an outside interruption, threatening the survival of their ongoing mystical endeavor, rather than an internal development enhancing it. Moreover, the extent to which irenic authors from among the Sufis did find ways to present their mysticism as being theoretically compatible with scholastic Islam still falls short of any evidence to assume that Sufism is based on it, let alone that to be "genuine Sufis" they must be wholly constrained by its formulated limits. At the same time, however, the particular understanding of mysticism shared by Rumi and most other Sufis, with its emphasis on divine verbal communication that can produce inspired books, and also direct the control of the mystic's actions, could hardly be more distinctive of the mysticism found in the Qur'an and Muhammad's life-story.

Since the main problem with this debate lies in the narrowness of the definition of Islam, restricting it to the scholastic edifice developed centuries after its sacred history, one wonders whether Rumi's famous parable about the four men who fought over grapes might point toward a resolution.[14] That is to say, the use of a more inclusive definition of Islam which embraces all movements that took inspiration from the Qur'an and Muhammad's example, each according to its own interpretations, might satisfy both sides of the debate without resorting to ahistorical and essentialist arguments. On the one hand it would not gloss over Rumi's low estimation of juridico-theological Islam from a mystical perspective, while on the other it would not strip Rumi of his own religious background. At the same time, this could contribute to fulfilling the urgent need for a more nuanced understanding of Muslims in general, beyond individuals programmed above all else to follow the laws and dogmas formulated by religious scholars.[15] After all, Rumi's popularity has itself been unrivalled across a huge swath of the Muslim heartlands for several centuries, rather than belonging to a secretive minority.

The main aim of this study has been to examine Rumi's teachings about Friendship with God, which represents the major preoccupation of his writings, and to clarify their relationship with the theoretical prose manuals that have frequently been treated as normative, as well as the wider Islamic religious system. A close examination of those manuals in comparison with both the theoretical works that preceded them as well as Rumi's didactic writings has provided insight into the kinds of dilemmas and concerns Muslim mystics grappled with at a time when the juridico-theological system was consolidating its authority. It has also highlighted some important developments in Sufi theory as a result of this challenging process. If insight into the direct influences on Rumi's teachings is sought instead, this could be gained by considering the treatment of these same topics in the mystical writings of the twelfth and early thirteenth centuries C.E., closer to his lifetime. Rumi was after all far from being alone during this period in expounding teachings that contrast with the irenic manuals. Though the twelfth-century Sufis Aḥmad Ghazālī, ᶜAyn al-Quḍāt Hamadānī, Ḥakīm Sanāʾī, Rūzbihān Baqlī, and Farīd al-Dīn ᶜAṭṭār may not have left any extended theoretical discussions directly confronting the issue of Friendship with God, recent studies on them indicate that such a project could still prove a rewarding endeavor.[16] However, that is a subject for another book.

Notes

INTRODUCTION

1. Barks, *The Essential Rumi*, p. 36. A more literal version of the full quatrain (no. 395 in Furūzānfar's edition of Rumi's *Kulliyāt-i Shams-i Tabrīzī*) in English quatrain form is:

   Beyond Islam and infidelity
   There is a place where we feel ecstasy;
   When mystics reach it they prostrate, because
   It is beyond Islam, unbelief, and even locality.
2. The union of a Sufi with God is referred to as a "wedding" (Arabic "*ᶜurs*"), most commonly in relation to his or her passing. For instance, in Konya the annual commemoration of Rumi's passing is still referred to as the "*şeb-i arus,*" or "wedding night."
3. Barks, *The Essential Rumi*, p. 261.
4. Coleman Barks is by far the most widely read translator of Rumi, and it is largely due to his renderings that Rumi has become so popular in recent decades. Barks translates through previous literal translations rather than from the original Persian directly, which has made his work vulnerable to suggestions that it may not represent Rumi accurately (e.g., see Gamard, "Corrections of Popular Versions").
5. This term is also frequently vocalized as "*wilāya,*" but not without semantic differences. Since this study concentrates on spiritual closeness to God rather than any outward exercise of authority based on that, "*walāya*" is the vocalization chosen here, notwithstanding the variability in usage and the "yin and yang relationship" between the terms that Vincent Cornell has insightfully elaborated on in the introduction of his *Realm of the Saint*, pp. xvi–xxi.

6. See further Renard, *Friends of God*, p.260; Morris, "Situating Islamic Mysticism," p. 317.
7. See further Elmore, *Islamic Sainthood*, pp. 112–18.
8. For a brief overview, see "Walāyah," in Eliade, ed., *The Encyclopedia of Religion*, pp. 9660–62 (H. Landolt); "Walī; 1. General Survey," in EI2 (B. Radtke).
9. E.g. see p. 58 below regarding ʿAlī Hujwīrī's comments about "*walāya*" being the foundation of Sufism. The theorist ʿAbd al-Karīm al-Qushayrī asserts that the term "*taṣawwuf*" began to be used for Muslim Mystics only in around 200 A.H. (815 C.E.). His account about how Sufis were identified before then is, however, a theological construct (R, p. 34; Calder, Mojaddedi and Rippin, eds. and trs., *Classical Islam*, p. 244). See further p. 132 below.
10. See further Morris, "Situating Islamic Mysticism," pp. 293–95. For the significance of "*walāya*" (and "*wilāya*") in early Twelver Imami Shīʿism, see Dakake, *The Charismatic Community*.
11. See pp. 28–30 below.
12. See pp. 63–64 below.
13. See p. 91 below.
14. This is an issue I have explored in relation to the biographical traditions of Abū Yazīd al-Basṭāmī (d. ca. 261/875) and Abū 'l-Qāsim al-Junayd (d. 297/910) in *The Biographical Tradition in Sufism*.
15. My differentiation between "practical" and "theoretical" Sufi writings follows the classification in James W. Morris, "Situating Islamic Mysticism," pp. 299–313.
16. See p. 6.
17. E.g. the editor and translator of Rumi's *Masnavi*, Reynold A. Nicholson, also edited Sarrāj's *Kitāb al-Lumaʿ* and translated Hujwīrī's *Kashf al-maḥjūb*, while his student A. J. Arberry translated Kalābādhī's *Kitāb al-Taʿarruf* as well as Rumi's *Fīhi mā fīh* (see bibliography).

CHAPTER ONE: THE SOURCES

1. Other Sufi manuals are not examined in the same detail in this study because they do not include extended theoretical engagements with the same juridico-theological concerns, even though they may contain material relevant to the topic (e.g., the Sufi traditionalist Abū Ṭālib al-Makkī's [d. 386/996] *Qūt al-qulūb*).
2. See further pp. 28–30. The main study of Rumi's biographical tradition is Lewis, *Rumi, Past and Present, East and West*.
3. This is because so many of Rumi's shorter poems, as well as his magnum opus, *The Masnavi*, indicate through their content that they originated without doubt after his meeting with Shams-i Tabrīzī in Konya less than thirty years before his own passing.

4. See further below concerning its inclusion of a verse from *The Masnavi* without reference to its source, and how that may be interpreted.
5. Other prose writings by Rumi have survived, namely his letters (*Maktūbāt*, ed. T. Subḥānī, Tehran, 1371/1992) and the seven Friday sermons he delivered (*Majālis-i sabᶜa*, ed. T. Subḥānī, Tehran, 1365/1986). However, their genres make them less suitable for this study. Many of Rumi's shorter poems may arguably be considered teaching poems as well, but their brevity means that their value for this kind of study would remain very limited. Needless to say, the teachings attributed to Rumi in his later biographies are less reliable than his own works, and can only be validated by confirmation in the latter, rather than serving as independent sources. Moreover, the heavy citation from Rumi's *Masnavī* in his most celebrated biography, Aflākī's *Manāqib al-ᶜĀrifīn*, suggests that much of it could even be exegetical in origin.
6. See further my analysis of Anṣārī's *Ṭabaqāt al-Ṣūfiyya* in Mojaddedi, *The Biographical Tradition*, chap. 3. For examples of similar book production among early jurisprudential circles, see Calder, *Studies in Early Muslim Jurisprudence*, chap. 7.
7. This mysterious looking title may have been derived from the following verse by Muḥyī 'l-Dīn Ibn ᶜArabī (d. 638/1240): *Kitābun Fīhi mā fīhi/badīᶜun fī maᶜānīhi//idhā ᶜayanta mā fīhi/raᵓayta 'l-durra yaḥwīhi* (A book which contains what it contains/ Novel in its meanings// If you examine what is inside it/ You will see that it contains pearls), which is found in his *al-Futūḥāt al-Makkiya* (vol. 2, p. 777), and is cited in Badīᶜ al-Zamān Furūzānfar's introduction to the *Fīhi mā fīh* (p. yb [introduction]). Given that Rumi shows little inclination toward reading Ibn ᶜArabī's works, if it was derived from this verse the title *Fīhi mā fīh* itself is likely to have been chosen by his students after his passing, as they in contrast soon became very influenced by such works.
8. The oldest surviving manuscript (Fetih no. 2760) was completed on the first day of Dhū'l-Ḥijja 716 according to its colophon, that is forty-four years after Rumi's death on 5 Jumādī al-Ukhra 672 (1273 C.E.). The second oldest manuscript (Fetih no. 5308) was completed on 4 Ramadan 751, under the title *al-Asrār al-Jalāliyya* ("Jalāl's [Rumi's] Secrets"). The former manuscript comprises only forty-two chapters, corresponding fairly closely to the first forty-five of the seventy-one chapters that make up the latter manuscript, and the familiar edition of the text based on that one. Since the later of these two manuscripts includes all of the seventy-one chapters recognized today as representing the complete work, it appears that thirty-eight additional chapters were included in it, nearly all of which were simply added where the earlier manuscript ends.
9. See for instance Ṣādiqī, ed. *Maqālāt-i Mawlānā*, p. xv. Furthermore, Ṣādiqī proposes identifying Rumi's son Sulṭān Walad, who died five years before the date given on the colophon of the oldest manuscript, as the individual compiler.

10. F, p. h (introduction).
11. See F, p. z (introduction).
12. However, they may have been omitted by the scribe of the oldest manuscript because they are in Arabic. The oldest manuscript contains only forty-two of the initial forty-five chapters found in the other manuscripts (chapters 1–21, 23–33, 35–42, 44, and 45). All the material here is in Persian. Chapters 22, 34, and 43, the ones that appear to have been inserted among existing chapters in all the subsequent manuscripts, are in Arabic, and they are not the only Arabic chapters among the seventy-one chapters of the longer recension. Rather than being tagged on after all the chapters found in the first manuscript like the other Arabic chapters (chapters 47, and 48), they appear to have been inserted among the existing chapters due to associations between their contents and those already found there. For instance, chapter 22 in Arabic has been inserted immediately after the only other chapter that mentions Rumi's deputy Ṣalāḥ al-Dīn. In fact, chapter 22 (F, pp. 95–96) is taken up almost entirely with a severe condemnation of opposition to Ṣalāḥ al-Dīn's instructions by a "Ibn Chāwush." This makes it likely that it was originally private and part of a written correspondence since there was no expressed reason for Rumi to talk in Arabic. The same can be assumed for the other Arabic chapters, two of which also contain severe criticisms (chapters 34, and 43). The only chapter in Arabic not accounted for above is the very last chapter; it includes the conventionally Arabic colophon, which takes up more than half of this extremely short entry, and probably determined the language used. It should be noted that many other chapter juxtapositions can be accounted for by virtue of associations between their contents, one prominent example being that between chapters 52, 53, and 54, all of which begin with poetry.
13. Thackston, tr., *Signs of the Unseen*, p. xiv.
14. See Mojaddedi, *The Biographical Tradition*, pp. 91–92, regarding "the box" (*jaʿba*) at Anṣārī's school, and the kinds of material among his miscellany, which included "diary writings" (*rūznāmahā*) and "loose notes" (*juzʾhā*).
15. See further the descriptions of these texts in, respectively, W. Chittick, tr., *Me and Rumi*, pp. xix-xxii, and Walad, *Maʿārif*, pp. *kt-mb*.
16. E.g., F, p. 46 (chapter 11) and p. 92 (chapter 21), where one finds very similar use of the same image of men collaborating to construct and erect a tent. References to the *Fīhi mā fīh* include the mention of the chapter where a passage appears, usually in the main text rather in these notes, in order to facilitate the use of one of the translations available, since chapter demarcations are the same in them (see further the bibliography).
17. E.g., F, p. 24 (chapter 6) and pp. 224–25 (chapter 63), where one finds the same joke about a jester and the king looking at the image of a cuckold in the stream.

18. E.g. F, p. 44 (chapter 11) and p. 73 (chapter 16), where one finds the same explanation and defense of the statement "I am God" (*anā 'l-Ḥaqq*), using the image of a drowned man (but not naming Ḥallāj, who is mentioned later in the work in relation to his famous ecstatic statement [p. 193, chapter 52]).
19. F, p. 117 (Chapter 26).
20. F, p. 35
21. F, p. 11.
22. F, p. 1.
23. F, p. 50; see also F, p. 240 (notes), and Lewis, *Rumi, Past and Present*, pp. 279–81.
24. Although Rumi does not give the obvious impression through his references to them that he valued the visits of these dignitaries so highly that he would only start a teaching-session for their sakes, his letters show that he was concerned to maintain influence over them. This makes it likely that he would not have failed to put in an appearance without good reason if a dignitary visited (see the notes on people mentioned in the letters in Rumi, *Maktūbāt*, pp. 247–304; and Lewis, *Rumi, Past and Present*, p. 295).
25. See p. 112 below concerning the nature of the madrasa Rumi inherited from his father.
26. F, p. 97. See further pp. 38–39 below.
27. F, p. 19 (Chapter 5).
28. F, p. 52.
29. F, p. 156.
30. Regarding the attacks on Ṣalāḥ al-Dīn and evidence for a murder plot, see Lewis, *Rumi, Past and Present*, pp. 209–11. Regarding the evidence for a plot to murder Shams-i Tabrīzī, see ibid., pp. 185–93.
31. F, p. 212.
32. F, p. 212. See further chapter 37, where similar insults are aimed at those philosophers who believe in the eternity of the world (F, pp. 212–13).
33. F, p. 193.
34. F, p. 228.
35. F, p. 47.
36. F, p. 47.
37. See pp. 67–72 below regarding Rumi's conviction that his words are divinely inspired.
38. F, p. 196 (chapter 53), where one finds the following couplet found in Rumi's *Masnavi*, Bk. 2, v. 278 ("Brother, your worth lies in your thoughts alone; / Apart from them you're only skin and bone").
39. M, Bk. 2, v. 7.
40. E.g., F, pp. 101–2 (chapter 23) cf. M, Bk. 1, vv. 1498–1503, where Rumi contrasts Adam and Satan's opposite attitudes toward accountability for their errors.

41. For instance, Rumi is quoted by Aflākī as referring before his disciples to the importance of *The Masnavi*, by comparing it with the Qur'an, and Aflākī includes references to the position of "*Masnavi*-reciter" (*mathnawī-khwān*) among the offices at Rumi's madrasa already in the aftermath of his death (e.g., MA, pp. 767–769, 777).
42. MA, pp. 739–41.
43. To begin with, Qāḍī ᶜIzz al-Dīn (d. 656/1258) is referred to as being alive in one of the chapters, and Shaikh Ṣadr al-Dīn arrived in Konya from Malatya only in 652/1254.
44. F, pp. 95, 96 (Chapter 22).
45. See further pp. 63–64 below.
46. Concerning manuscripts, see Lewis, *Rumi, Past and Present*, pp. 303–9.
47. The most celebrated among which are Sanāʾī's (d. 525/1131) *Ḥadīqat al-ḥaqīqat*, and Farīd al-Dīn ᶜAṭṭār's (d.ca. 618/1221) *Manṭiq al-ṭayr*.
48. The meter of Rumi's *Masnavi* is the *ramal* meter in apocopated form (–v– –/–v– –/–v–), a highly popular meter.
49. For further references to this process of composition, see EIr, s.v. "Ḥosam al-Dīn Chalabī" (M. Estelami).
50. See MA, pp. 496–97, 741–42.
51. See further Burton, *The Collection of the Quran*.
52. ᶜAṭṭār, *Manṭiq al-ṭayr*. It is well-known in the English translation by Afkham Darbandi and Dick Davis, entitled *Conference of the Birds*.
53. Richter, *Persiens Mystiker Dschelal-eddin Rumi*, pp. 27–49; Dabashi, "Rumi and the Problems of Theodicy," pp.112–35.
54. In a private discussion at the May 2007 UNESCO Conference in Istanbul to commemorate the 800th anniversary of Rumi's birth, Abdolkarim Sorush suggested to me that Rumi may have chosen to continue his final story of book 3 in book 4, rather than complete it in book 3, out of a reluctance to write an excessively long component book. Book 3 has more than 4,800 verses as it stands, making it the second longest book after the sixth and final book (more than 4,900 verses), which presumably could not have a continuation.
55. See Karamustafa, "Speaker, Voice and Audience," pp. 36–45.
56. Safavi and Weightman, *Rumi's Mystical Design*, pp. 3–8.
57. For instance, the excursus on good manners (*adab*) toward the beginning of the first story in Book 1 of the *Masnavi* is said to be parallel to the section where the king's attendants lure the goldsmith to his palace, but the association through the contrast between contentment and greed does not seem to explain their respective positions in the story any better than a linear reading (see ibid., pp. 70–73, 75).
58. It arguably depicts his poem as something resembling G. I. Gurdjieff's *Beelzebub's Tales to His Grandson*. That twentieth-century European work seems to have deliberately made severe cerebral demands of the reader, something

which runs counter to what we learn about Rumi by looking at his own actual writings. Safavi and Weightman base their study on Reynold A. Nicholson's initial Persian edition of the text of book 1, and without taking into account the corrections which Nicholson himself made to it retrospectively midway through his edition of the entire work, after discovering an older manuscript. This is no small matter because the discrepancies between the manuscripts include differences in the positioning and number of the section headings, which are all-important for the Safavi-Weightman theory, and which they repeatedly describe as being remarkably precise.

59. This is acknowledged by the authors themselves, although they still maintain that their synoptic reading is the one designed for mystic wayfarers, while, in contrast, a linear reading is superficially "worldly" (ibid., pp. 230–31).
60. See ibid., pp. 42–43; Baldick, "Persian Sufi Poetry," pp. 112–32.
61. See further Knysh, *Islamic Mysticism*, pp. 56–60.
62. Saab, "Ṣūfī Theory and Language," pp. 24–69.
63. She refers to "al-Kharrāz, Abū Saʿīd," in EI2 (W. Madelung). The same interpretation is repeated in Knysh, *Islamic Mysticism*, p. 59.
64. Saab, "Ṣūfī Theory and Language," pp. 76–77.
65. See further Arberry, ed. and tr., *The Book of Truthfulness (Kitāb al-Ṣidq)*.
66. See the introduction to the printed edition of these short treatises: KB, pp. 14–24.
67. See further KB, p. 31, and pp. 46–49 below.
68. KB, p. 16.
69. Nwyia, *Exégèse coranique*, pp. 239–42; Saab, "Ṣūfī Theory and Language," p. 105.
70. See further Radtke and O'Kane, *The Concept of Sainthood*, p. 5. As Radtke points out, Hujwīrī is the only manual author who acknowledges Tirmidhī. However, although he gives him high praise and proceeds to discuss Friendship with God extensively in the context of describing his followers, he does not do so in a way that corresponds accurately with Tirmidhī's own theory about it, failing even to mention the rank of "Seal of Friendship with God" in his hierarchy (see further pp. 58–59 below). In contrast, while Sarrāj omits any mention of Tirmidhī, he nonetheless shows signs of having been influenced by his writings (see further p. 149 below). All of this suggests that the harmonizing theorists found Tirmidhī a problematic figure to negotiate.
71. For a list of Tirmidhī's major works, see ibid., pp. 2–5. Their translation of his autobiography is in the same volume (ibid., pp. 13–36).
72. See further ibid., pp. 10–11. Radtke and O'Kane's *The Concept of Sainthood* includes a richly annotated translation of the *Sīrat al-awliyāʾ* based on the critical edition that Radtke had already published in his work *Drei Schriften des Theosophen von Tirmiḏ* (pp. 1–134 [Arabic text]). Since the critical edition and translation are divided into corresponding paragraphs, all references to this work will be to its paragraphs, thereby enabling reference to both in a precise and economical way.

73. Sarrāj's contemporary Abū Ṭālib al-Makkī (d. 386/996) wrote a heavily traditionalist compendium on Sufism entitled the *Qūt al-qulūb* ("Nourishment of Hearts") at around the same time, but this does not include an extended discussion of the theory of Friendship with God in relation to juridico-theological issues and is therefore not one of the main works discussed in this study (see further Karamustafa, *Sufism*, pp. 87–89).
74. Ibid., pp. 66–9.
75. E.g., see his discussions of theopathic utterances made by Abū Yazīd al-Basṭāmī and Abū Bakr al-Shiblī in the *Luma*ᶜ, pp. 380–98.
76. Karamustafa, *Sufism*, p. 47.
77. Ibid., pp. 69–71.
78. Baghdādī, *Taʾrīkh*, Vol. 11, p. 83.
79. Fārisī, *al-Siyāq*, BII, ff. 49a–51a.
80. See further Knysh, tr., *al-Qushayrī's Epistle*, pp. xxi–xxvii.
81. See my *The Biographical Tradition*, pp. 121–22
82. R, p. 121.
83. See further my *The Biographical Tradition*, pp. 133–34.
84. See further my "Extending the boundaries of Sufism."

CHAPTER TWO: FRIENDSHIP WITH GOD IN RELATION TO PROPHETHOOD

1. MA, pp. 86–87.
2. Jāmī, *Nafaḥāt al-uns*, p. 468.
3. MA, p. 87.
4. See MA, pp. 618–19.
5. F, 168–69.
6. F, pp. 69–70.
7. It should probably also be noted here that when Rumi's analogy relates leaving the realm of infidels for the realm of Muslims with leaving the higher spiritual realm for the lower physical one, he is simply trying to offer an analogy that his audience could relate to through their experience of slaves being brought to their Muslim community from conquered non-Muslim lands.
8. M, Bk. 1, vv. 3474–77.
9. Rumi illustrates the way this potential can be fulfilled by his audience with the famous story about the painting competition between the Chinese and the Greeks, which follows immediately after the above passage. The Greeks are victorious because instead of painting, they polish their walls so cleanly that they reflect in a more dazzling way the colorful paintings of their Chinese competitors. In the conclusion of that story, Rumi clarifies that the Greeks are the ones who had completely purged their hearts of their own attributes, so that they would then fulfill their potential to reflect divine light, and that they represent perfected Sufis: The Greeks stand for the

Sufis, you should note: / Without skills or book-learning based on rote / They've polished their breasts, so they now shine bright / Free from all stinginess, desire and spite (M, Bk. 1, vv. 3497–98).

10. F, p. 171. This passage occurs toward the beginning of chapter 45, which begins with a reference to someone named *Sayf al-Dīn* ('Sword of the Religion'), hence the sword imagery.
11. The only instance where Rumi presents a hierarchy of Friends of God in his didactic writings actually serves as a polemical passage against Shii notions of the Imam (M, Bk. 2, vv. 820–29). Yet still in this context, Rumi ends by suggesting that the lowest members of the hierarchy, "those who cannot bear much light due to being squint-eyed," can potentially improve their vision and rise to higher levels: "Impaired sight can improve eventually:/Once you've passed every veil you'll reach the sea" (M, Bk. 2, v. 829).
12. M, Bk. 5, vv. 742–43.
13. This is the way the verse is explained by Mohammad Estelami in the notes to his edition of *The Masnavi*.
14. M, Bk. 1, vv. 1953–59.
15. The passage is found in a break from the narrative of the famous story about the old harpist. It immediately precedes a further teaching of the Prophet Muhammad regarding the arrival of divine communication and grace through breezes (*nafaḥāt*), among many passages embedded in this story about divine communication reaching the senses (M, Bk. 1, vv. 1923–2233).
16. When discussing succession involving Prophets and those who come after them, the most striking of these passages is found towards the beginning of the second book of *The Masnavi* (M, Bk. 2, vv. 908–33). Here, a chain of succession begins appropriately with Adam, the first Prophet of Islam, reminding of the universalist emphasis among Muslims on the continuity of Prophethood as far back as even the first human. But what is most interesting for the present discussion is that it continues seamlessly through the Prophets Seth, Noah, Abraham, Ismael, David, Solomon, Jacob, Joseph, Moses, Jesus, and Muhammad, the rightly guided Caliphs, and major early Sufis. God's Qur'anic lightning flash (*sanā barqih;* Qur'an 24/43) is described here as being passed on through millennia, and, since Muhammad is closer to the time of the last members of the succession, one assumes that its radiance does not diminish. See further my article "Negāh-i Mawlawī bi-Ṣūfiyān-i Mutaqaddim," pp. 103–14.
17. F, pp. 66–67.
18. F, p. 176.
19. Rumi, like most commentators, considers Khiḍr a Friend of God rather than a Prophet (e.g., see M, Bk. 3, v. 4305).
20. See pp. 42–46 below.
21. M, Bk. 6, vv. 173–74.

22. Regarding the *ḥadīth qudsī* see further Graham, *Divine Word and Prophetic Word.*
23. F, pp. 105–6.
24. See further Rubin, "Pre-existence and light," pp. 62–119; Schimmel, *And Muhammad is the Messenger of God*, pp. 123–43. Schimmel refers here to a biographical report about Rumi in Aflākī's *Manāqib al-ᶜĀrifīn* where in the course of interpreting Ikhtiyār al-Dīn Imām's dream, he is quoted as saying: "That endless ocean is the greatness of God, and that huge tree is the blessed existence of Muhammad and the branches of this trees are the ranks of the Prophets and the stations of the saints, and those big birds are their souls, and the different tunes they sing are the mysteries and secrets of their tongues" (MA, p. 131). It is worth noting that Prophets and Friends of God (translated as "saints" by Schimmel) are once again grouped together in this image.
25. F, p. 105. This chapter begins with the declaration that Muhammad was the most humble of all in consequence of his primordial role, and then ten lines further down Rumi attributes the same qualities to Adam.
26. This was in itself a play on a saying of Muhammad, which is actually cited in another chapter of the *Fīhi mā fīh* (p. 12).
27. These phrases are formulae repeated in the Muslim prayer ritual.
28. See EQ, s.v. "ᶜĀd" (R. Tottoli) and "Thamūd" (R. Firestone).
29. Qur'an 3/97.
30. F, pp. 224–25.
31. F, p. 106. Muhammad has the distinction of having this role for all humanity and not just his own contemporaries
32. F, pp. 226–27.
33. Since the recognition of the Prophethood of Muhammad is a major part of what distinguishes Muslims from Christians, it is worth recalling Rumi's comments regarding the value of his sessions with non-Muslims: When questioned by his own students about how such people could possibly understand what he was saying even though few Muslims were able to, Rumi explains that they understand the original purpose of his speech even if they cannot understand the words, because every path is aiming for the same goal. He expands on this point using the analogy of pilgrims on different paths heading for Mecca, and accusing each other of being misguided until they all arrive at the Kaaba, where "inner beings (*darūnhā*) have a strong connection, love (*ᶜishq*), and affection (*maḥabbat*), for there is no room there for dispute; that connection is neither infidelity (*kufr*) nor faith (*īmān*)" (F, p. 97).
34. One mystic who expresses this view is Rumi's contemporary Najm al-Dīn Rāzī (see Rāzī, *Mirṣād al-ᶜIbād*, p. 237).
35. M, Bk. 5, v. 1237. See further pp. 72–73 below regarding Rumi's argument in the conclusion of this story for the continuation of *waḥy* communication after Muhammad.

36. Schimmel, *The Triumphal Sun*, p. 280. It is true that emphatic reverence of the Prophet Muhammad as a historical personality is characteristic of many manifestations of Sufism, such as prominent streams of Indian Sufism in the last few centuries, in which Schimmel herself specialized. However, it is inaccurate to assume the same for someone who lived in an entirely different historical context.
37. See further Davis, "Narrative and doctrine."
38. Renard, *All the King's Falcons*, p. 151.
39. Ibid., p. 11.
40. Chittick, *The Sufi Path of Love*, pp. 119-20.
41. See p. 35 above.
42. Lewis, *Rumi: Past and Present*, p. 408. Though the point of the reference he provides here is unclear (M, Bk. 1, vv. 1944–46, corresponding to Lewis's reference of Bk. 1, vv. 1934–36 of the Nicholson edition), it is worth noting that it mentions veiled and unveiled communications as well as Mary; Prophets and Friends of God are mentioned earlier in the same section, but no distinction is made by Rumi when it comes to their speaking "with the voice of God" (M, Bk. 1, vv. 1923–36). See further pp. 64–74 below.
43. Friedmann, *Prophecy Continuous*, p. 51. The Qur'an of course does not list 124,000 Prophets, but it leaves the total number open by declaring that it has mentioned only some of them to Muhammad ("We have sent Apostles (*rusul*) before you-some of them we mentioned to you, and some we did not mention to you" Qur'an 40/78).
44. See further Friedmann, *Prophecy Continuous*, p. 50.
45. E.g., Qur'an 16/36: "We have sent a messenger to every community, saying, 'Worship God, and avoid idolatry!'" See also 10/47, 13/7, 35/24.
46. See further Friedmann, *Prophecy Continuous*, pp. 49–82. A shorter version of these chapters was published previously by Friedmann as "Finality of Prophethood in Sunni Islam." The Qur'anic verse concerned is 33:40: "Muhammad is not the father of any of your men, but the Apostle of God and the Seal of the Prophets (*khātim al-nabiyīn*)."
47. Ibid., pp. 59–64,70–71. The main topic in these hadiths is whether or not Muhammad's son Ibrāhīm would have been a Prophet, if he had survived him. The oldest creeds which incorporate the dogma date from the tenth century C.E. In contrast, the early creeds include a statement requiring belief in Prophets before Muhammad and not him alone (see further Wensinck, *The Muslim Creed*, pp. 103, 114–15).
48. Friedmann, *Prophecy Continuous*, p. 77–80.
49. See ibid., pp. 68–69.
50. Regarding claims to Prophethood after Muhammad, see ibid., pp. 64–68. Regarding the *ridda* wars in general, see Donner, *The Early Islamic Conquests*; Idem, tr., *The History of al-Ṭabarī*, X.

51. See Friedmann, *Prophecy Continuous*, p. 68.
52. E.g., see Crone and Hinds, *God's Caliph*, pp. 26–28.
53. In his recent book *Muhammad Is Not the Father of Any of Your Men*, David S. Powers has also pointed to fear of succession to leadership of the community after Muhammad (by a potential subsequent Prophet) as the factor determining the "Sealing of Prophethood" verse (Qur'an 33/40).
54. See further Lowry, *Early Islamic Legal Theory*.
55. Musa, "Al-Shafi'i, the Hadith, and the Concept of Duality of Revelation."
56. Dreams are even deemed "a part of Prophethood" (*juzʾ min al-nubuwwa*) which continues after Muhammad. See further Friedmann, *Prophecy Continuous*, pp. 83–85. Another continuing source of divine communication which is extrapolated from the hadith literature and alternative readings of the Qur'an by Friedmann is the "*muḥaddath*," or prophet-like individual who receives communication from God (pp. 86–92).
57. Concerning overlapping esoteric concerns among early Sufis and early Shī'is, see Amir-Moezzi, *The Divine Guide in Early Shī'ism*.
58. See further Amir-Moezzi, "Notes à propos de la *walāya* imamite," pp. 722–41. The earliest sources do not give any clues about relationships between early Sufis and Shī'is. This is probably due to the Caliph al-Mutawakkil's (r. 232–47/847–61) anti-Shī'ism policies.
59. In the same period, the ruling house of the Umayyads maintained a similar understanding of their position as Caliph (*khalīfa*), whom they viewed not only as a political leader but as an intermediary with God; he gave rulings on God's authority, and was not only independent of the Prophet Muhammad, but, in the view of some Umayyads, superior. Crone and Hinds also witness that Muhammad is not singled out in the texts of the Umayyad period as having a supreme position distinguished from the other Prophets. (See Crone and Hinds, *God's Caliph*, pp. 26–28).
60. See pp. 20–24 above for background information about these individuals and their writings.
61. KB, p. 31.
62. KB, p. 37.
63. KB, p. 33.
64. KB, p. 37.
65. KB, p. 31.
66. KB, p. 37. Nada A. Saab has pointed out that elsewhere in his writings Kharrāz uses the term "*ishāra*" to mean "a state of being totally absorbed" in one's focus on God, and "the spiritual temperament which the *awliyāʾ* inherit from Him and proclaim in physical existence" (Saab, "Ṣūfī Theory and Language," p. 127).
67. Qur'an 18/60–82.
68. He also identifies the story of Solomon and Āṣaf as a Qur'anic story (27/16-44) that has been misinterpreted by them with the same consequence. See KB, p. 32.

69. This knowledge of Khiḍr came to be commonly described as "*ʿilm ladunnī*" (derived from the Qur'anic (18/65) phrase: "*ʿallamnāh min ladunnā ʿilman*" ("We taught him a knowledge from Our presence"), and was equated with divine communication (*ilhām*) in the Qur'anic exegesis of Qushayrī (see Halman, "Where Two Seas Meet," p. 168; Qushayrī, *Laṭāʾif al-ishārāt*, Vol. 4, p. 79).
70. Qur'an 18/78–82. See further Halman, "Where Two Seas Meet," especially pp. 63–67, where he provides a useful compiled story based on the hadith reports which add flesh to the Quranic account. I have been informed by the author that a revised version of this dissertation is in the process of being published by Fons Vitae.
71. KB, p. 32.
72. KB, p. 36.
73. See further N. Saab, "Ṣūfī Theory and Language," p. 147, note 406.
74. KB, p. 32.
75. See further pp. 81–82 below, where Sarrāj uses an argument with the same structure regarding the divine communication received by Prophets and Friends of God.
76. S, paras. 105–6. See also the notes to para. 106 in Radtke and O'Kane's translation of this work, *The Concept of Sainthood*, for an explanation of Tirmidhī's use of the term *qurrāʾ*, especially to mean "hypocritical ascetics" (see further EI, s.v. "kurrāʾ" [T. Nagel]). Tirmidhī's description of the latter here in the *Sīra* portrays them as competing religious devotees who had not gained the same divine gifts as the Friends of God, and denied their possibility for anyone due to this reason, rather than due to scriptural or theoretical interpretations.
77. See further pp. 23–24 above.
78. This is putting it mildly, because he refers to the interpretation of "seal" as meaning "final" to be "the interpretation of ignorant fools" (*hādhā taʾwīl al-bulh al-jahla*; S, para. 62).
79. S, para. 61.
80. S, paras. 53, 56, and 64. Tirmidhī implies that he had attained the rank of the Seal of *walāya*, and also that the end of time was imminent, so his alternative interpretation could be intended simply to emphasize that while "Seal" does not mean "final," he and Muhammad would be the last Friend of God and Prophet respectively because time happened to be ending (paras. 148, 153, 159).
81. S, paras. 106–7. See pp. 50–51 below.
82. Regarding the difficulty in translating the term "ḥaqq" in Tirmidhī's variable and idiosyncratic usage, see Radtke and O'Kane, *The Concept of Sainthood*, pp. 43–44, note 1, and pp. 213–18.
83. S, para. 47.
84. It is possible that before his treatise, the title "*walī*" (pl. *awliyāʾ*; Friend(s) of God) may have been used more loosely to refer to mystic seekers, leading

Tirmidhī to define an elite group from among the mystics in order to exclude lesser individuals who would aspire to such a title. In this regard, it is worth noting that his contemporary Kharrāz refers to his readership at the end of his *al-Kashf wa'l-bayān* (KB, p. 37) as "*awliyā*ʾ" (Friends of God). Tirmidhī's innovative differentiation would then have the potential to restrict any descriptions of Friends of God that were very lofty and Prophet-like exclusively to this elite group who have fully realized Friendship with God. This is because he gives them the generic-sounding title "*walī Allāh*," and to the mystics aspiring to achieve the same status the alternative title of "*walī Ḥaqq Allāh*" (Lesser Friend of God), which had probably never been used before let alone been the subject of lofty descriptions and claims. He could also have had further polemical reasons: Among Tirmidhī's opponents are those whom he could thereby demote to the rank of Lesser Friend of God, a rank which leaves them unable to fathom the higher rank of Friend of God which he and other mystics have achieved.

85. See Karamustafa, "*Walāya* according to al-Junayd," p. 65. Regarding Junayd's image in the eyes of posterity, see my "Narratives about al-Junayd."
86. His unusual strategy of using an alternative reading of the Qur'an, which he clearly identifies as such, as a proof in an argument indicates his considerable self-confidence in these matters rather than a deficiency, as the extensive list of his works can further corroborate (see further Radtke and O'Kane, *The Concept of Sainthood*, pp. 2–5).
87. See further pp. 73–74 below.
88. S, para. 69.
89. S, para. 61.
90. Radtke, *The Concept of Sainthood*, p. 114, note 1.
91. S, para. 91.
92. See M. Chodkiewicz, *Seal of the Saints*, regarding the ideas of Ibn ʿArabī.
93. S, para. 106.
94. In this paragraph he refers to "*qurrā*ʾ," regarding whom see note 76 above.
95. Tirmidhī's subsequent attempt at giving reassurance to the interlocutor itself remains ambiguous, however. This is because he remarks that others cannot be superior to Prophets due to the excellence of their Prophethood and their "location" (*maḥall*). But, according to the abovementioned hadith, the reason why Prophets envy these special servants of God is said to be their "proximity" (*qurb*) and their "place" (*makān*). The usually comprehensive Tirmidhī does not clarify here whether there is a substantial difference between "location" and "place," whether he rejects the hadith in question, or whether it is just a matter of semantics. Commenting on the writings of an author from over a millennium ago and in a very difference social and intellectual context, I make the last suggestion only with a great amount of circumspection. I am reassured by the fact that Rumi boldly says that similar matters are just a matter of

semantics, that my reaction to reading such passages may have been similar to those much closer to Tirmidhī's time and intellectual tradition. See pp. 65–67 below.

96. See S, para. 86.
97. See S, para. 159, where the Seal of Friendship with God is said to be the closest to Muhammad when it comes to sovereignty (*mulk*).
98. See further Karamustafa, "*Walāya* according to al-Junayd," p. 67.
99. Ahmet Karamustafa suggests that in writings attributed to him, Junayd "may have come close to collapsing *nubuwwa* and *walāya* into a single phenomenon" (see further ibid., p. 67).
100. See Böwering, *The Mystical Vision of Existence*, pp. 238–39. As Gerhard Böwering points out, Tustarī specifies that while Prophets are always at God's throne, Friends of God can also reach it, and the difference in their roles is that the former must also propagate teachings for God, while the latter serve simply as reminders of God's presence (p. 240).
101. For background information about Sarrāj and Kalābādhī, see pp. 24–25 above.
102. See EI2 s.v. "al-ṣiddīk" (A. Rippin).
103. L, p. 424. The view that Prophethood is superior was one Sarrāj clearly felt was important to reiterate whenever discussing Friends of God, because elsewhere in the *Lumaʿ* where he argues for their existence, he offers the following reassurance: "[Prophets] are distinguished from [other holy people] by their being favored by God with the *waḥy* form of communication, their specific mission and the miraculous evidences of their Prophethood, in which no one else can compete with them. God knows best." (*faʾinnahum yanfaridūna ʿan hāʾulāʾi bi-takhṣīṣ al-waḥy wa'l-risāla wa-dalāʾil al-nubuwwa fa-lā yajūzu li-aḥad an yuzāḥimahum fī dhālika wa'Llāh aʿlam;* L, p. 17).
104. L, p. 422.
105. L, p. 424.
106. L, pp. 2–3.
107. See further chapter 3 below on divine communication.
108. T, p. 69. Kalābādhī ends this chapter with comments by Tustarī, Abū Yazīd, and Ibn ʿAṭāʾ which support this viewpoint albeit without specifically mentioning the actual terms *walāya* or *walī*. They are preceded by a hadith in which the Prophet is quoted as informing his disciple and son-in-law ʿAlī that his older companions Abū Bakr and ʿUmar are the highest ranking members of paradise after the Apostles and Prophets. The point made here is that Apostles and Prophets are above everyone else, though it probably had polemical origins.
109. See further chapter 5 below on miracles, pp. 151–3.
110. T, p. 74.
111. T, p. 75. Most of the remainder of this chapter is taken up with the implications of the Friend of God's relationship to his deeds and their future consequences, matters relevant to chapter 4 of this book.

112. T, p. 79.
113. L, p. 423.
114. Al-Makkī, *Qūt al-qulūb*, p. 143.
115. For biographical information about Qushayrī, see pp. 25–27 above.
116. In the much shorter chapter on Friendship with God, Qushayrī presents Friends of God as possessors of a direct, two-way relationship with God without the mediation of Prophets or any other individuals or texts. The implications of the discussion in this chapter for the religious scholars' juristic formulations will be discussed in chapter 4.
117. R, p. 488.
118. R, p. 488.
119. See further pp. 153–56 below.
120. For background information about Hujwīrī, see p. 27 above.
121. KM, p. 265.
122. KM, p. 303.
123. KM, p. 286.
124. KM, p. 305.
125. Concerning Hujwīrī's lengthy chapter on this topic, see further Renard, *Friends of God*, pp. 265–66.
126. See further Karamustafa, *Sufism*, pp. 66–69.
127. Regarding the special importance of Abū Yazīd for Rumi, see my article "Nigāh-i Mawlawī bi-Ṣūfiyān-i Mutaqaddim," pp. 103–14.
128. See note 9 of the introduction.
129. Elmore, *Islamic sainthood*, p. 159. It is worth noting that while Ibn Arabi famously says that "*walāya*" can be superior to "*nubuwwa*" in the case of a Prophet's *walāya* being superior to his own *nubuwwa* (in his view Prophets possess both; *Fuṣūs al-ḥikam*, p. 135), his exceptionalization of Muhammad does not merely facilitate parity between Friends of God and the other Prophets, but enables the Friends of God who follow after Muhammad to surpass them. See also Chodkiewicz, *Seal of the Saints*.
130. Rāzī, *Mirṣād al-ʿIbād*, p. 131. This saying is followed by details about the six reasons.
131. Rāzī, *Mirṣād al-ʿIbād*, p. 237.
132. See pp. 160–61 below.

CHAPTER THREE: DIVINE COMMUNICATION

1. Muʿīn, *Farhang-i Fārsī*, s.v. "Mathnawī."
2. The earliest textual recording of this verse was recently traced by Franklin Lewis and Alan Godlas on the Adabiyat listserve to the late nineteenth-century Indian commentary of *The Masnavi* (Muḥammad, *Sharḥ-i Mathnawī*, p. 3), where it is used to emphasize the poem's magnificence.
3. See pp. 67–71 below.

4. See EQ s.v. "Revelation and inspiration" (Daniel Madigan).
5. I have decided to use the term "communication" in preference to alternatives such as "inspiration" or "revelation." The term "*waḥy*" is notoriously difficult to translate and has taken on two dimensions of meaning in relation to Prophets because of the importance of its origin as well as its verbal expression (see further "*waḥy,*" in EI2 (A. J. Wensinck [and A. Rippin]). The terms used to designate the equivalent for Friends of God are clearly designed to share with *waḥy* a verbal expression, rather than a mere internal prompting, even when the term "*ilhām*" is used for this purpose. This is evident from the fact that in Sufi literature alternative terms are used for non-verbal promptings and inspirations.
6. MA, pp. 741–43. See also ibid., p. 291.
7. M, Bk. 1, v. 2997.
8. Rumi, *Kulliyāt*, Poem Nr. 463 (p. 212).
9. F, p. 81 (Chapter 18).
10. See further chapter 5.
11. M, Bk. 4, vv.1852–56.
12. See EI2 s.v. "al-lawḥ al-maḥfūẓ" (A. J. Wensinck [and C. E. Bosworth]).
13. See pp. 74–83 below.
14. Rumi alludes here to the sacred tradition in which God says, "The heavens and the earth could not contain me, but the heart of a believer can," which is cited in Ibn Ḥanbal's *Kitāb al-Zuhd*, p. 81.
15. Rumi also uses the term *waḥy-i dil* in the story about the man who claimed to be a Prophet which is found in the fifth book of the *Mathnawī* (vv. 1121–43; see further pp. 72–73 below).
16. F, p. 128.
17. E.g., Sulamī presents this hadith about the miraculous insight (*firāsa*) of the believer, as a transmission by the most widely accepted early Sufi, Abu'l-Qāsim al-Junayd (d. 297/910). See Sulamī, *Kitāb Ṭabaqāt al-Ṣūfiyya*, p. 142.
18. M, Bk. 3, vv. 4230–94.
19. M, Bk. 3, vv. 4273–84. The Qur'anic verse referred to here is 34/10.
20. M, Bk. 3, vv. 4285–94.
21. See Karamustafa, "Speaker, voice and audience," pp. 36–45.
22. Reynold A. Nicholson punctuates the passage differently: he extends the speech of the Qur'an until the beginning of the final couplet, that is until "on your grave as well."
23. F, p. 213.
24. See further EQ s.v. "Revelation and inspiration" (Daniel Madigan).
25. E.g., KM, p. 327.
26. Qur'an 16/68.
27. Qur'an 17/70.
28. M, Bk. 5, vv. 1228–33.

29. See pp. 22–33 above for the background information on Kharrāz and his writings.
30. KB, p. 32.
31. See further pp. 47–48 above.
32. KB, p. 37.
33. KB, p. 36.
34. KB, p. 35.
35. Wansbrough, *Quranic Studies*, p. 34. See also, pp. 34–36, 61–63.
36. In this context, the "emissary" has been identified by exegetes as the Angel Gabriel, who provides the angelic mediation.
37. Wansbrough, *Quranic Studies*, pp. 34–35, where he refers to the writings of Muḥammad al-Kalbī and Muqātil b. Sulaymān.
38. See pp. 23–24 above for the background information on Tirmidhī and his writings.
39. Regarding Tirmidhī's use of the term "*ḥaqq*" see note 82 in chapter 2.
40. S, para. 67.
41. E.g., S, para. 80, where "*ilhām*" is listed in Tirmidhī's response to the question "What is the outward sign of the Friend of God?" but "*ḥadīth*" is not.
42. Not only does Kharrāz imply this, as shown above, but the discussions by Sarrāj and Kalābādhī only a century later suggest that "*ilhām*" was then understood as unmediated divine communication (see pp. 80–83 below), making this a strong possibility.
43. S, para. 67. See further the commentary on this paragraph in Radtke and O'Kane, *The Concept of Sainthood*.
44. S, para. 78.
45. S, para. 71.
46. One could also interpret Tirmidhī's distinction between the sources of those divine communications and the forms in which they reach their recipients as his way of dealing with the overlapping usage of these terms as both inspiration and speech of some kind. See furthermore EI2 s.v. "Waḥy" (A. Wensinck [and A. Rippin]).
47. See pp. 24–25 above for the background information on Sarrāj and his writings.
48. L, pp. 1–2.
49. E.g., see the chapter on "spiritual stations (*maqāmāt*) and states (*aḥwāl*)" (L, pp. 41–72).
50. See pp. 53–54 above.
51. L, pp. 423–24.
52. See p. 25 above for the background information on Kalābādhī and his writings.
53. T, p. 90.
54. T, pp. 150–55.
55. See p. 55 above for Kālābādhī's use of this method while discussing the relationship between Prophets and Friends of God.

56. See pp. 25–27 above for the background information on Qushayrī and his writings.
57. See pp. 148–9 below.
58. R, p. 33.
59. R, p. 160.
60. R, p. 160. Curiously, Qushayrī says that the type which comes from an angel is "*ilhām*." He does not name the type that comes from God Himself.
61. See p. 27 above for the background information on Hujwīrī and his writings.
62. KM, pp. 162–63.
63. Anṣārī, *Manāzil al-sā'irīn*, pp. 361–64.
64. Mojaddedi, "Rumi," pp. 362–72. See also the prose introduction of the second book of *The Masnavi*, where he dismisses the final clause in Qur'an 5/54 ("and they love Him"), asserting that "'He loves them' is complete [as it is]" (*yuḥibbuhum tamām-ast*).
65. MA, p. 291.
66. Rāzī, *Mirṣād al-ʿIbād*, p. 366.
67. See Izutsu, *God and Man in the Koran*, pp. 152–53, 166.
68. M, Bk. 2, vv. 160–66. See also p. 69 above.
69. Rumi offers only the following ray of hope to scholars, which implicitly dismisses the merit of their learning: "Although this group who are stuck with letters and sounds cannot attain [the mystic's] states, nonetheless they gain nourishment from him and grow, and find peace in him, like a child that does not understand all aspects of its mother" (F, p. 156).
70. See EI2 s.v. "furkān" (R. Paret).
71. Bahā Walad, *Maʿārif*, Vol.1, pp. 152–53.
72. E.g., Qur'an, 20/62–76.
73. See further M, Bk. 1, vv. 2165–71.

CHAPTER FOUR: THE FRIEND OF GOD AND THE SHARIAH

1. MA, vol. 2, p. 640.
2. Regarding Rumi's own acknowledgment that scholars are scared to study with him, see pp. 14–15 above.
3. In writings of Islamic jurisprudence, these are the minimum amounts of water necessary to be considered impervious to pollution and therefore appropriate for use in ritual ablutions. It implies that the Sufi master cannot be harmed by any impurity.
4. M, Bk. 2, vv. 3319–21. A fourth verse is included by Aflākī immediately after this, but that one is taken instead from book 1 of *The Masnavi:* "If Friends of God drink poison it tastes lovely/ If students drink it then their minds turn murky" (Bk. 1, v. 2615).

5. See EI2 s.v. "ḥadd" (B. Carra de Vaux-[J. Schacht]).
6. See p. 96 below.
7. For an introduction to the early historical development of jurisprudence in Islam, see Hallaq, *The Origins and Evolution of Islamic law*; Melchert, *The Formation of the Sunni Schools of Law*.
8. While the healer is introduced from the start as a representative of God, by the conclusion of this story Rumi describes the king also as a Friend of God.
9. M, Bk. 1, vv. 223–38.
10. See further pp. 47–48 above regarding the story of Moses and Khiḍr in the debate about the status of Prophets and Friends of God.
11. M, Bk. 1, vv. 3817–22.
12. F, p. 148 (Chapter 39).
13. Another famous story about Bāyazīd which makes the same general point is the story about his pilgrimage in the second book of *The Masnavi* (vv. 2224–57), where he makes spiritual progress by circumambulating a Sufi shaikh rather than continuing his journey to Mecca. See further pp. 101–2 below and Safi, "On the Path of Love Towards the Divine," pp. 24–27.
14. M, Bk. 1, vv. 1473–74.
15. Qur'an 18/18.
16. M, Bk. 1, vv. 394–96.
17. M, Bk. 1, vv. 1775–80.
18. M, Bk. 2, vv. 2825–30.
19. See note 3 above.
20. Qur'an 28/88.
21. M, Bk. 2, vv. 3319–20, 3334–37.
22. M, Bk. 2, vv. 3421–26.
23. M, Bk. 2, vv. 3427–38. This is actually based on the hadith "*Law kānat al-dunyā daman ʿabīṭan lā takūnu qūt al-muʾmin illa ḥalālan,*" cited in Furūzānfar, *Aḥādīth-i Mathnawī*, p. 69. Rumi frequently cites this kind of legal exception under duress, including also in this same story: "When helpless, even carcasses are clean" (M, Bk. 2, v. 3431).
24. M, Bk. 2, vv. 3223–30.
25. M, Bk. 2, vv. 3379–412.
26. M, Bk. 2, vv. 2250–55.
27. F, p. 12 (Chapter 3).
28. E.g., in addition to the next citation from *The Masnavi* below about Muhammad's advice to ʿAlī, see the many references to the greater importance of the inner dimension of prayer over its outward form in the *Fīhi mā fīh*, (e.g., pp. 75, 143–44, 147–48, 174).
29. Qur'an 18/78.
30. Qur'an 48/10.
31. M, Bk. 1, vv 2972–93.

32. For another passage where he explicitly articulates this viewpoint, see also M, Bk. 5, vv. 236–446.
33. For further examples of this teaching, see e.g., M, Bk. 1, vv. 1539–56, M, Bk. 2, vv. 2168–71.
34. A sacred hadith included in Suyūṭī, *Jāmiᶜ Ṣaghīr*, vol. 1, p. 82.
35. This is a hadith of the Prophet which is also cited in L, p. 45. See further Furūzānfar, *Aḥādīth-i Mathnawī*, p. 188.
36. F, p. 49.
37. F, p. 136.
38. M, Bk. 1, vv. 3374–3409.
39. M, Bk. 1, vv. 3398–99.
40. M, Bk. 2, vv. 2614–2835.
41. F, p. 149.
42. M, Bk. 5, pp. 7–8.
43. Elsewhere, it is explained that this is because the Friend of God is directly commanded by God (see pp. 96–7 above). It is worth noting that Rumi extends this immunity to what "was gold originally" (*yā khud az aṣl zar būd*) and therefore has no need for alchemy. According to the analogy, this could refer to Prophets and angels, and perhaps also those drawn up to God through an immediate attraction (*majdhūb*).
44. One translator has even inserted this into his earliest translation as a parenthetic interpretation (see Chittick, *The Sufi Doctrine of Rumi*, pp. 20–21; but see also p. 111 below regarding his later revision of this translation).
45. Denny, *Introduction to Islam*, p. 98.
46. Tirmidhī and Hujwīrī also use *sharīᶜa(t)* to refer more broadly to religion than to the law (see pp. 116, 129 below) as do later scholars, including those writing in Arabic (e.g., see Chittick, *The Sufi Path of Knowledge*, pp. 170–72).
47. M, Bk. 5, v. 1243. There are passages in book 5 that appreciate the value of law (*sharᶜ*) for social cohesion, but they do not relate law to any spiritual benefit (e.g., M, Bk. 5, vv. 1212–17).
48. Chittick, *The Sufi Doctrine of Rumi*, p. xiv.
49. Ibid., p. 20.
50. Ibid., p. 19.
51. Chittick, *The Sufi Path of Love*, pp. 10–11. This is more truncated than it may at first appear, as a comparison with my translation above will clarify. However, Chittick does include here the analogy with medicine, stating that "the Truth is to find everlasting health and to have no more need for theory and practice."
52. Ibid., p. 10.
53. Ibid., p. 10.
54. Schimmel, *The Triumphal Sun*, p. 28.
55. Ibid., p. 298.

56. Ibid., p. 357.
57. Lewis, *Rumi, Past and Present*, p. 95. As Lewis has shown, there were already precedents for places called "*madrasa*" to function as centers for the practice and study of Sufism, and Rumi's *madrasa* certainly qualifies as one of these.
58. F, p. 156 (Chapter 42).
59. See pp. 18–19 above.
60. Lewis, *Rumi, Past and Present*, p. 407.
61. Ibid., p. 407.
62. For background information on Kharrāz and his work, see pp. 22–23 above.
63. For background information on Tirmidhī and his work, see pp. 23–24 above.
64. M, Bk. 1, vv. 3069–114.
65. KB, p. 34.
66. See Melchert, "Baṣran origins," p. 225. While Kharrāz does not express much interest in jurisprudence, it seems that Tirmidhī had disagreements with jurists because of his conviction that his contemporaries were straying from the intentions of the founders of the discipline, towards an all-encompassing understanding of their legal formulations (see p. 117 below).
67. Saab, "Ṣūfī Theory and Language," p. 2.
68. Ibid., pp. 139–40. See also pp. 76–77 and 90.
69. This is not a literal translation, but represents the point of Tirmidhī's distinction, which is to separate Friends of God who are drawn up by Him, from those who still aspire to such a goal but must struggle against their carnal souls. See further note 82 in chapter 2 above.
70. S, para. 134.
71. S, para. 92. This title literally means "The ten who received good tidings." See further EI2 s.v. "al-ʿashara al-mubashshara" (A. J. Wensinck).
72. S, para. 96. The issue of whether or not a worshipper is able to transcend fear of God was significant in the Ghulām Khalīl Trial of 264/877, for which see Melchert, "The transition from asceticism to mysticism."
73. S, para. 47.
74. See further S, para. 20.
75. Karamustafa, "*Walāya* according to al-Junayd," p. 66, where Karamustafa cites Junayd's letter to Yūsuf b. al-Ḥusayn al-Rāzī.
76. See further EI2 s.v. "farḍ" (Th. W. Juynboll).
77. See note 5 above in this chapter.
78. S, para. 16.
79. S, paras. 14 and 15. See also para. 37.
80. S, para. 99.
81. S, para. 43.
82. S, para. 102.
83. S, para. 73.
84. Böwering, *The Mystical Vision of Existence*, p. 235.

85. See EI, s.v. "kurrāʾ" (T. Nagel).
86. See p. 51 above.
87. See Radtke, "al-Ḥakīm al-Tirmidhī on miracles," pp. 291–93.
88. For background information about Kalābādhī and his work, see p. 25 above.
89. T, p. 84.
90. T, p. 58–59.
91. T, p. 131.
92. Ismāʿīl b. Muḥammad al-Mustamlī (d. 434/1043), the author of a commentary on Kalābādhī's *Taʿarruf*, unsurprisingly makes this specific assertion as his interpretation of the aforementioned comment on duties imposed by God: "The gist of this discourse is that the servant [of God] can never fall short of any of the customs of the Shariah. He also said that there is no station (*maqām*) where the customs of the Shariah can be no longer incumbent on him, and no matter how high the station or close to God, nothing forbidden (*ḥarām*) can become permissible (*ḥalāl*) for the servant, and nothing compulsory (*farīḍā*) can be removed without a legitimate excuse (*ʿadhr, ʿillat*)" (T, p. 329).
93. For background information about Sarrāj and his work, see pp. 24–25 above.
94. L, p. 431.
95. See note 5 above in this chapter.
96. L, p. 431.
97. L, p. 431.
98. See e.g., Böwering, *The Mystical Vision of Existence*, pp. 237–40.
99. Regarding later Muslim reflection on the theoretical status of acts before the revelation of God's laws, see Reinhart, *Before Revelation*.
100. L, p. 425.
101. See further Sulamī, *al-Futuwwa*.
102. L, p. 425.
103. E.g. see Sulamī, *Jawāmiʿ ādāb al-ṣūfiyya*.
104. L, p. 102.
105. For background information on Qushayrī and his work, see pp. 25–27 above.
106. R, p. 34. See further the analysis of this biographical section and its relation to the other sections of the *Risāla*, in my *The Biographical Tradition in Sufism*, chapter 4.
107. R, p. 541.
108. R, p. 552.
109. R, p. 159.
110. R, p. 137.
111. R, p. 137.
112. R, p. 137.
113. R, p. 122.
114. R, pp. 407–8.

115. R, pp. 122–23. In his definition of the term "moment" (*waqt*), Qushayrī specifies that God's command and law (*sharʿ*) cannot be neglected as a result of being directed by the moment, while in his definition of the station (*maqām*) he is more ambiguous.
116. The same of course applies to his biographies, which are made up of the same building-blocks of transmitted reports, but to a more limited extent there since he selects those that stress the role of the Shariah and following the sunnah of the Prophet, as indicated by the full heading of the biographical section noted above on p. 125.
117. R, p. 374.
118. R, p. 375.
119. For background information on Hujwīrī and his work, see p. 27 above.
120. KM, p. 268.
121. KM, p. 269.
122. KM, p. 275.
123. See pp. 114–5 above.
124. KM, p. 270.
125. R, pp. 16–7.
126. For a sign that Qushayrī was familiar with Tirmidhī's *Sīra*, see Radtke, "al-Ḥakīm al-Tirmidhī on miracles," p. 298, and Gramlich, *Das Sendschreiben al-Qushayris*, p. 359.
127. F, p. 17.

CHAPTER FIVE: MIRACLES

1. MA, pp. 124–25.
2. Jabre, ed. and tr., *al-Munqid*, pp. 35–40 (Arabic Text); English translation in Calder et al., eds. and trs., *Classical Islam*, pp. 228–32.
3. See pp. 65–67 above.
4. See further EI2 s.v. "Uways al-Karanī" (J. Baldick); Hussaini, "Uways al-Qaranī and the Uwaysī Sufis," pp. 103–13; Baldick, *Imaginary Muslims*, pp. 15–21.
5. M, Bk. 4, v. 1827.
6. The commentary which he provides at the end of the story is presented on p. 65 above.
7. F, p. 118.
8. M, Bk. 6, vv. 1306–11. "*Moon which was split*" is taken from Qur'an 54/1.
9. Renard, *All the King's Falcons*, pp. 43–44.
10. The saying "Let whoever wishes to sit with God sit with the Sufis" is even a title of a section in the first book of *The Masnavi* (vv. 1539–56).
11. M, Bk. 2, vv. 2161–71. This anecdote is loosely based on a saying of the Prophet Mohammad, which describes God as asking Mankind this question at the

Resurrection. Mankind is bewildered by the suggestion that they could have visited God when He was sick, and so God explains that if they had visited the sick people whom they had ignored they would have found Him there. Appropriately perhaps for this context, a variant of this hadith identifies Moses rather than all Mankind as the person being addressed by God (see further Furūzānfar, *Aḥādīth-i Mathnawī*, p. 57).

12. M, Bk. 1, vv. 3481–3513; F, pp. 44 (chapter 11), 73 (chapter 16) and 193 (chapter 52).
13. F, p. 41.
14. M, Bk. 1, vv. 1425–36.
15. F, p. 41.
16. M, Bk. 1, 2503–7.
17. M, Bk. 1, vv. 1939–44.
18. M, Bk. 1, vv. 1679–83. The citation is from Qur'an 2/106, which is commonly used in relation to the principle of abrogation of early Qur'anic verses by later ones.
19. M, Bk. 2, vv. 379–447.
20. M, Bk. 2, vv. 382.
21. M, Bk. 2, vv. 3221–29, 3236–42.
22. F, p. 184.
23. See pp. 22–23 above for the background information on Kharrāz and his writings.
24. KB, p. 35.
25. For all the terms used to mean "miracle" here, see EQ s.v. "Miracles" (Denis Gril).
26. See pp. 23–24 above for the background information on Tirmidhī and his writings.
27. "[The exoteric scholars] claim that those are the miracles of the Messengers (*āyāt al-mursalīn*), and if we affirm that they are also for those of a lower rank we will then nullify the proofs (*ḥujaj*) of the Messengers" (S, para. 105). Concerning the Mu'tazilites' disagreements with Sufis over the possibility of non-Prophetic miracles, see Sobieroj, "The Mu'tazila and Sufism," pp. 90–92.
28. S, para. 105.
29. There is no hint in these texts of any link to jurisprudential concerns, or even relevance to the latter, to support Florian Sobieroj's suggestion that legal issues were at the root of the Mu'tazilite denial of miracles, on the basis of their doctrine of "prescribing right and forbidding wrong" (see Sobieroj, "The Mu'tazila and Sufism," pp. 91–92).
30. See pp. 24–25 above for background information about Sarrāj and his writings.
31. L, p. 323.
32. L, p. 318.
33. Sarrāj achieves this by means of the citation of a comment by Ibn Sālim, in which he defines the four "pillars" (*arkān*) of faith, and then explains that belief in God's power means belief in His *karāma* (L, pp. 315–16).

34. These differences are identified in the course of the following discourse: L, pp. 318–320.
35. L, p. 315.
36. L, pp. 320–32.
37. See p. 25 above for background information about Kalābādhī and his writings.
38. T, p. 71.
39. See EI2 s.v. "Iʿdjāz" (G. E. Von Grunebaum).
40. T, p. 72. A minority of exegetes classified Mary as a Prophet, although the dogma that all Prophets must be male limited such interpretations. See further Schleifer, *Mary, the Blessed Virgin of Islam.*
41. T, p. 72.
42. T, p. 72.
43. T, p. 73.
44. T, p. 73.
45. See p. 67 above.
46. See pp. 25–27 above for background information about Qushayrī and his writings.
47. R, p. 485.
48. R, p. 486.
49. This reasoning begs the question how then a Prophet could possibly have a *karāma* miracle, though clearly this is not of any significance to Qushayrī's own agenda.
50. R, pp. 487–88.
51. R, p. 488.
52. e.g. R, pp. 507–8. Here Dhū'l-Nūn is described as filling a tree with dates after his companions expressed a wish for them.
53. See p. 27 above for background information about Hujwīrī and his writings.
54. KM, p. 279.
55. KM, p. 276.
56. KM, pp. 278, 282.
57. KM, p. 286.
58. KM, p. 288–89. Regarding Hujwīrī's special interest in drunkenness and intoxication, see my "Getting drunk with Abū Yazīd or staying sober with Junayd."
59. Rāzī, *Mirṣād al-ʿIbād*, pp. 313–14.
60. Ibid., p. 314.
61. Ibid., pp. 219–20.
62. See pp. 28–30 above.

CONCLUSION

1. M, Bk. 2, vv. 1725.
2. M, Bk. 2, vv. 1763–64.
3. M, Bk. 2, vv. 1774.

4. See further M, Bk. 5, vv. 1142–72.
5. M, Bk. 1, v. 3428.
6. Karamustafa, *Sufism*, pp. 68–69.
7. See further my "Extending the boundaries of Sufism."
8. See Radtke, "A forerunner of Ibn ᶜArabī."
9. Lumbard, "From *ḥubb* to *ᶜishq.*"
10. Ibid., p. 375.
11. See further the introduction to Ḥallāj's poetry in the forthcoming collection of translations by Carl W. Ernst.
12. See further Ernst, *The Shambhala Guide to Sufism*, pp. 8–18.
13. See further Karamustafa, "Islam: A civilizational project in progress," pp. 98–110.
14. M, Bk. 2, vv. 3697–3715.
15. See further Ernst, *Following Muhammad*, pp. 28–36.
16. See further Safi, "On the Path of Love Towards the Divine."

Bibliography

Abdel-Kader, Ali Hassan. *The Life, Personality and Writings of al-Junayd*. London: Luzac, 1976.

Aflākī, Shams al-Dīn. *Manāqib al-ʿĀrifīn*. Ed. T. Yazıcı, 2 vols. Tehran: Dunyā-yi Kitāb, 1362/1983.

Amir-Moezzi, Mohammad A. *The Divine Guide in Early Shi'ism: The Sources of Esotericism in Islam*. Trans. D. Speight. Albany: State University of New York Press, 1994.

———. "Notes à propos de la *walāya* imamite (Aspects de l'imamologie duodécimaine, x)." *Journal of the American Oriental Society* 122/4 (October–December 2002), pp. 722–41.

Anṣārī, ʿAbd Allāh. *Manāzil al-sāʾirīn ilā al-ḥaqq al-mubīn*. Ed. ʿAbd al-Ḥafīẓ Manṣūr. Tunis: Dār al-Turkī lil-Nashr, 1989.

ʿAṭṭār, Farīd al-Dīn. *Manṭiq al-ṭayr*. Ed. Muḥammad Shafīʿī-Kadkanī. Tehran: Sukhan, 2004.

———. *The Conference of the Birds*. Trans. Afkham Darbandi and Dick Davis. Harmondsworth: Penguin, 1984.

Baghdādī, al-Khaṭīb. *Taʾrīkh Baghdād*. 14 Vols. Cairo: Maktabat al-Khanjī, 1931–.

Baldick, Julian. *Imaginary Muslims: The Uwaysi Mystics of Central Asia*. London: I. B. Tauris, 1993.

———. "Persian Sufi Poetry up to the Fifteenth Century." In George Morrison, ed., *History of Persian Literature: From the Beginning of the Islamic Period to the Present Day*. Handbuch der Orientalistik 4.2.2. Leiden: E. J. Brill, 1981, pp. 112–32.

Barks, Coleman. *The Essential Rumi: New Expanded Edition*. New York: HarperCollins, 1995.

Böwering, Gerhard. *The Mystical Vision of Existence in Classical Islam: The Qur'anic Hermeneutics of the Ṣūfī Sahl at-Tustarī (d. 283/896)*. Berlin: De Gruyter, 1980.

———. "Early Sufism between Persecution and Heresy." In Bernd Radtke and Frederick De Jong, eds., *Islamic Mysticism Contested: Thirteen Centuries of Controversies and Polemics*. Leiden: E. J. Brill, 1999, pp. 45–67.

Burton, John. *The Collection of the Quran*. Cambridge: Cambridge University Press, 1977.

Calder, Norman. *Studies in Early Muslim Jurisprudence*. Oxford: Oxford University Press, 1993.

Calder, Norman, Jawid Mojaddedi, and Andrew Rippin, eds. and trans. *Classical Islam: A Sourcebook of Religious Literature*. London: Routledge, 2003.

Chittick, William C. *Me and Rumi: The Autobiography of Shams-i Tabrīzī*. Louisville: Fons Vitae, 2004.

———. *The Sufi Doctrine of Rumi*. Bloomington: World Wisdom, 2005.

———. *The Sufi Path of Love: The Spiritual Teachings of Rumi*. Albany: State University of New York Press, 1983.

———. *The Sufi Path of Knowledge: Ibn al-Arabi's Metaphysics of Imagination*. Albany: State University of New York Press, 1989.

Chodkiewicz, Michel. *Seal of the Saints: Prophethood and Sainthood in the Doctrine of Ibn ᶜArabī*. Trans. Liadain Sherrard, Cambridge: Islamic Texts Society, 1993.

Cornell, Vincent. *Realm of the Saint: Power and Authority in Moroccan Sufism*. Austin: University of Texas Press, 1998.

Crone, Patricia, and Martin Hinds. *God's Caliph: Religious Authority in the First Centuries of Islam*. Cambridge: Cambridge University Press, 1986.

Dabashi, Hamid. "Rumi and the Problems of Theodicy: Moral Imagination and Narrative Discourse in a Story of the Masnavi." In A. Banani, R. Hovannisian, and G. Sabagh, eds., *Poetry and Mysticism in Islam: The Heritage of Rumi*. Cambridge: Cambridge University Press, 1994.

Dakake, Maria M. *The Charismatic Community:Shi'ite Identity in Early Islam*. Albany: State University of New York Press, 2007.

Davis, Richard. "Narrative and doctrine in the first story of Rumī's Mathnawi." In G. R. Hawting, Jawid Mojaddedi, and A. Samely, eds., *Studies in Islamic and Middle Eastern Texts and Traditions in Memory of Norman Calder*. Oxford: Oxford University Press, 2000, pp. 93–104.

De Bruijn, J. T. P. *Persian Sufi Poetry: An Introduction to the Mystical Use of Classical Poems*. Richmond: Curzon, 1997.

Denny, Frederick M. *An Introduction to Islam*. New York: Macmillan, 1985.

Donner, Fred M. *The Early Islamic Conquests*. Princeton: Princeton University Press, 1981.

———, trans. *The History of al-Ṭabarī, X (The Conquest of Arabia: The Riddah Wars A.D. 632–3/A.H. 11)*. Albany: State University of New York Press, 1993.

Elmore, Gerald T. *Islamic Sainthood in the Fullness of Time:Ibn al-ᶜArabī's Book of The Fabulous Gryphon*. Leiden: E. J. Brill, 1997.

Ernst, Carl W. *Following Muhammad: Rethinking Islam in the Contemporary World*, Chapel Hill: University of North Carolina Press, 2003.

———. *The Shambhala Guide to Sufism*. Boston: Shambhala Publications, 1997.

———. *Words of Ecstasy in Sufism*. Albany: State University of New York Press, 1985.

Fārisī, ᶜAbd al-Ghāfir. "Al-Siyāq li-Taʾrīkh Nīsābūr." In Richard Frye, ed., *The Histories of Nishapur*. Cambridge, Mass: Harvard University Press, 1965.

Friedmann, Yohanan. *Prophecy Continuous: Aspects of Ahmadi Religious Thought and Its Medieval Background*. New Delhi: Oxford University Press, 2003.

———. "Finality of Prophethood in Sunni Islam." *Jerusalem Studies in Arabic and Islam* 7 (1986), pp. 177–215.

Furūzānfar, Badīᶜ al-Zamān. *Aḥādīth-i Mathnawī*. Tehran: Intishārāt-i Amīr Kabīr, 1347/1968.

Gamard, Ibrahim. "Corrections of Popular Versions." Available: http://www.dar-al-masnavi.org/corrections_popular.html. January 26, 2011.

Graham, William A. *Divine Word and Prophetic Word in Early Islam: A Reconsideration of the Sources, With Special Reference to the Divine Saying or Hadith Qudsi*. The Hague: Mouton, 1977.

Gurdjieff, Georges I. *Beelzebub's Tales to His Grandson: All and Everything*. New York: Arkana, 1992.

Hallaq, Wael. *The Origins and Evolution of Islamic Law*. Cambridge: Cambridge University Press, 2005.

Halman, Hugh T. "Where Two Seas Meet: The Qur'anic Story of Khiḍr and Moses in Sufi Commentaries as a Model for Spiritual Guidance." PhD diss., Duke University, 2000.

Hujwīrī, ᶜAlī. *Kashf al-maḥjūb*. Ed. Valentin Zhukovski. Tehran: Intishārāt-i Ṭahūrī, 1371/1992.

———. *Kashf al-maḥjūb*. Reynold A. Nicholson, trans., *The Kashf al-Maḥjūb of Al-Hujwīrī*. London: Luzac, 1911.

Hussaini, A. S. "Uways al-Qaranī and the Uwaysī Sufis." *Muslim World* 57 (1967), pp. 103–13.

Ibn al-ᶜArabī, Muḥyī'l-Dīn. *Al-Futūḥāt al-Makkiya*. Cairo: Bulaq, 1911; reprint, Beirut, Dār Ṣādir, n.d.

Izutsu, Toshiko. *God and Man in the Koran*. Salem, NH: Ayer, 1987.

Jabre, Farid, ed. and trans. *al-Munqid min aḍalāl (Erreur et délivrance)*. Beirut: Commission Libanaise pour la traduction des chefs-d'oeuvre, 1969.

Jāmī, ᶜAbd al-Raḥmān. *Nafaḥāt al-uns min ḥaḍarāt al-quds*. Ed. Maḥmūd ᶜAbidī, Tehran: Intishārāt-i Iṭṭilāᶜāt. 1373/1994.

Kalābādhī, Abū Bakr. *Kitāb al-Taᶜarruf*. Ed. Muḥammad J. Sharīᶜat. Tehran: Intishārāt-i Asāṭīr, 1371/1992.

———. *The Doctrine of the Sufis*. Trans. Arthur J. Arberry. Cambridge: Cambridge University Press, 1993.

Karamustafa, Ahmet. *God's Unruly Friends: Dervish Groups in the Islamic Later Middle Period, 1200–1550*. Salt Lake City: University of Utah Press, 1994.

———. "Islam: A Civilizational Project in Progress." In Omid Safi, ed., *Progressive Muslims*. Oxford: Oneworld, 2003, pp. 98–110.

———. "Speaker, Voice and Audition in the Koran and the *Mathnawi*." *Sufi* 79 (January–June 2010), pp. 36–45.

———. "Walāya according to al-Junayd (d. 298/910)." In Todd Lawson, ed., *Reason and Inspiration in Islam: Theology, Philosophy and Mysticism in Muslim Thought, Essays in Honour of Hermann Landolt*. London: I. B. Tauris, 2006.

Kharrāz, Abū Saʿīd. "Kitāb al-Kashf wa'l-bayān." In Qāsim al-Sāmarrāʾī, ed., *al-Rasāʾil*., Baghdad, 1967.

———. *The Book of Truthfulness (Kitāb al-ṣidq) by Abū Saʿīd al-Kharrāz*. Ed. and Trans., Arthur J. Arberry. Oxford: Oxford University Press, 1937.

Knysh, Alexander D. *Islamic Mysticism: A Short History*. Leiden: E. J. Brill, 1999.

Landolt, Hermann. "Walāyah." In Mircea Eliade, ed., *The Encyclopedia of Religion*. New York: Macmillan, 1995.

Lewis, Franklin D. *Rumi, Past and Present, East and West*. Oxford: Oneworld, 2000.

Lowry, Joseph E. *Early Islamic Legal Theory: The Risāla of Muḥammad ibn Idrīs al-Shāfiʿī*. Leiden: E. J. Brill, 2007.

Lumbard, Joseph E. B. "From *ḥubb* to *ʿishq*: The Development of Love in Early Sufism." *Journal of Islamic Studies* 18.3 (2007), pp. 345–85.

Makkī, Abū Ṭālib. *Qūt al-qulūb fī muāʿmalat al-maḥbūb wa-wasf ṭarīq al-murīd ilā maqām al-tawḥīd*. Beirut: Dār Ṣādir, n.d.

Malamud, Margaret. "Sufi Organisations and Structures of Authority in Medieval Nishapur." *International Journal of Middle Eastern Studies* 26 (1994), pp. 427–42.

Massignon, Louis. *Essay on the Origins of the Technical Language of Islamic Mysticism*. Trans. Benjamin Clark. Notre Dame: University of Notre Dame Press, 1997.

McAuliffe, Jane D., ed. *The Encyclopaedia of the Qur'an*. Leiden: E. J. Brill, 2001–6.

Meier, Fritz. *Essays on Islamic Piety and Mysticism*. Trans. John O'Kane. Leiden: E. J. Brill, 1999.

Melchert, Christopher. *The Formation of the Sunni Schools of Law, 9th–10th Centuries C.E.* Leiden: E. J. Brill, 1997.

———. "Baṣran origins of classical Sufism." *Der Islam* 82 (2005), pp. 221–40.

———. "The Transition from Asceticism to Mysticism at the Middle of the Ninth Century C.E." *Studia Islamica* 83 (1996), pp. 51–70.

Mojaddedi, Jawid. *The Biographical Tradition in Sufism: The Ṭabaqāt Genre from al-Sulamī to Jāmī*. Richmond: RoutledgeCurzon, 2001.

———. "Extending the Boundaries of Sufism: Hujwīrī's *Kashf al-mahjūb*." *Sufi* 35 (1997), pp. 45–49.

———. "Getting Drunk with Abū Yazīd or Staying Sober with Junayd." *Bulletin of the School of Oriental and African Studies* 66.1 (2003), pp. 1–13.

———. "Narratives about al-Junayd." In John Renard, ed., *Tales of God's Friends: Islamic Hagiography in Translation*. Berkeley: University of California Press, 2009, pp. 79–91.

———. "Nigāh-i Mawlawī bi-Ṣūfiyān-i Mutaqaddim." *Iran Nameh, A Persian Language Journal of Iranian Studies* 25.1–2 (Spring–Summer 2009), pp. 103–14.

———. "Rumi." In Andrew Rippin, ed., *The Blackwell Companion to the Qur'an*. Oxford: Blackwell, 2006.

Morris, James W. "Situating Islamic Mysticism: Between Written Traditions and Popular Spirituality." In R. Herrera, ed., *Mystics of the Book: Themes, Topics and Typologies*. New York: P. Lang, 1993, pp. 293–334.

Muḥammad, Walī. *Sharḥ-i Mathnawī*. 2 vols. Lucknow, 1894.

Muᶜīn, Muḥammad. *Farhang-i Fārsī*. Tehran: Intishārāt-i Amīr Kabīr, 1371/1992.

Musa, Aisha Y. "Al-Shafi'i, the Hadith, and the Concept of Duality of Revelation." *Islamic Studies* 46.2 (2007), pp. 163–215.

Nicholson, Reynold A. *Studies in Islamic Mysticism*. Cambridge: Cambridge University Press, 1967.

Nwyia, Paul. *Exégèse coranique et langage mystique: Nouvel essai sur le lexique technique des mystiques musulmans*. Beirut: Dar el-Machreq [distribution: Librairie orientale], 1970.

Powers, David S. *Muhammad Is Not the Father of Any of Your Men: The Making of the Last Prophet*. Philadelphia: University of Pennsylvania Press, 2009.

Pourjavady, Nasrollah, ed. *Majmūᶜa-yi āthār-i Abū ᶜAbd al-Raḥmān al-Sulamī*. 2 vols. Tehran: Nashr-i Dānishgāhī, 1369/1990.

Qushayrī, Abū'l-Qāsim. *Al-Risāla al-Qushayriyya*. Ed. ᶜAbd al-Ḥalīm Maḥmūd and Maḥmūd Ibn al-Sharīf. Reprint, Tehran, 1374/1995 [2 vols., Cairo: Dār al-Kutub, 1956].

———. *Al-Risāla al-Qushayriyya*. Trans. Alexander D. Knysh as *al-Qushayrī's Epistle on Sufism*. Reading: Garnet, 2007.

———. *Al-Risāla al-Qushayriyya*. Trans. Richard Gramlich. Weisbaden: Steiner, 1989.

———. *Laṭāʾif al-ishārāt*. Ed. Ibrāhīm Basyūnī. 6 vols. Cairo: Dār al-Kātib al-ᶜArabī, 1968.

Radtke, Bernd. *Drei Schriften des Theosophen von Tirmiḏ*. Beirut: Franz Steiner, 1992.

———. "al-Ḥakīm al-Tirmidhī on miracles." In Denise Aigle, ed., *Miracle et karāmā: Hagiographies Medievales compares*. Turnhout: Brepols, 2000, pp. 287–99.

———. "A Forerunner of Ibn ᶜArabī: Ḥakīm Tirmidhī." *Journal of the Muhyiddin Ibn ᶜArabi Society* 8 (1989), pp. 42–49.

Radtke, Bernd, and John O'Kane, trs. *The Concept of Sainthood in Early Islamic Mysticism*. Richmond: Curzon, 1996.

Rāzī, Najm al-Dīn. *Mirṣād al-ᶜIbād*. Ed. Muḥammad A. Riyāḥī. Tehran: Intishārāt-i ᶜIlmī wa-Farhangī, 1375/1986.

———. *The Path of God's Bondsmen*. Trans. H. Algar. Delmar, NY: Caravan Books, 1982.

Reinhart, A. Kevin. *Before Revelation: The Boundaries of Muslim Moral Thought*. Albany: State University of New York Press, 1995.

Renard, John. *All the King's Falcons: Rumi on Prophets and Revelations*. Albany: State University of New York Press, 1994.

———. *Friends of God: Islamic Images of Piety, Commitment and Servanthood*. Berkeley: University of California Press, 2008.

Richter, Gustav. *Persiens Mystiker Dschelal-eddin Rumi: Eine Stildeutung in drei Vortraegen*. Breslau: n.p., 1933.

Rubin, Uri. "Pre-existence and Light: Aspects of the Concept of Nūr Muḥammad." *Israel Oriental Studies* 5 (1975), pp. 62–119.

Rumi, Jalāl al-Dīn. *Kitāb Fīhi mā fīh*. Ed. Badīᶜ al-Zamān Furūzānfar. Tehran: Intishārāt-i Amīr Kabīr, 1330/1951.

———. *Kitāb Fīhi mā fīh*. Trans. Arthur J. Arberry as *Discourses of Rumi*. London: J. Murray, 1961.

———. *Kitāb Fīhi mā fīh*. Trans. W. M. Thackston, Jr. as *Signs of the Unseen: The Discourses of Jalaluddin Rumi*. Boston: Shambhala, 1994.

———. *Kulliyāt-i Dīwān-i Shams-i Tabrīzī*. Ed. Badīᶜ al-Zamān Furūzānfar. Tehran: Intishārāt-i Amīr Kabīr, 1358/1979.

———. *Majālis-i sabᶜa*. Ed. Tawfīq Subḥānī. Tehran: Markaz-i Nashr-i Dānishgāhī, 1375/1986.

———. *Maktūbāt*. Ed. Tawfīq Subḥānī. Tehran: Intishārāt-i Kayhān, 1371/1992.

———. *Maqālāt-i Mawlānā (Fīhi mā fīh)*. Ed. Jaᶜfar Mudarris Ṣādiqī. Tehran: Nashr-i Markaz, 1373/1994.

———. *Mathnawī*. Ed. M. Istiᶜlāmī. 7 vols. Tehran: Intishārāt-i Zuwwār, 1369/1990.

———. *The Masnavi: Book One*. Trans. Jawid Mojaddedi. Oxford: Oxford University Press, 2004.

———. *The Masnavi: Book Two*. Trans. Jawid Mojaddedi, Oxford: Oxford University Press, 2007.

Saab, Nada A. "Ṣūfī Theory and Language in the Writings of Abū Saᶜīd Aḥmad ibn Īsa al-Kharrāz (d. 286/899)." PhD diss., Yale University, 2003.

Safavi, Seyed G., and Simon Weightman. *Rumi's Mystical Design: Reading The Mathnawī, Book One*. Albany: State University of New York Press, 2009.

Safi, Omid. "On the Path of Love towards the Divine: A Journey with Muslim Mystics." *Sufi* 78 (2009/10), pp. 24–27.

Sanāʾī, Ḥakīm. *Ḥadīqat al-ḥaqīqat wa-sharīᶜat al-ṭarīqat*. Ed. Mudarris Raḍawī. Tehran: Chāpkhāna-yi Sipihr, 1329/1950.

Sarrāj, Abū Naṣr. *Kitāb al-Lumaᶜ fi'l-taṣawwuf*. Ed. Reynold A. Nicholson. Leiden: E. J. Brill, 1914.

Schimmel, Annemarie. *And Muhammad Is the Messenger of God: The Veneration of the Prophet in Islamic Piety*. Chapel Hill: University of North Carolina Press, 1985.

———. *The Triumphal Sun: A Study of the Works of Jalāloddin Rumi*. 2nd ed. Albany: State University of New York Press, 1993.

Schleifer, Aliya. *Mary, the Blessed Virgin of Islam*. 3rd ed. Louisville: Fons Vitae, 1997.

Smith, Grace M., and Carl W. Ernst, eds. *Manifestations of Sainthood in Islam*. Istanbul: Isis Press, 1993.

Sobieroj, Florian. "The Mu'tazila and Sufism." In Bernd Radtke and Frederick De Jong, eds., *Islamic Mysticism Contested: Thirteen Centuries of Controversies and Polemics*. Leiden: E. J. Brill, 1999, pp. 68–92.

Sulamī, Abū ʿAbd al-Raḥmān. *al-Futuwwa*. Ed. Iḥsān al-Thāmirī and Muḥammad al-Qadḥāt. Amman: Dār al-Rāzī, 2002.

———. *Jawāmiʿ ādāb al-ṣūfiyya and ʿUyūb al-nafs wa-mudāwātuhā*. Ed. Etan Kohlberg. Jerusalem: Jerusalem Academic Press, 1976.

———. *Kitāb Ṭabaqāt al-Ṣūfiyya*. Ed. Johanes Pedersen. Leiden: E. J. Brill, 1960.

Tirmidhī, Ḥakīm. *Sīrat al-awliyāʾ*. In Bernd Radtke, *Drei Schriften des Theosophen von Tirmiḏ*. Beirut: Franz Steiner, 1992, pp. 1–134 (Arabic text).

Walad, Bahāʾ al-Dīn. *Maʿārif: majmūʿa-yi mawāʿiẓ wa-sukhanān-i sulṭān-i ʿulamāʾ Bahā al-Dīn Walad*. Ed. Badīʿ al-Zamān Furūzānfar. 2 vols. Tehran: Intishārāt-i Ṭahūrī, 1352/1973.

Wansbrough, John. *Quranic Studies: Sources and Methods of Scriptural Interpretation*. Oxford: Oxford University Press, 1977.

Wensinck, Arent J. *The Muslim Creed: Its Genesis and Historical Development*. Cambridge: Cambridge University Press, 1932.

Index

miracles distinguished from Friends of God's miracles, 149–50
miracles of, 146–47
Muhammad as greatest, 36, 39, 44–45, 62
number of, 42, 179n43
qualities of, 44, 73
Qushayrī on Friends of God and, 57–60
ranks of, 55
Rumi on Friends of God and, 30–42
Sarrāj on, 183n103
Sarrāj on Friendship with God and, 53–57
successors, 31, 43, 46, 83–84, 177n16
as superior to Friends of God, 47, 58–59, 60, 84–85
Tirmidhī on, 46–53
tongue of, 83, 85
trials of, 47
Tustarī on Friends of God and, 183n100
union and, 59
Prophethood
as bonus honor, 48
cycle of, 45
in early Islam, 42–46
gap in cycle of, 42
limited to males, 194n40
start of, 58–59
Prophetic Hadith, 80
Prophetless era, 43, 45
punctuation, 70–71

al-Qaranī, Uways, 65, 138
Qur'an
authority of, 73
as divine communication, 44, 63
outward appearance of, 68
The Masnavi referred to as, 63, 86, 87
al-Qushayrī, ʿAbd al-Karīm, 25–27
on divine communication, 83–85
on Friends of God and Prophets, 57–60
on miracles, 57–58, 153–56, 164
on return to authenticity, 132–33
on Shariah, 125–31
on spiritual moment, 126–27
Qūt al-qulūb (Makkī), 57, 171n1, 176n73

Radtke, Bernd, 23, 51–52, 117, 175n70, 175n72, 181n76
rasūl, 147, 183n108. *See also* Messenger of God; Prophet(s); *specific Apostles*
Rāzī, Najm al-Dīn "Dāya"
on divine communication, 87–88
on Khiḍr, 62
on miracles, 158
on Moses, 62
religious scholarship, 14
Rumi on, 15, 112–13, 134–35, 187n69
Tirmidhī on, 147–48
Renard, John, 41
on miracles, 140
Resurrection, 192n11
Revealing of the veiled (Hujwīrī). *See* *Kashf al-maḥjūb*
Richter, Gustav, 19
Rightly-Guided Caliphs, 83
al-Risāla fī ʿilm al-taṣawwuf (Qushayrī), 25–27, 57–60, 83–85, 125–31, 153–56
introduction to, 131–32
omissions in, 26–27
sections of, 26
theological section, 83
Rumi, Jalāl al-Dīn, 5, 6, 10–22, 63, 171n7, 174n41, 174n48
access to, 13